THE

POLITICS

AND

TECHNOLOGY

OF

NUCLEAR

PROLIFERATION

THE
POLITICS
AND
TECHNOLOGY
OF
NUCLEAR
PROLIFERATION

Robert F. Mozley

UNIVERSITY OF WASHINGTON PRESS

Seattle and London

Library of Congress Cataloging-in-Publication Data
Mozley, Robert Fred
The politics and technology of nuclear proliferation / Robert F. Mozley.
        p.   cm.
Includes bibliographical references and index.
ISBN 0-295-97725-6 (alk. paper).
ISBN 0-295-97726-4 (pbk. : alk. paper)
1. Nuclear nonproliferation.   I. Title.
JZ5675.M69   1998   98-12070
        327.1'747—dc21   CIP

Contents

Illustrations

Acknowledgments

The help of my wife, Anita Ventura, was essential to the completion of this book. She encouraged the work and participated in its composition. Her detailed editorial scrutiny at all stages of the writing vastly improved the manuscript.

The book benefited greatly from reviews of the manuscript by Frank von Hippel and David Fischer. They identified many errors but are of course not responsible for any they may have missed, or for the instances in which I did not follow their advice. George Bunn was a continual source of advice and knowledge during the preparation of the manuscript.

I was helped by my friendly reception at Stanford University's Center for International Security and Arms Control. My conversations there with Michael May and John Harvey were particularly useful.

My early work on the organization of the book was greatly stimulated by a residency at the Rockefeller Foundation's Bellagio Study and Conference Center at the Villa Serbelloni in Bellagio, Italy.

THE

POLITICS

AND

TECHNOLOGY

OF

NUCLEAR

PROLIFERATION

Introduction

From the beginning, the development of nuclear weapons was an international achievement.[1] It started in Italy in 1934, when Enrico Fermi, together with Edoardo Amaldi, Franco Rasetti, and Emilio Segre, bombarded uranium with neutrons and produced the first, though then misunderstood, indications of fission. Studies continued in France at the laboratory of Irène and Frédéric Joliot-Curie and, more conclusively, in Germany with the research of Lise Meitner, Otto Hahn, and Fritz Strassman. The idea of fission was first developed and understood by two physicists—Lise Meitner and her nephew Otto Frisch—during a 1938 Christmas visit he made to her in Sweden, to which she had fled from Nazi Germany the previous July.

Germany was the center of physics research in the years before the Second World War, with physicists from many countries immigrating there for graduate education. The Nazis ended this flow: by 1941 about one hundred physicists had migrated from Germany to the United States, and a lesser number to Great Britain. With this influx of the most talented of the German physicists, Great Britain and the United States took the lead in nuclear research.

Physicists from other countries participated in the development as well, particularly physicists from Hungary. Among them were the German-trained Edward Teller, Eugene Wigner, and Leo Szilard and the mathematician John von Neumann—all Hungarian natives. Szilard, a brilliant gadfly, worked first in Great Britain and then in the United States. He was possibly the first scientist to recognize the dangers of nuclear-weapons development. In 1939, with the help of Wigner, he was instrumental in persuading Albert Einstein to write a letter to President Franklin Roosevelt pointing out both the benefits and the terrible hazards of atomic energy. This letter sparked the U.S. government's interest in the possibility of developing an atomic bomb. Szilard seemed at times clair-voyant in his understanding: as early as the 1930s he had taken out patents on the nuclear chain reaction.

By 1940, studies of nuclear fission were being made in Russia, Japan,

France, Great Britain, and the United States. A year later, American and emigré scientists, with a great deal of help from the British, had pushed the United States into a serious program of nuclear-energy development. Work on nuclear weapons continued in Germany; fortunately, it never got the support or the management it needed to achieve success. Japan and the Soviet Union did not have the resources to do more than study the problem.

By the spring of 1942, the United States had embarked on a crash program to develop nuclear weapons, driven by the fear that Germany might obtain them first. The decision was made to attempt the production both of plutonium, using a nuclear reactor, and of highly enriched uranium, using three methods of enrichment: the centrifuge, gaseous-diffusion, and electromagnetic (calutron) methods. The production reactors and chemical-separation units for plutonium were built at Hanford, Washington, while the main production work on uranium enrichment was soon concentrated at Oak Ridge, Tennessee.

Detonating a uranium weapon appeared to be so straightforward that a test using the precious enriched uranium was not thought necessary. On the other hand, the difficulty of properly imploding a plutonium weapon made a test of such a weapon imperative. Both the test and the test site, in a remote region of New Mexico, were called "Trinity" by Robert Oppenheimer, director of nearby Los Alamos, the government's center for developing the atomic bomb. At 5:30 A.M. on July 16, 1945, the first atomic weapon, of plutonium, was exploded, yielding an explosive effect equivalent to that of 18,600 tons of TNT.

Enrichment of uranium proceeded at Oak Ridge, both in the calutrons and at the gaseous-diffusion plant. The amount of enriched uranium needed for the first uranium weapon was produced both by calutron alone and by gaseous diffusion (to produce low-enriched uranium, which was then further enriched by calutron).

The first uranium bomb, previously untested, was exploded over Hiroshima at 8:16 A.M. on August 6, 1945; the second plutonium bomb was exploded over Nagasaki three days later at 11:02 A.M. World War II ended on August 15, 1945.

At the war's end, scientists of Great Britain, as well as those of the United States, understood the technology of producing nuclear weapons. The United States, however, was the only country with operating plants for the production of plutonium and enriched uranium and with facilities for the design of nuclear weapons. French and Canadian scientists, though they had helped in some of the design work, were not as intimately involved as were the British. Some Soviet scientists who were working on the processes for enriching uranium and producing plutonium had been helped by spies inside the U.S./British effort, the most important being Klaus Fuchs, a German refugee physicist who worked in the British theoretical design group from 1942 to 1949.

The United States has consistently tried to prevent the spread of nuclear weapons to other nations. It did not help Great Britain develop them, even though the British were its partners in developing the first ones. It did not help France, which made its weapons independently. It actively tried to prevent the Soviet Union from making a nuclear weapon. All of these nations, having since become nuclear powers, have tried to prevent the spread of nuclear-weapons technology to the rest of the world. In the pages that follow I discuss the reasons for this attempt, the technologies involved, the degree of success of the attempt, and the possible consequences of its failure.

1

Nuclear Confrontation

DANGERS DURING THE COLD WAR

There is a popular belief, based on the nuclear standoff between the United States and the Soviet Union during the Cold War, that the possession of nuclear weapons makes nations so careful in their dealings with one another that war of any sort between them can be avoided. Some international-relations theorists even propose increased nuclear proliferation as a method for reducing the risk of conventional war. They assume that all governments are rationally controlled and therefore would not order a nuclear first strike against an enemy or engage in conventional military confrontations that might escalate to nuclear conflict.

These proposals ignore many practical realities. Even if all leaders were rational, it does not necessarily follow that their governments and nations would act rationally, nor is it certain that no situation could exist in which it would be rational to launch nuclear weapons against a nuclear-armed enemy.

Few national leaders have subordinates who carry out their orders in perfect detail; delegated authority must be exerted through people who may disagree and who make mistakes. The technology used may break down. The result in either case can be actions that are unrelated to the wishes of the person or agency in nominal control, actions that are compounded of the habits and desires of the leaders and those of the people who must put the actions into effect. Even more dangerous is the possibility of war started accidentally or through misunderstanding.

Controlling nuclear weapons is a particularly demanding problem. Obviously, no rational leader would start a nuclear war with a hostile nation if that nation could retaliate with its own devastating nuclear attack. He would not even start a war with conventional weapons if it might easily escalate into a nuclear conflict. There can, however, be no reliance on a nation's not taking an opportunity to conquer an opponent by a sudden nuclear attack that would remove any chance of retaliation. During the Cold War, the United States and the Soviet Union maneuvered in order to be able to retaliate for a nuclear attack, leading to the position that came to be known as *mutually assured destruction* (MAD), in which each nation could survive a nuclear attack with enough nuclear weapons intact to exact devastating destruction on the attacker.

There is evidence, however, that the position of MAD was very hazardous during the years of the Soviet-U.S. confrontation. In his book *The Logic of Accidental Nuclear War*, Bruce G. Blair describes a situation that occurred shortly before the end of the Cold War, in which the military commands of both the United States and the Soviet Union were not sure whether their command and control systems would survive a first strike.[1] In this situation, their nuclear-armed missiles, however well protected, would not have been able to respond effectively. The United States attempted to strengthen its command and control by delegating the ability to launch nuclear weapons to commanders well below the presidential level. The Soviets, on the other hand, tried to protect the central command by elaborate defenses, such as establishing control bunkers 1,000 feet below Moscow (the conservative military had doubts about command safety even at this depth). For those controlling the ICBMs on both sides, this development led to policies of launch on warning. These policies were not publicized, and both sides emphasized the need of making the ICBMs themselves able to survive a nuclear attack.

During the early days of the Cold War, a launch-on-warning posture would have allowed considerable examination of the warning and debate about its validity during the many hours required by attacking bombers to make their way over the pole to their targets. With the advent of ballistic missiles, however, the time available shrank to less than half an hour, or, for submarines launching weapons off the shores, to a few minutes.

To make even half an hour's warning available, great technological development was necessary. Normal radar works in a line-of-sight manner. Thus, because of the earth's curvature, radar would be able to sight oncoming missile warheads only about halfway through their trajectories, allowing only about fifteen minutes for a decision to be made and counterstrike missiles fired. For this reason, the United States developed an over-the-horizon (OTH) radar that has sufficient range to detect the missiles as they are launched. This system's radar signals, though moving in straight lines, bounce off of the ionosphere and, possibly, the sea to overcome the earth's curvature and obtain a very long range. The reliability of this system is affected by changes in the height and character of the ionosphere. To make it reliable, changes in the ionosphere must be monitored and compensated for. During a nuclear war, the explosion of a weapon in space could affect ionization in space and prevent this system (and many satellite communications systems) from working. Until recently, the Soviets were unable to develop OTH radar technology successfully.

The United States also has developed early-warning satellites that carry infrared sensors, which can detect the radiation from the exhaust plume of a missile as it is launched. Such satellites, in geosynchronous orbit 21,000 miles above the earth, remain in one spot over the equator and have a range that extends to most of the Soviet Union. (The Soviets also had difficulty with this technology, because their infrared sensors were unreliable.)

Both of these technologies are now in use by the United States and Russia, and would provide the principal early warning of a nuclear attack. There are, however, other ways of getting an indirect indication that an attack is being planned: satellites can carry electronics for intercepting radio communications (no matter whether these can be decoded, the volume of traffic can give an indication that something is up); movements of troops can be observed by satellite; and of course spies, however old-fashioned, continue to be helpful. This secondary information is used, together with the general state of relations between the two countries, to indicate how seriously the information from the radar and infrared sensors should be taken.

The sensors do not always work reliably. Blair describes a retired Soviet general's recollection of once witnessing signals from space-based sensors warning of the launch of U.S. Minuteman missiles against the Soviet Union: "A 'competent operator,' the general recalled with relief, determined that the supposed missile exhaust plumes were in fact merely patches of sunlight."[2] Moreover, the Soviet over-the-horizon radar worked so badly in its early development that it could be relied on only to detect the launch of a group of missiles. It was used primarily to confirm data from satellite sensors.

Scott D. Sagan lists in his book *The Limits of Safety* other types of accidents that have occurred with the U.S. system.[3] A ballistic-missile early-warning system (BMEWS) is installed in northern Greenland at the Thule base. On November 24, 1961, all communication with the base went dead. This event could have been interpreted either as the technical communications failure that it was, or as the result of an attack on the base. The incident caused a major alert until a B-52 bomber, on a checkup flight over the Thule base, reported that the base was safe.

Alerts that may involve nuclear-armed interceptor planes, and even bring all branches of the nuclear-defense triad into a state of readiness, are far from risk-free. An accidental detonation of an American nuclear missile during such an alert could be interpreted by us as a nuclear strike by the Russians and thus start a nuclear war. Great efforts have been made to assure that American nuclear weapons will be safe in case of an accident, but only recently have calculations (performed with the aid of more powerful computers than were available during the weapons' design) shown that an accident that might cause a conventional explosive of one of the American weapons now in use to detonate could not, even under special circumstances, cause a nuclear explosion.

The special use of a B-52 to monitor the Thule BMEWS station in order to prevent the misinterpretation of a failure of communications is a reasonable way of increasing the reliability of a complex system. Even so, Sagan points out, this could in itself have led to the accidental start of a nuclear war.[4] On January 28, 1968, the B-52 monitoring the Thule station, which carried nuclear weapons, caught on fire and crashed about seven miles from the station. It flew over the station just before it crashed. Had it crashed closer to Thule and had one of its weapons detonated, the control system of the United States would have observed a communications blackout at Thule, and ground sensors would have sent information that a nuclear explosion had taken place there. This would have been enough to cause a retaliatory strike against the Soviet Union.

Frank von Hippel, in an article in the *Bulletin of the Atomic Scientists,* describes other errors: in one instance, early-warning radar signals were caused by a low-orbiting rocket body. And two or three times a year, a computer or a piece of communications equipment transmitted false information that suggested a missile attack.[5] Fortunately, these incidents occurred at a calm time in U.S.-Soviet relations. There were a number of much more dangerous accidents during the Cuban missile crisis. A frightening one described by Sagan occurred on October 28,

1962. Just before 9 A.M., the Moorestown, New Jersey, radar station picked up what appeared to be a missile launch from Cuba against the United States, and immediately reported it over the voice hot line to the North American Aerospace Defense Command (NORAD) center in Colorado. Moorestown predicted an impact point eighteen miles west of Tampa at 9:02 A.M. The operators were asked to recheck their data; it appeared unambiguous. The NORAD officers passed on the warning to the Strategic Air Command (SAC) base in Omaha. No detonation was noted. Moorestown finally reported that a test tape had somehow gotten into the system and that they had simultaneously picked up a satellite passing in the field of view.[6]

Blair describes a normal sequence of the launch-on-warning procedure:[7]

	Total elapsed time
Enemy missile launch	0 minutes
Missile launch observed by satellite detectors	½ minute
Transmittal to ground station	½ minute
Computer processing and evaluation	¾ minute
Transmittal to NORAD, SAC, Pentagon	1 minute
Conference for evaluation between the above	—
Check by NORAD with ground operators about equipment malfunction	assessment period
Evaluation of strategic position	—
NORAD determination of possible attack: no, medium, or high confidence (if medium or high, contact by Pentagon of chairman JCS, who notifies secretary of defense)	4 minutes
Depending on outcome of NORAD determination, conference of president, defense secretary, JCS chairman, and up to all twelve nuclear commanders, plus NORAD and SAC	8 minutes
Additional information from radar	9 minutes
Deliberation leading to decision	20 minutes

The situation for the Soviets was even more urgent because they had more difficulty in gathering information and it took them longer, in general, to launch their missiles. It is inconceivable that either side could have come to a reasonable decision given such a schedule.

The United States experienced many tests of this system. They were triggered by Soviet test launches (488 Soviet missile launches in 1984), sensor anomalies, defective computer chips, false data, and other problems. Blair states that from 1977 through 1984 there was an annual average of 2,598 routine assessments of unusual warning indications; about 5 percent of them required further evaluation.[8]

In a period of calm between the United States and the Soviet Union this system might have been secure enough, but during a crisis U.S. policy was to err on the side of getting the missiles launched, and the personnel involved would have been less critical of data. We have survived a hazardous time. Nations that now get nuclear weapons will confront situations that are even more dangerous.

DANGERS FROM NEW PROLIFERATION

The United States and the Soviet Union started their competition at a time when nuclear weapons were delivered by bombers. With the distances involved, several hours of warning time were available before the bombs would strike. This was enough time for the intended victim nation to get its bombers into the air, which meant that many of those bombers would survive a first strike. As the Cold War progressed, however, each side developed increasingly sophisticated weapons and warning systems and became more experienced in their use.

Although only a few nations are now actively trying to acquire nuclear weapons, a serious change in the international security system could produce many other prospective owners. Most of these nations are in close proximity to their antagonists. Although many of them are still able to deliver weapons only by bombers, missiles are now commercially available, and the accuracy of these missiles is improving. With the short distances involved, even a relatively inaccurate guidance system might be sufficient to make possible a first strike that could destroy an opponent's nuclear forces. In almost any kind of conflict, the need for a preemptive strike may be compelling for both sides.

When they developed their nuclear weapons, both the United States and the Soviet Union were stable states with a secure power structure. There was good communication between them: they had diplomatic ties; each had groups studying and trying to understand the other; they eventually had hot lines to be used in case of a dangerous situation. Most of these conditions do not obtain today for a number of countries that might attempt to get nuclear weapons if the international situation changed and pressures against proliferation relaxed.

A lack of technical proficiency in less-developed nations can result in unstable bombs. Normally, a nuclear weapon is made to produce a nuclear explosion by the detonation of conventional explosives, which in turn compresses a shell or sphere of uranium or plutonium to a much higher density, of supercritical value. This conventional explosion must be brought about with very accurate timing. A nation unable to master this technology can compensate by using more fissile material, which makes the weapon more nearly critical before detonation. Such a weapon will of necessity be more easily set off by a detonation of its conventional explosive, which could occur if it were dropped and would certainly happen if a plane carrying a weapon were to crash. A *New York Times Magazine* article reported on the findings of U.N. inspectors when they examined the design of the nuclear bomb the Iraqis had developed:

> The inspectors found out one other thing about the Iraqi bomb—
> it is highly unstable. The design calls for cramming so much
> weapon-grade uranium into the core, they say, that the bomb
> would inevitably be on the verge of going off—even while sitting
> on the workbench. "It could go off if a rifle bullet hit it," one
> inspector says, adding: "I wouldn't want to be around if it fell off
> the edge of this desk."[9]

The explosion of a weapon, even one's own, can seem like a nuclear strike by an enemy. Nuclear explosions leave nothing behind to indicate who was responsible. Also, the satellite and radar technology helpful in making informed decisions about such events is not readily available to less-developed nations.

If a nation's territory is large, it may be able to survive a few nuclear explosions without losing its ability to function as a nation, but small countries may be completely disrupted. One thing is sure: if a nation has nuclear weapons, it can easily become a target for others with nuclear weapons. Without nuclear weapons, a nation may be susceptible to blackmail by those nations that have them, but it will not be the target of a possible preemptive strike.

Ideally, a system in which warheads are separated from delivery systems might, if adopted by all antagonists, reduce the destabilizing effect of nuclear weapons. It is believed that India and Pakistan not only keep their warheads separate from their delivery vehicles but maintain the warheads apart from the fissile component. One hopes that Israel's weapons are maintained in the same way.

Such a storage system would make it difficult for an enemy to mount a preemptive attack on the weapons themselves, though not on the delivery systems. The length of time that such a nation would require to make its nuclear weapons operational would lessen the threat to its neighbors of a surprise attack. Under these circumstances there would also be much less chance of an accidental launch of a weapon, and bureaucratic controls could be more easily put in place to prevent an unauthorized launch. There would, however, be the necessity of exercises in arming the delivery systems to make sure that the weapons were operational. If such an exercise were to take place during a time of great tension, it might be perceived as a first step in using the weapons, or the nation performing the exercise might use it as a signal of determination.

THE THREAT OF ANONYMOUS ATTACK

An additional hazard exists: the possibility that nuclear weapons may be used anonymously, even by terrorists. There is a group of nations that regard themselves as harmed by the world's present security system (dominated by the United States and other powers) and so they often support terrorism. If one of these maverick states, such as Iraq, Iran, Libya, Syria, or North Korea, acquired nuclear weapons and decided to use them, it would want to use them anonymously. Yet such a nation would find it impossible to operate anonymously in a situation where it was the only possible author of a nuclear strike. However, if two or more nations that possessed nuclear weapons could be viewed as the initiators, the target country would be faced with the difficult choice of not responding at all or of striking multiple attackers.

An anonymous attack might be considered unlikely because no such attack has occurred over the long period during which the United States, the Soviet Union, and China have had nuclear weapons. But the reason has less to do with the moral scruples of the national leaders involved than with the enormous risk of discovery of an act from which little could be gained considering the physical size and power of these three nations and the fact that only one or two weapons could be used anonymously. Terrorist-sponsoring nations, on the other hand, would not require a major change in the power structure as the result of such an attack—only that a perceived enemy be hurt and its people frightened. Only with an understanding of the psychology of each of these nations can one say with any assurance that none of them will expand its terrorist horizons if given the opportunity.

The anonymous use of nuclear weapons, even by stable democratic nations, is possible whenever such use would appear to be in a nation's interest. For example, an anonymous attack might be made to prevent proliferation. Let's say that Israel might one day be faced with the threat that an antagonist country, such as Iran, will obtain nuclear weapons. An air attack by Israel with conventional weapons (such as that country's attack on the Iraqi nuclear reactor) might not be effective. Instead, Israel might consider an anonymous attack. It could get a truck carrying a concealed nuclear weapon into Iran and then explode this weapon in the midst of key atomic installations, with the explosion appearing to be the result of an accident involving one of the weapons being built in the region attacked.

The advantage of an anonymous attack over a missile or regular air attack is the possibility of denying responsibility. The denial would not have to convince the victim (unless it were itself a nuclear power), but it would have to be plausible enough to cast serious doubt in the international community as to who was responsible. There might even be circumstances in which a powerful and stable nation would consider using this method.

Thus either of two conditions is required for an anonymous strike. A nuclear power must have a need to, without angering the international community, (1) attack a stronger nuclear power or (2) attack a nonnuclear or an incipient nuclear power.

PROPONENTS OF PROLIFERATION

There are analysts who, extrapolating from the Cold War experience of the United States and the Soviet Union, reach the conclusion that the possession of nuclear weapons by an increasing number of nations prevents large-scale conventional war without adding any real risk of a nuclear one. These proliferation proponents range from Kenneth N. Waltz, who urges increased nuclear proliferation, through Bruce Bueno de Mesquita and William H. Riker, who attempt to develop a mathematical model describing a situation where more proliferation is better, to Steven J. Rosen and John J. Mearsheimer, who make detailed analyses of selected situations in which they feel that additional ownership of nuclear weapons might be beneficial.

All of these men share the assumption that the U.S.-Soviet confrontation was without appreciable risk. In their theoretical scenarios they have no place for the very real risk of preemption or of accident, although they use qualifying phrases to take these risks into account.

Kenneth N. Waltz, who over a decade ago published *The Spread of Nuclear Weapons: More May Be Better,* has been very influential.[10] In that paper he concluded that general proliferation would create a more stable situation among nations. His only qualification of this argument is the suggestion that the proliferation be gradual. His paper is comprehensive in its discussion of the dangers of proliferation. However, through his best-case analysis of these dangers, he reached the conclusion that more proliferation was better. Waltz's paper ignores the limitations of a generalization based on the single example of the Cold War. He is not bothered by the knowledge that each situation of conflict is different. He assumes that all national decisions are made rationally and that nations actually carry out the wishes of their leaders. He does not allow for errors, incompetence, or insubordination. In the case of nuclear war, this omission is particularly significant. In a situation in which a national leader does not want to start a conventional war, and finds that some of his directives are being ignored by the national bureaucracy, he will generally have time, measured in weeks, to correct any national actions he did not intend. If he is trying to correct actions that lead to nuclear war, he may have only a few minutes.

In furthering his argument with regard to the more unstable third-world nations, Waltz points to the restraint that many third-world leaders have used in the past when faced with truly dangerous military situations, and emphasizes that the huge uncertainty about the result of the use of nuclear weapons against even a nonnuclear foe would make any power, no matter how aggressive, hesitate to use them. Similar considerations would, he feels, prevent anonymous use.

These arguments for increased nuclear proliferation would be more credible had Waltz made it clear that he was merely pointing out the most probable result of proliferation in the many situations he examines. When considering the fate of nations, however, even improbable worst-case scenarios should be taken into account. The terrible consequences of a nuclear war should deter policy makers from putting a nation at any risk, however small.

In their article "An Assessment of the Merits of Selective Nuclear Proliferation," Bruce Bueno de Mesquita and William H. Riker attempt to derive a mathematical expression of a situation in which the additional proliferation of nuclear weapons might be desirable.[11] Their degree of success is to some extent irrelevant, because the accuracy of the input data available lends itself more to hand-waving arguments than to mathematical analysis.

Their paper is sensibly restrictive and comprehensive in describing the multiple interactions that must be examined between the would-be proliferant and its adversaries. But, like everyone who argues for more proliferation, they underestimate the risks of accidental nuclear war. The search for a mathematical model does have the beneficial effect of making necessary a clear statement of all of the ways in which a conflict could begin, but Bueno de Mesquita and Riker's model does not include terms expressing the risk of accidental or preemptive war. Their model does lead, however, to a comparison of the risks associated with nuclear warfare and those associated with conventional warfare. Using data on wars and on opportunities to start wars between 1816 and 1974, they find that of all the calculations that have led to war, the ratio of the seemingly rational and correct to the either irrational or erroneous is over forty to one. According to Bueno de Mesquita and Riker, these figures imply that with somewhat controlled nuclear proliferation, one might be able to prevent forty conventional wars for every miscalculated or irrational nuclear exchange. Taking into account the forty most recent conventional wars, "this analysis implies that a nuclear exchange in the third world would have to kill several tens of millions of people before some proliferation would be unjustified by yielding a higher expected loss of life."[12] Putting aside other objections, this information is of little use because the underlying assumption is that the hypothetical nuclear war would not have occurred accidentally and that only one such war might occur during the time in which forty conventional wars did occur.

There are a number of analysts who make sensible attempts to show that in special situations the acquisition of nuclear weapons by one or more nations would have a beneficial effect. It is difficult to prove that no such situation can exist; one must examine each situation individually. Without exception, all of the analysts who posit such situations seriously underestimate the possibility of accidental or preemptive nuclear war.

Steven J. Rosen suggests in an article in the *American Political Science Review* that the possession of nuclear weapons by all the nations of the Middle East might bring about stability in that region.[13] He argues that a negotiated settlement is unlikely and that if only conventional weapons are used, continuing wars between Israel and the Arabs are inevitable; eventually the Arabs will win. He then makes the assumption, a common one among proliferation proponents, that nuclear weapons would produce a benign standoff. His paper was written long before the recent Israeli-Palestinian accord. Clearly, he does not understand the nature of the risks of accidental war; but his most serious omission is any consideration of terrorist attacks in a region that has developed them to a high art.

The most persuasive of the proponents of proliferation is John J. Mearsheimer. He proposed in 1990 that a more secure Europe would evolve if Germany had nuclear weapons.[14] His logic is driven by his analysis, which shows that a bipolar conflict between nations of somewhat comparable strength leads to a more stable situation than any multipolar one and is less likely to erupt into warfare.

He also makes the interesting observation that deterrence with nuclear weapons can be much less expensive than with conventional weapons and therefore less likely to cause those in charge to resort to hypernationalism in order to make their populations willing to accept the costs of armaments. He points out that theories that rely on an interdependence of nations for preventing war have a difficult time accounting for the start of World War I, because the period before 1914 saw greater European interdependence than ever before. The suggestion that democracies do not go to war with other democracies he believes to be more valid, although not well tested. As for Europe, he points out that we do not know whether most of the nations of Eastern Europe will become securely democratic. It is difficult to see how the terrible and irrational conflict in the former Yugoslavia would fit into this analysis.

Mearsheimer's ideal prescription for a stable Europe would involve a toned-down version of the Cold War, with Russia and the United States participating. Accepting this vision as unrealistic, he nevertheless deplores the situation that seems to be leading to what he considers a "nuclear vacuum" at the heart of Europe. He writes:

> First, the caution and the security that nuclear weapons impose would be missing from the vast center of Europe. The entire region between France and the Soviet Union, extending from the Arctic in the north to the Mediterranean in the south, and comprising some eighteen significant states would become a large zone thereby made "safe" for conventional war.[15]

His solution to this dilemma is for the existing nuclear powers to give nuclear weapons to Germany. This, he says, should be done in such a way that adequate controls existed at all times. Yet he admits that such a controlled introduction has little chance of occurring.

Mearsheimer lists many dangers and difficulties inherent in the possession of nuclear weapons but, like the other proliferation proponents, does not appear to understand the dangers of accidental nuclear war. This lack of understanding as well as an insufficient discussion of the effect on the other nations in Central Europe of Germany's having nuclear weapons constitute two major flaws in Mearsheimer's analysis. A third is the omission of any consideration of the dangers of nuclear weapons themselves. The chance of war, even conventional war, may be lessened if nuclear weapons are present, but even when sophisticated nations are involved, accidental or preemptive war is still a finite possibility. Mearsheimer is so reasonable in much of his analysis that, when he proposes conditions on the method by which nuclear weapons should be introduced to Germany, he concedes that these conditions would never be met; he certainly does not make a convincing case for proliferation to Germany.

In the summer of 1993, Mearsheimer proposed that it would be best for Ukraine to keep its nuclear weapons in order to avoid a disastrous conflict with Russia.

Although the question of Ukraine's nuclear weapons is now resolved, with its June 1996 transfer of the last of the strategic weapons on its territory to Russia, an examination of Mearsheimer's arguments with regard to this issue is useful. Mearsheimer's proposal was made in the journal *Foreign Affairs,* in the form of a debate with Steven E. Miller, director of studies at the Center for Science and International Affairs at the John F. Kennedy School of Government.[16] Here Mearsheimer went into much more detail about the situation faced by Ukraine than he did in his discussion of Germany. His main point was that Ukraine would inevitably come into conflict with Russia, and that it did not have enough resources to defend itself with conventional weapons against its more powerful neighbor. He made much of the nuclear standoff that he said would produce peace between the two nations.

Miller pointed out that a nuclear deterrent would not inevitably prevent conventional conflict over issues like the Crimea, and that the expenditures needed for the nuclear deterrent would inevitably make Ukraine's conventional forces less effective. A defeat could then lead to nuclear war. He pointed out the risk of instant proliferation were Ukraine to seize the Soviet weapons now in its territory. Such a development would be particularly dangerous, he said: not having experienced the buildup of weapons over many years that is typical of other nuclear powers, Ukraine would not have personnel trained in safety procedures.

Much of Miller's analysis was confirmed by William H. Kincade's assessment, in the journal *Arms Control Today,* of the situation in Ukraine.[17] Kincade stated that the armaments in Ukraine were still in Russian custody. Guidance-system software in the cruise missiles carried by bombers located in Ukraine had been removed after the Soviet Union dissolved. The SS-19 and SS-24 missiles were disabled. There were safeguards against unauthorized use of the weapons, similar to the permissive-action links (PALs) of the United States. All of these things meant that even if Ukraine were to get custody of the weapons, it would not immediately be able to use them. Redirecting the trajectories of the missiles to Russian targets would be very difficult, because they were designed for the six thousand-mile trip to the United States. Moreover, Ukraine had no satellites giving it information about Russia and no accurate targeting data. Maintenance of the SS-19s would be necessary, as would that of the bombers. Ukraine would own and have to maintain nuclear weapons it could not use, making it an inviting target for a preemptive strike by Russia. Even if Ukraine could become an operational nuclear power, its relationship with Russia would be very difficult. Russia had detailed information on the missiles and emplacements. Russia's missiles could be very accurate over the short distances involved in an attack on Ukraine, making a secure second-strike force unlikely. The country would have no nuclear submarines as secure emplacements for its missiles.

If Ukraine had taken over the nuclear weapons, its action would have had a damaging effect on the arms-control agreements that apply to Russia and Ukraine. The START agreements would obviously have been affected, and, more important, the tension of the nuclear move would have undone the Conventional Forces in Europe agreement, the Helsinki Confidence and Security Building Measures agreements, and the Open Skies Treaty. All of these measures improved Ukraine's military security. It is hard to see, even from a Ukrainian perspective, how having nuclear weapons would have made Ukraine more secure.

There may be other proponents of nuclear proliferation whose writings I have not discussed. Though their arguments may differ from those cited here, I believe it is likely that any such arguments will be similar in their underestimation of the dangers inherent in nuclear confrontation.

2

Introduction
to the Technology

The following analysis of the technology needed for producing nuclear weapons examines key components that could be denied to
countries in the less technically developed world.

To produce nuclear weapons without outside assistance, a country
must have a highly developed technological infrastructure and must be
proficient in a broad range of technologies. By definition these are quali-
ties that less-developed countries do not have, although such countries
do exhibit a range of capabilities; for example, some (such as Libya)
would require turnkey plants, whereas others (such as Iran) already have
some technology base.

Major changes in technology have occurred over the past fifty years;
new materials, such as metal composites and special ceramics, have been
developed, as well as new vacuum pumps, lasers, transistors, computer
chips, and computers themselves. Many of these new technologies, however, are not available in developing countries. With regard to the manufacture of nuclear weapons, then, those countries find themselves in a
situation similar to that of the United States in the early days of World
War II. Therefore, in the following discussion I shall occasionally refer to
the experience of the United States during that war to illustrate the
technical difficulties that developing countries must overcome if they
intend to manufacture nuclear weapons. Developing countries today,
however, lack an infrastructure and resources comparable to those of the
United States at that time. Commenting on work at Los Alamos during
the Second World War, Robert Serber, then a young theoretical physicist
working for J. Robert Oppenheimer, says: "I remember someone at Los
Alamos saying that he could order a bucket of diamonds, and it would
go through Purchasing without a question, whereas if he ordered a type-
writer he would need (because of wartime rationing rules) to get a priority number and submit a certificate of need."[1] To understand the
strength of the claim that nuclear-weapon development had on U.S.

resources during the war, one need only look at the fact that the coils of electromagnetic isotope-separation units were made of bar silver from the country's silver reserve. The precious metal helped to produce a more efficient magnet design.

Nor do developing countries have the many trained scientists that were available for the atomic-bomb project. The best scientists of Europe had migrated to the United States to escape Hitler, and many of them worked on the project. Among them were at least fifteen Nobel Prize winners or future winners, along with an equal or greater number of scientists with the same abilities.

On the other hand, those few effective scientists the developing countries do have can reap the benefits of hindsight: they will know which of the many paths of development that were explored have proved effective. These countries may even have the plans of current operating equipment. Some of their scientists may have hands-on experience with some of the technologies, and many of them will have been educated at those European or American universities that offer the most advanced technological training. A great deal of literature on U.S. nuclear-weapon development is declassified and available. (Once it became evident that the Soviet Union had mastered this technology, secrecy was considered unnecessary; in addition, it was felt that because many of the technologies involved have other, nonsecret uses, the enforcing of secrecy among developed nations would be impossible.)

Most important for this discussion is the fact that developing nations may be able to buy critical equipment and design assistance from the developed world. Efforts to slow nuclear-weapon proliferation to less-developed nations by controlling the flow of hardware and knowledge will vary in effectiveness according to circumstances. Preventing a country from building only a few weapons is much more difficult than keeping it from becoming a major nuclear power. A small-scale production facility can be hidden and can use technologies that would be too expensive to use in a major nuclear-weapons program.

Uranium 235 and plutonium 239 are the two materials most suitable for producing fission weapons. In general, it is simpler to obtain plutonium than U-235 but more difficult to construct a weapon from it. Plutonium is produced from the uranium in the fuel of a nuclear reactor during its operation and can be separated from the uranium chemically after the fuel has been removed from the reactor. The radioactivity of the fission products in the fuel makes this a very hazardous operation. Because fashioning a weapon from the plutonium once it has been obtained is a more complex task than making a weapon from U-235, less-developed countries may prefer to try to produce enriched uranium, complex though that process is. China, for example, produced its first nuclear weapons from enriched uranium.[2] Thus it is necessary to control access both to the technology for producing plutonium and separating it from reactor fuel, and to the technology for enriching uranium such that its content of U-235 is raised from the 0.7% that occurs in nature to the approximately 90% needed for a useful nuclear weapon.

In the chapters that follow I shall consider, in addition to the technological difficulties of producing the plutonium or uranium needed for a fission bomb, the problem of fashioning this material into an effective and deliverable weapon. It should be understood, however, that even a poorly constructed weapon, or one made of a large amount of lower-grade uranium, could, despite its messiness and inefficiency, prove to be an incredibly destructive device.

A knowledge of the technology needed for weapon construction makes it possible to develop methods for detecting some of the activities involved. This knowledge may in some cases also make it possible to restrict access to the materials and equipment that a country needs to produce a nuclear weapon, and thus slow the development of nuclear weapons there. A discussion of the types of possible controls and their utility appears in chapters 6 and 9.

REQUIREMENTS FOR PRODUCING A NUCLEAR WEAPON

The primary material used in fission weapons is plutonium 239. This is produced from the uranium 238 used in nuclear-reactor fuel when it absorbs a neutron to become U-239 and then experiences two nuclear decays. In the first decay, U-239 emits an electron, producing neptunium 239; the neptunium 239 then itself decays in a similar way, producing plutonium 239. If the plutonium remains in the reactor fuel and is subject to a large flux of neutrons, it, in turn, can absorb a neutron and become Pu-240. The presence of this contaminant, which produces a great many neutrons by spontaneous fission, makes it difficult to trigger a plutonium weapon and to produce a strong explosion. If a reactor is being used to produce plutonium for weapons, the U-238 that is either present in the fuel rods or placed in the reactor to be converted to plutonium should be removed after a relatively short exposure—one that is long enough to allow the production of some plutonium but short enough to avoid its conversion into Pu-240.

The separation of plutonium from material that has been exposed to high irradiation in a reactor is very difficult because of the high radioactivity of the material from which the plutonium is being separated. Also, the plutonium is extremely poisonous; inhaling even a microgram can be deadly.

To produce a plutonium weapon, it is necessary to take the following steps:

1. *Mine or obtain uranium.* Geologists, mining engineers, and equipment are needed. Uranium is found in useful quantities in many parts of the world: in the Americas, Africa, Europe, and Asia. It can occur in oxides, hydrous oxides, phosphates, and organic compounds.[3]

2. *Process uranium.* Chemical engineers and a complex plant are needed. The process includes preconcentration, the crushing and grinding of ores, leaching with acid or alkali, and extraction from leach liquors by direct precipitation or ion-exchange processes—leading to the production of a compound such as yellowcake (usually U_3O_8) that can be used in further production.

3. *Refine uranium.* Chemical engineers and a complex plant are needed. The end product of the refining may be uranium dioxide, UO_2; or, if the product is to be used as nonenriched reactor fuel, uranium metal; or, if it is to be further enriched by isotope separation, uranium metal, uranium tetrachloride, or uranium hexafluoride.

4. *Produce plutonium.* Obtain heavy water or pure graphite for the moderator of a reactor that can operate with natural uranium, or obtain 3%-enriched U-235 for use in a standard light-water-moderated reactor. Operate the reactor to produce plutonium.

5. *Separate plutonium from the uranium and fission products.* An elaborate chemical plant is needed because of the radioactivity of the fission products.

6. *Manufacture a weapon.* Requirements include, among other things, the ability to machine highly toxic plutonium and beryllium, the design and construction of focusing explosive lenses, the construction of an electrical firing system for the explosives that is accurate to a fraction of

a microsecond, and a triggered neutron source to assure a source of neutrons at the time of firing.

7. *Produce a weapon-delivery system.* The weapon can be delivered by missile, plane, truck, or boat.

To produce a uranium weapon, a country must follow the first three steps just described for the production of a plutonium weapon—that is, **mine, process, and refine uranium.** It must then enrich the uranium; various methods of enrichment will be discussed later. It must **manufacture the weapon,** in a process similar to that for a plutonium weapon, but less demanding in many ways. Finally, it must **produce a weapon-delivery system.**

A less-developed country may already have a high-power research or power reactor. Generally, the reactor will have been bought under the conditions of the Nuclear Non-proliferation Treaty and thus will be subject to safeguards such as periodic inspections to assure that none of the plutonium produced by the reactor is being diverted to make nuclear weapons. Even if such a country could find ways of avoiding these controls, the difficulties involved in the use of plutonium might cause it to choose uranium instead.

NUCLEAR PHYSICS

A little knowledge of elementary nuclear physics is needed for an understanding of the technology that I describe here. In writing this section, I have assumed that readers know something of the vocabulary and physics principles involved. The following discussion is intended to help refresh the reader's memory.

Atoms and Nuclei

Atoms, although very small, are immense in comparison to the nuclei at their centers. The lightest atom, hydrogen, has a radius of about 5×10^{-9} cm, whereas its nucleus, the proton, has a radius about fifty thousand times smaller (10^{-13} cm). One of the heaviest atoms, uranium, has an atomic radius about five times smaller than that of hydrogen and a nuclear radius about nine times larger than hydrogen's. Hydrogen consists of a single positively charged proton as a nucleus and a single negatively charged electron distributed over a sphere

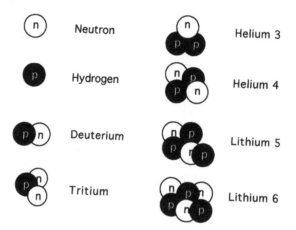

FIG. 1. Light nuclei

5×10^{-9} cm in radius around the proton. Uranium, instead of having only one electron around its nucleus, has ninety-two. If I were to draw a circle that filled this page to represent the atomic diameter of uranium, the nucleus would have to be a dot about 20 microns in diameter. The smallest dot I can have printed here has a diameter of about 100 microns. Atoms are mostly void.

There are other nuclear particles of almost the same mass as protons but without any charge. These are called neutrons. Discovered by the physicist James Chadwick in 1932, they were at first thought, because of their neutral charge, to be a combination of a proton and an electron. Later understanding, however, made it clear that the neutron is an independent particle. Protons and neutrons are now grouped together and referred to as nucleons. They have similar masses, each about two thousand times the mass of an electron.

Nuclei consist of protons and neutrons bound together by the very strong force, called the nuclear force, that comes into play when nucleons are close together. The number of negatively charged electrons surrounding the nucleus of an atom is equal to the number of positively charged protons in the nucleus, and as a result the atom as a whole is neutral, uncharged. The characteristics of any of the elements, such as their chemical reactions, are caused by the electrons, whereas any direct effect of the nucleus is, ordinarily, almost unobservable. Of course, its

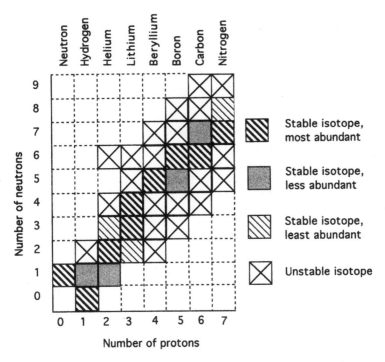

FIG. 2. Nucleons in the light nuclei

charge is what attracted the electrons there in the first place. One can think of the nucleus of each of the elements as made up of a number of protons and neutrons. Nuclei of a single element can have different numbers of neutrons. These different nuclei are called isotopes (from the Greek for "equal place") of the same element. Chemically, isotopes are almost exactly the same, but their atoms have different weights. Hydrogen, deuterium, and tritium are all isotopes of hydrogen; they could also be called hydrogen 1, hydrogen 2, and hydrogen 3. Almost all elements have several isotopes. The lightest nuclei are illustrated in figure 1; isotopes of hydrogen are among them.

A more complete plot of the light isotopes is given in figure 2, with the number of protons shown horizontally and the number of neutrons vertically. Each column represents a different element and its isotopes, while the rows show the number of neutrons in each isotope. The number of neutrons and the number of protons in a light nucleus are always

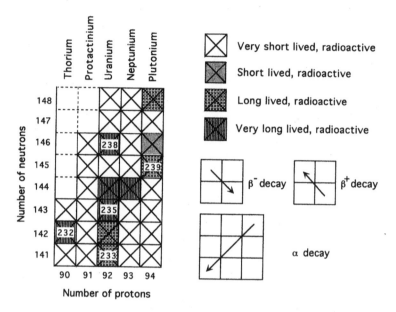

FIG. 3. Nucleons in some of the heavier nuclei.
Alpha and beta decay proceed in the direction indicated by the arrows.

close to being equal. Variations do occur: heavy hydrogen or deuterium (an isotope of hydrogen) has a nucleus with one proton and one neutron; tritium or hydrogen 3, which is unstable, has a nucleus with one proton and two neutrons. (It decays in about twelve years by emitting an electron and, because the lost electron was negative, becomes more positively charged, changing into a helium isotope with two protons and one neutron.)

As the nuclei get heavier, the number of neutrons in a stable isotope becomes larger than the number of protons; when we reach uranium, the principal isotope has a total of 238 nucleons—92 protons and 146 neutrons. The standard nomenclature for elements gives the number of protons as a subscript before the symbol for the element and the number of nucleons as a superscript after it—as, for example, $_{92}U^{238}$. Figure 3 shows the number of protons and the number of neutrons in some of the heavier nuclei. All of the nuclei shown are radioactive, and many, because of their short lifetimes, do not exist in nature and must be created artificially.

Radioactive Decay

Some nuclei are unstable and change by emitting helium nuclei, positive or negative electrons, or x-rays—or, sometimes, by absorbing an electron. These emissions have been given different names for historical reasons. When they were first observed at the end of the nineteenth century, their identity was unknown, but it was known that they were of three kinds, which were given the names *alpha* (α), *beta* (β), and *gamma* (γ). It was only later that these emissions were identified as helium nuclei, positive or negative electrons, and x-rays, respectively, but their Greek-letter names are still used when they are the result of radioactive decay. (Note that the term *x-ray* also shows the discoverer's uncertainty about the nature of this radiation. X-rays are now known to be the very-short-wavelength part of the electromagnetic spectrum; radio waves and light are longer-wavelength parts of this spectrum.) One would suppose that if there were enough energy, the emission of α and β particles and γ-rays might occur immediately. The electrons and γ-rays, however, do not exist inside the nucleus, but are produced when rearrangements of the protons and neutrons inside the nucleus happen. When the β particles (or electrons) and the α particles (or helium nuclei) are emitted, the nucleus changes its character completely. Figure 3 shows how these emissions change the elements: β^- emission adds one proton to the nucleus and removes a neutron; β^+ emission does the opposite; α emission removes two protons and two neutrons. The α particle can be considered as existing inside the nucleus but being too tightly bound by the nuclear forces to be able to escape easily, even though escape is energetically possible. The situations that allow the nuclei to change, possibly by the emission of α or β particles, occur in a completely random manner; it may take a microsecond, a second, a year, or a million years for the emission to take place. What is generally quoted for any radioactive isotope is its half-life: the time it takes for half of the nuclei in a large amount of the isotope to change by the emission of a particle or a ray.

The radioactive nuclei found in nature usually have very long half-lives—about a billion years. They were more plentiful when the earth was first created. U-235 has a half-life of 700 million years, while the half-life of U-238 is 4.5 billion years. These figures mean that a couple of billion years ago the percentage of U-235 in natural uranium was several times higher than it is now. In fact, there is evidence that about 1.8 billion years ago there was a natural reactor in Gabon in Africa. At that time, U-235 would have made up about 3% of natural uranium rather than 0.7% as it does today. Its presence is smaller now because it has decayed much faster than the more plentiful U-238.

Nuclear Energy

Nuclear forces bind the nucleons very tightly together, whereas the positive charges on some of the nucleons cause them to repel each other and tend to force them apart. Some nucleon combinations are held together much more strongly than others; nuclear power is derived from these differences.

To understand where the energy of nuclear interactions comes from, it is necessary to consider Einstein's formula for the relation between mass and energy, $E = mc^2$. Here E is the energy, m is the mass, and c is the velocity of light. The latter, c, is a constant, so this formula states that energy can be considered as proportional to mass. This implies that if, for example, you were to measure the mass of a relaxed spring, and if you then stretched it and measured its mass again, you would find the mass increased by an amount proportional to the amount of energy needed to stretch the spring. (This mass increase would be immeasurably small under any circumstances.) In the case of nucleons, if the force between them is attractive, and they mutually pull each other together, the total mass of the two nucleons when they are pulled together will be smaller than the mass of the two nucleons when they are apart. Pulling them apart against the nuclear force would be like stretching a spring and would result in increased mass.

The more attractive the forces, the more stable the nucleus. Knowing the mass of all nuclei, one can calculate how much less total mass (or energy) each nucleus has compared with the total mass of the individual nucleons of which it is made (or the nuclear binding energy). A useful way of displaying the results for a variety of nuclei is to take the total energy change for each nucleus (if it were broken up into its individual nucleons) and divide it by the number of nucleons in that nucleus to get the change of energy per nucleon. As figure 4 shows, this change, or apparent mass loss, as nucleons are combined to make a nucleus, is greatest in nuclei with about 50 to 100 nucleons. The energy figures in

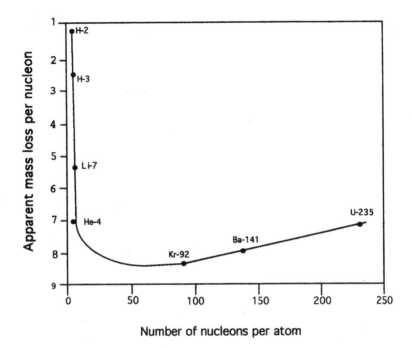

FIG. 4. Apparent loss per nucleon

From R. H. Flowers, "How Reactors Work," in W. Marshall, ed.,
Nuclear Power Technology, vol. 1, *Reactor Technology* (Oxford:
Oxford University Press, 1983), p. 7, fig. 1.3.
Reprinted by permission of Oxford University Press.

the chart are given in millions of electron volts, a unit very often used by nuclear physicists in discussing energy. (The standard term is *joule.*)

Energy is equal to a force applied over a distance. The size of the unit joule can be seen by the fact that a mass of one kilogram, moving at a velocity of one meter per second, has a kinetic energy of one-half joule. One *electron volt*, a very much smaller unit, is the kinetic energy that an electron would acquire in falling through a potential of one volt. (Electric voltage is also called potential because it expressed the potential work that an electric charge can do. The greater the voltage or potential, the more work the charge can do.) One electron volt (1 eV) is equal to 1.6×10^{-19} joules. It is a very small number, used primarily in calculations dealing with very small things. When dealing with atoms, energies are generally measured in electron volts, whereas with nuclei, millions of electron volts (MeV) are most often used (thousands of electron volts, or keV, are also commonly used units).

Referring again to figure 4, we see something very interesting: U-235 nucleons have about 7.2 MeV binding energy each, while those in the region of krypton and barium have about 8.2 MeV. If U-235 could be made to break up into krypton and barium, about 200 MeV of energy would be available. The krypton isotope produced could have a total of 92 nucleons—36 protons and 56 neutrons. The barium isotope could have a total of 141 nucleons—56 protons and 85 neutrons. Such a change can indeed take place; if you add one neutron to U-235 to make it U-236, it will become unstable and will often break into two parts or undergo fission. In the case of the example involving krypton and barium, three extra neutrons are also emitted. This type of fissioning is the source of the nuclear energy for reactors and for a uranium or plutonium bomb. Fission of fissile heavy elements results in a whole variety of elements; the krypton and barium used in the illustration are only a single pair of the possible fission products containing the number of protons and neutrons that might result from the fissioning of U-235. The distribution of these elements or fission fragments is shown in figure 5.

The final nuclei, such as krypton, are usually produced as very unstable isotopes. In about three seconds krypton 92 decays by emitting an electron and becomes rubidium 92. This similarly decays in about six seconds to become strontium 92. Strontium decays in about 2.7 hours to become ytrium, which decays in 3.5 hours to become zirconium, a stable element.

Cross Section

The fact that energy can be obtained from the fissioning of a nucleus is useful for producing nuclear energy only if we know how to cause that fissioning to occur. In the case just considered, a neutron must be added to U-235 to make it fission. If this addition takes place, the resulting fission might produce three extra neutrons, one of which might find its way to another U-235 nucleus to cause another fission and so on. The probability of any neutron's causing a nucleus to fission can be expressed by the concept of cross section. First, we consider total cross

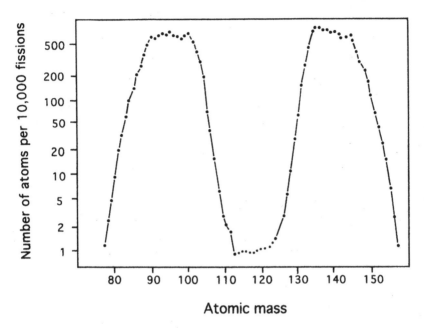

FIG. 5. Mass distribution of fission fragments

From R. H. Flowers, "How Reactors Work," in W. Marshall, ed.,
Nuclear Power Technology, vol. 1, *Reactor Technology* (Oxford:
Oxford University Press, 1983), p. 19, fig. 1.11 (a).
Reprinted by permission of Oxford University Press.

section. Imagine the nucleus as an object like a billiard ball, and a neutron as a marble. On a billiard table with several nuclei (billiard balls), one could estimate the probability of a marble's hitting one of them if it was shot across the table at random. This probability would be related to the combined diameters of the billiard balls and the marble. If, on the other hand, the billiard balls (nuclei) were suspended in space, the probability of a collision by a marble thrown through them would be related to the area of a circle with a radius equal to the sum of the radii of the marble and billiard ball. The cross section is the area of that circle. This billiard-ball analogy to the cross section for a neutron reaction cannot be taken literally, though it works fairly well when the size attributed to the neutron is very much smaller than that of the nucleus with which it is colliding.

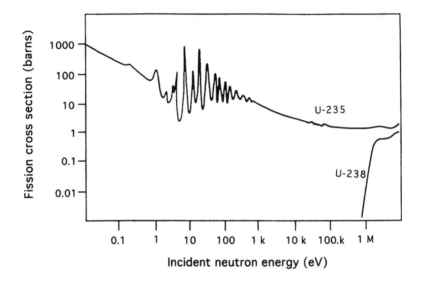

FIG. 6. Fission cross section of uranium
as a function of the energy of the incident neutrons

From R. H. Flowers, "How Reactors Work," in W. Marshall, ed.,
Nuclear Power Technology, vol. 1, *Reactor Technology* (Oxford:
Oxford University Press, 1983), p. 11, fig. 1.5 (a).
Reprinted by permission of Oxford University Press.

The term *partial cross section* is also used; one might think of a partial cross section as related to the probability that if a small area of one of the billiard balls were hit, this event would cause some reaction to occur. (This illustration cannot be taken literally.) The total cross section can then be thought of as made up of a combination of all the partial cross sections. In figures 6 and 7, two partial cross sections are shown as they change when the energy of the incident neutron is varied. These cross sections, the first being that for causing uranium to fission and the second that for the absorption of an incident neutron by uranium, are crucial to the process of producing usable nuclear energy.

When three neutrons are emitted from U-235, their chances of hitting another U-235 nucleus and causing another fission are therefore related to the cross section of U-235 for fission and the number of other nuclei around. Earlier, I gave a value for the radius of a uranium nucleus

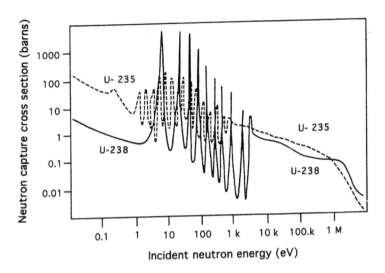

FIG. 7. Absorption cross section of uranium
as a function of the energy of the incident neutrons

From R. H. Flowers, "How Reactors Work," in W. Marshall, ed.,
Nuclear Power Technology, vol. 1, *Reactor Technology* (Oxford:
Oxford University Press, 1983), p. 11, fig. 1.5 (b).
Reprinted by permission of Oxford University Press.

as about 9×10^{-13} cm. Its total area would then be a bit smaller than 3×10^{-24} or 3 barns. (The unit of area *barn* probably got its name as a joking reference to its size: "as big as a barn door.") If we again look at figure 6, we can see how the cross section of U-235 for fission varies as a function of the energy of the incoming neutron; there we find values of nearly 1,000 barns, and these values are only for the partial cross section. The reason for this confusing latter fact is that in calculating the total cross section we must also take into account the size of the incident neutron: at low energies this becomes huge.

One of the consequences of quantum mechanics is that in dealing with the interactions of particles one must associate a wavelength with the moving particle; one cannot localize the particle to closer than its wavelength divided by 2π. The rule is $\lambda = h/p$, where λ is the wavelength, h is Planck's constant, and p is the momentum of the moving

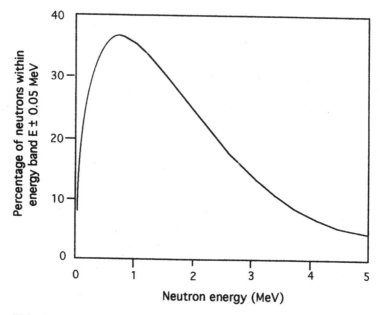

FIG. 8. Energy spectrum of neutrons emitted by fissioning U-235

From R. H. Flowers, "How Reactors Work," in W. Marshall, ed.,
Nuclear Power Technology, vol. 1, *Reactor Technology* (Oxford:
Oxford University Press, 1983), p. 12, fig. 1.7.
Reprinted by permission of Oxford University Press.

particle. (Planck's constant is at the heart of any quantum-mechanical evaluation.) λ effectively gives a minimum radius to the colliding particle, and a measurement of nuclear interactions can result in nuclear areas very much larger than those mentioned earlier as characteristic of the hydrogen and uranium nuclei.

The chance of a neutron's hitting a U-235 nucleus and causing it to fission is much greater if the neutron is very slow. Figure 8 shows the energy spectrum of neutrons emitted by fissioning U-235. We see that the neutrons are emitted at energies that vary from zero to over 5 meV, but that the largest number are emitted at an energy a little below 1 MeV. Because large cross sections occur at much lower energies, it is desirable to slow down the emitted neutrons.

Slowing Down Neutrons

A neutron can be slowed down by causing it to collide with a nucleus, thereby giving the nucleus some of its energy. As an illustration, consider the neutron and the nucleus it hits to be perfectly elastic. If the neutron hits a very heavy nucleus head-on, it will act like a ball hitting a brick wall. The neutron will bounce back with the same energy it had before it hit. If it hits a nucleus of exactly the same weight as itself, it can lose a lot of energy; if it does not give it a glancing blow, but hits it head-on, it will lose all of its energy to the other nucleon, just as occurs with billiard balls when one hits another. This special case of a head-on collision can be expressed with a simple mathematical expression:

$$E_1'/E_1 = (M_1 - M_2)^2/(M_1 + M_2)^2.$$

Here E_1 is the neutron's energy before the collision, E_1' the energy after the collision, and M_1 and M_2 are the masses of, respectively, the neutron and the particle it hits. It can be seen that for $M_1 = M_2$, E_1' is zero. This would be the case for a neutron that hits a proton. If it were to hit a deuteron with twice its mass, $E_1'/E_1 = (-1)^2/3^2 = 1/9$. If it were to hit carbon, whose mass is 12 times as big, $E_1'/E_1 = (-11)^2/13^2 = 0.72$. See figure 9. If it hits uranium, whose mass is about 238 times as big, $E_1'/E_1 = 0.98$; that is, only 2% of the energy is lost. To slow down neutrons by causing only a small number of collisions, a light element is needed, called a *moderator*.

Absorption

A neutron would be slowed down after making a few hundred collisions with uranium nuclei, but even so, each time it hit it would still have a chance of producing a reaction other than that of fission or an elastic bounce. In particular, there is very little chance for neutrons below an energy of about 1 MeV to cause U-238 to fission, but there is a cross section of about ⅓ barn for the neutron to be captured by the U-238, thus causing it to become U-239. This chance (cross section) of capture would rise to a few barns at what are called thermal energies. Thermal energies are energies so low that the average neutron energy is the same as the heat energy of the atoms of the material it is hitting. (Every atom

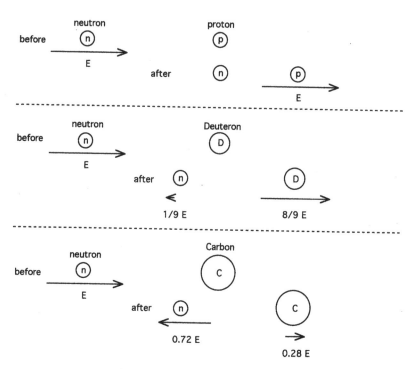

FIG. 9. Energy and direction of a neutron
after a head-on collision with a nucleus

in a material can be thought of as moving randomly, with the energy of movement increasing as the material becomes hotter.) If a neutron were to bounce off of U-238 nuclei many times, there would be a good chance that it would be absorbed by one of the nuclei it hits and never survive to cause more fissions or a chain reaction. From the point of view of a nation trying to build an atomic bomb, however, this absorption is of interest for producing plutonium. The U-239 produced by the absorption decays by emitting an electron and becomes neptunium 239, which in turn decays to become the desired plutonium 239.

All sorts of materials can capture neutrons. The stainless steel that might be used in the construction of a reactor can capture them, and so can the hydrogen that is a part of the water used to cool a reactor. Heavy hydrogen (deuterium) and carbon can capture neutrons, but only with very small cross sections.

Chain Reactions

There are many chemical chain reactions. A wood fire in the fireplace is one example. If wood is heated until it is very hot, it will emit gases that burn and heat it even more, producing more gases. Placing two logs together allows the heat of one log to heat the other. Having the fire in an enclosure like a stove or fireplace allows the walls to reflect the heat back and contribute to the chain reaction.

When the German scientists Otto Hahn and Lise Meitner discovered fission in 1938, it became crucial to find out how many neutrons were emitted in each occurrence. The average number, it was later found, was slightly more than two; had the average been less than one, there would have been no way of ever producing a nuclear chain reaction.

Let us examine a crude example, in which U-235 fissions, emitting two neutrons, both of which survive to be absorbed by other U-235 nuclei, and so forth. In eighty generations, requiring a time of about a microsecond, 1.2×10^{24} fissions would have taken place (if there were enough U-235), producing an energy equivalent to that of about 9,000 metric tons of explosive. Actual uranium bombs are not this efficient: they release only about 30% of the energy available.

The nuclei that are readily able to undergo fission and sustain a chain reaction, such as U-233, U-235, Pu-239, and Pu-241, are called fissile nuclei; those that can be converted into fissile nuclei by the absorption of a neutron, such as U-238 and thorium 232, are called fertile nuclei.

SOURCES OF URANIUM

In the years before the Second World War, uranium was processed for the radium that was found in it. A Czechoslovakian plant was started in 1904; ore from Colorado was processed in Denver beginning in 1913; in the 1920s a plant was built in the Congo region (Democratic Republic of Congo, known 1971–97 as Zaire); and the Canadian deposits at Great Bear Lake were first used in 1933. Aside from its value as a source of radium, uranium was a source of yellow and green color for ceramics and was used in steel alloys. Once it had been processed, most of the uranium mined for its radium content ended up in waste piles, which were to provide a valuable resource for the Manhattan Project during World War II.

At the end of the war, there was little knowledge of how widespread useful uranium-ore deposits were. Only certain types of pitchblende (UO_2 + UO_3) deposits were believed to contain it in useful quantities. For a short time, the United States attempted to monopolize the known deposits as a way of preventing proliferation of nuclear weapons. Because of the demand created by the use of nuclear power, methods were developed for obtaining uranium from the great variety of ore types that exist, and it became clear that a monopoly on all of these was not possible. Uranium occurs in various amounts everywhere in the world. The earth's crust contains about forty times as much uranium as silver, and about one-tenth as much as copper. Low-silica igneous rocks contain about 1 part per million (ppm); high-silica rocks, 4 ppm. Ocean water contains about 0.002 ppm.

Many sources of uranium in useful concentration are available. The major commercially useful types are pitchblende and uraninite (a similar ore with a different ratio of the oxides). These and other, less-common types are found in large quantities in northern Australia, Gabon, Niger, the Congo, the Czech Republic, France, Portugal, Spain, Canada, England, Argentina, Brazil, and several parts of the United States. Some of South Africa's ore is of low grade, mixed with its gold deposits, but it is commercially useful because it is a by-product of gold mining, which reduces its cost. Russia, Ukraine, Kazakhstan, China, and Korea have useful sources. Nations with commercially useful sources of uranium are listed in table 1. (Not all make commercial use of uranium ore.)

The extraction of uranium from ore is not technically demanding. For ores in which the uranium-bearing material is mixed with other minerals, the first step is sorting: lumps of the ore are spread on a slow-moving conveyor belt, and those with some radioactivity are selected. In some cases, this selection can be done by weight, using a crude centrifuge system.

Next, the radioactive ore is crushed into fine grains. The uranium is generally separated from its ore by leaching the ore with acid, usually sulphuric acid. (The reaction is $6H_2SO_4 + 3MnO_2 + 3UO_2 \rightarrow 3UO_2SO_4 + 3MnSO_4 + 6H_2O$.) If the uranium is contained in a mixture with a high lime content, an alkaline leach is used. After the uranium has been separated from other material in this way it must be precipitated out of the solution; this separation is sometimes accomplished with the use of

TABLE 1.

Nations with Economically Useful Uranium Reserves, 1981

Country	Estimated Uranium Reserves (thousands of metric tons)	Country	Estimated Uranium Reserves (thousands of metric tons)
Algeria	26	Kazakstan	—
Argentina	43	Korea, North	—
Australia	602	Korea, South	11
Brazil	200	Kyrgystan	—
Canada	1,020	Mexico	9
Central African Republic	18	Namibia	188
Chad	—	Niger	213
Congo	—	Portugal	11
Czech Republic	—	Russia	—
Denmark	43	Somalia	10
Estonia	—	South Africa	530
Finland	3	Spain	25
France	120	Sweden	82
Gabon	32	Tadjikstan	—
Germany	14	Turkey	5
Greece	13	Ukraine	—
India	57	U.K.	7
Italy	4	United States	1,700
Japan	8	Uzbekistan	—

Source: Data from Organization for Economic Cooperation and Development and International Atomic Energy Agency, *Uranium: Resources, Production and Demand* (Paris, 1982), pp. 18–19.

resins. What results is generally a complex solid of varying composition, called yellowcake; it may contain U_3O_8 or $Na_2U_2O_7$. This marketable commodity is then brought to another plant for further purification.

Pure uranium metal is not a good reactor fuel because of its unusual change in crystalline structure and density with variations in temperature and radiation: an orthorhombic structure occurs up to a temperature of 667°C, a tetragonal structure from 667 to 774°C, and a body-centered cubic structure from 774 to 1132°C; the last is of lower density than the lower-temperature material, whereas the first two expand directionally. Bare uranium metal is also attacked by water and evolves hydrogen—a process that can be very dangerous.

For most reactors, fuel in the form of sintered uranium dioxide, UO_2, is used. (To *sinter* is to heat a grainy material until the particles fuse into a solid.) This has a high melting point, 2760°C, and a cubic crystalline structure that gives it uniform expansion properties. It must be kept from contact with air because it can react with oxygen to form a higher oxide. In all of the fuel processing, a very high standard of purity must be maintained because any contaminants may be strong neutron absorbers and thus render the uranium fuel useless.

As pointed out earlier, commercially useful uranium ore is spread worldwide. Some of the less developed nations may market it only in the form of yellowcake; the more developed ones will also have it available in a purer form such as uranium metal, uranium dioxide, or uranium hexafluoride. Trade at the yellowcake level of processing is not controlled by the International Atomic Energy Agency (IAEA).

3

Plutonium Production
in Nuclear Reactors

PLUTONIUM AND NUCLEAR WEAPONS

Most nuclear weapons use the plutonium produced in a nuclear reactor as the fissile material. This plutonium is produced when a U-238 nucleus absorbs a neutron to become U-239, this nucleus decays in a short time by β^- emission to become neptunium 239, and this, in turn, decays to give Pu-239. Usually, nuclear reactors use the energy they produce to generate electrical power. These reactors, however, also produce plutonium whenever they operate.[1]

The difficulty of making a nuclear explosion from plutonium led the United States to make a test explosion in New Mexico on July 16, 1945, almost a month before a uranium weapon (a previously untested device) was exploded over Hiroshima and a second plutonium bomb set off over Nagasaki. The Soviet Union's first atomic bomb, made with plutonium, was tested on August 29, 1949. (The Soviets had a program for enriching uranium to produce a weapon, but difficulties they encountered in the gaseous-diffusion enrichment process delayed the test of a weapon with uranium in it for two years.) A second weapon, again with plutonium, was tested on September 24, 1951, and a third, with a mixed uranium-plutonium core, in October of the same year. Great Britain's first atomic bomb was also made of plutonium and was exploded at a test site on the Monte Bello Islands off the west coast of Australia in October 1952. France exploded its first nuclear weapon, using plutonium, in February 1960 at a test site in Algeria, and India exploded its first weapon, also of plutonium, in 1974. It has been postulated that the untested Israeli weapons are also made of plutonium, and that North Korea was at one point planning to make a plutonium weapon. Making a nuclear weapon using either enriched uranium or plutonium is very difficult. Using plutonium was apparently easiest for these nations.

Simplified Reactor Theory

The description of nuclear reactors that follows focuses largely on their use for plutonium production. Nations that want to secretly produce plutonium justify their construction of reactors by pointing to their need to produce isotopes for medical purposes or, possibly, to their need for electrical power. In reactors that fill the latter need, the heat caused by nuclear fission (instead of heat from burning coal, gas, or oil) is used to boil water to produce steam for producing electrical power. See figure 10.

In order to have a chain reaction, uranium with some content of U-235 is needed, and with most reactors, a moderator will be used to slow down the neutrons from fissioning U-235 to make them more effective. The neutrons are slowed to "thermal" energies, which means that the neutrons are of the same energy, the heat energy, as the atoms they hit. In the type of thermal reactor most commonly used, ordinary water serves as both the moderator and the method of carrying off the heat. Heavy water, made of deuterium and oxygen, D_2O rather than H_2O, can also be used. Heavy water is superior as a moderator because the deuterium does not readily absorb neutrons, whereas hydrogen can fairly easily absorb a neutron to become deuterium. With heavy water as a moderator, it is possible to operate a reactor using natural uranium, which contains only 0.7% uranium 235. In a reactor using ordinary water as a moderator, many of the neutrons are lost in the moderator, so not as many neutrons are available to carry on the chain reaction. To increase the chance that a U-235 nucleus will be hit by one of the reduced number of neutrons, it is necessary to use uranium with a content of U-235 larger than the 0.7% present in natural uranium—generally, 3–4%. Light water is preferred to heavy water because it is cheaper. Before World War II, heavy water sold for $14 an ounce, or $500,000 a metric ton. Although it is much cheaper now, about $60,000 a ton (or about what one would pay for a very expensive wine), some losses are inevitable, and its replenishment can add significantly to operating costs.

American commercial reactors invariably use light water as a moderator. The most commercially viable reactor moderated with heavy water is the Canadian-deuterium-uranium or CANDU reactor. A third type of reactor uses graphite as a moderator. The advantages of using graphite are similar to those of using heavy water: very pure graphite also has a

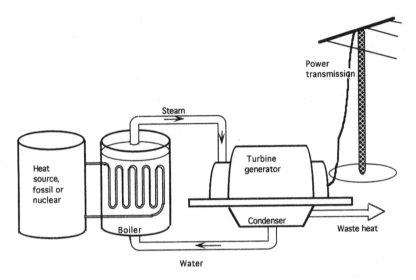

FIG. 10. Power plant

very low cross section for absorbing neutrons, and its use as a moderator also allows the use of natural uranium as a reactor fuel. The first reactor that Enrico Fermi brought into operation under the University of Chicago football stadium in 1942 used graphite as a moderator, as did the U.S. reactors used for the military production of plutonium, the infamous Chernobyl reactor, and many other reactors in the former Soviet Union. Whatever the type of reactor, all of those using uranium as a fuel produce plutonium as the neutrons from the chain reaction hit and are absorbed by the uranium 238.

The chain reaction by which the neutrons from one fissioning atom cause more than one other atom to fission must be controlled, or the reactor will melt down. Control of the fissioning action is maintained by inserting rods of neutron-absorbing material into the reactor's core of uranium and moderator to prevent neutron multiplication. Boron is most commonly used, although the use of cadmium, europium, or gadolinium is also possible. If the chain reaction does not cause at least one new nucleus to fission for every previous one, the number of neutrons will decrease, whereas if more than one is made to fission, the number of ensuing fissions increases, sometimes moving suddenly to a dangerously

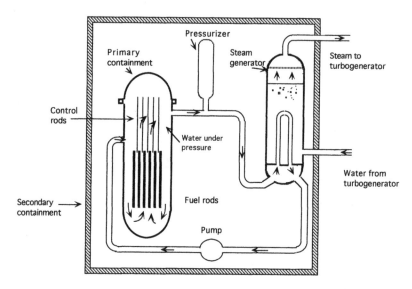

FIG. 11. Pressurized-water reactor

high level. The idea is to reach a high power and then keep the number of new fissions exactly the same as the old. This balancing act is made easier by the presence of what are called delayed neutrons. About 1% of the neutrons from fission are emitted a few seconds after the fissioning has taken place. They are not a result of the fissioning itself, but come from isotopes made as a result of fissioning. The control rods of reactors are set so that the number of new neutrons produced is slightly less than the old. The delayed neutrons then bring the ratio of new to old to exactly one. The delay gives time for the control rods, with their neutron-absorbing material, to make the necessary adjustment.

TYPES OF NUCLEAR REACTORS

Light-Water-Moderated Reactors

Light-water-moderated reactors are of two types: the pressurized-water reactor (PWR) and the boiling-water reactor (BWR). These reactors are typically designed to operate at a thermal power level of about 3,900 megawatts (MWt) yielding electrical power of about 1,300 megawatts (MWe). In both reactors, the uranium fuel is encased in tubing that can

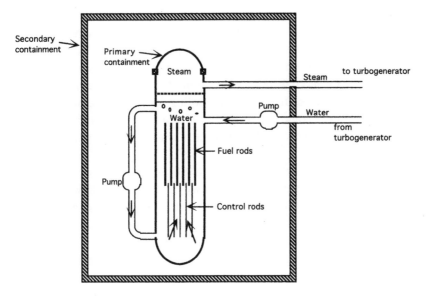

FIG. 12. Boiling-water reactor

withstand the high temperatures and severe neutron flux of the reactor. The tubing, generally a special stainless steel or an alloy of zirconium, prevents contamination of the moderator and coolant by the fission products. It must be strong enough to withstand the internal pressure of the expanding high-temperature uranium dioxide and the pressure of the gaseous fission products, such as krypton. Uranium dioxide, UO_2, is used instead of uranium metal, which would expand a great deal under the high temperatures used and the radiation present, and which furthermore undergoes a strong reaction when exposed to water.

Water is circulated past the encased uranium rods to cool them, and the same or additional water acts as a moderator to slow down the neutrons produced by fissioning U-235. The slower neutrons have a greater chance of interacting with other U-253 atoms they hit, and this causes more fissioning. In a PWR the hot water may be under a pressure of about 150 atmospheres, so that its boiling point is higher than the temperature at which the reactor operates (over 300°C). This hot water circulates past a heat exchanger, where it transfers its heat to water that is under a much lower pressure, possibly only 60 atmospheres. The high-pressure steam thus produced is used to power turbines to produce electricity.

High-temperature steam is needed to operate a turbine efficiently, and the temperature inside the uranium dioxide reactor fuel is very much higher still. The temperature available for the steam is, therefore, determined by the ability of the material that encases the uranium to withstand this very corrosive environment, and by the ability of the reactor to contain the high-pressure cooling water. If the temperature of the cooling water could be raised, the efficiency would be increased, but this would in turn raise the temperature of the fuel, possibly to a dangerous level.

The boiling-water reactor operates in the same way as the pressurized-water reactor, except that the water used for cooling is allowed to boil after it has removed the heat from the reactor, and the resulting steam is used to operate the turbines. The temperature at the surface of the encased uranium dioxide is lower than it is in a PWR.

The fuel in these reactors is, typically, enclosed in rods about a centimeter in diameter and about three meters in active length. The rods are assembled in bundles, and control rods are inserted into the bundles.

Because high pressure is required to prevent the cooling water from boiling when it comes into contact with the fuel rods, the whole reactor must be enclosed in a steel vessel that can withstand pressures of approximately 100 atmospheres, or 1,500 pounds per square inch. In the case of a high-power pressurized-water reactor, the steel reactor vessel may measure thirteen meters high, six meters in diameter, and over twenty centimeters thick.

Heavy-Water-Moderated Reactors

The CANDU reactor, the Canadian deuterium-moderated reactor, is of very different design. In a reactor, heavy water is superior to regular water because neutrons are absorbed by the deuterium much less often than they would be by the hydrogen of light water, so far fewer neutrons are lost as they are being slowed down. As a result, it is possible to use ordinary unenriched uranium (containing 0.7% U-235), rather than the 3–4%-enriched uranium needed for the operation of a light-water-moderated reactor. However, there is a penalty (in addition to the greater cost of the heavy water): heavy water is less effective in slowing neutrons than light water, and a larger volume of heavy water is therefore required. This means that, given similar reactor designs, with differences being merely of scale, the heavy-water reactor would need a much larger pressure vessel, which would be harder to make safe. To solve this problem, each fuel bundle of a CANDU reactor is surrounded separately by its own high-pressure cooling tube. This can be of reasonably small diameter and wall thickness. Neutrons can readily penetrate this tube to the low-pressure heavy-water moderator outside. The result is that very high pressure on the cooling system can be maintained safely, despite the large size of the whole structure.

Because the CANDU reactor uses unenriched uranium with about one-fourth the U-235 content of the enriched fuel used in light-water reactors, it uses up its fuel at a higher rate; this must be replaced regularly. In light-water reactors, about one-quarter of the most depleted fuel is replaced once a year. This involves shutting down the reactor, allowing it to cool off, removing the top of the pressure vessel, and changing a whole group of fuel rods. For the CANDU, the separate pressurizing tube for each fuel bundle makes it possible to change one fuel bundle at a time, and to do so without shutting down the reactor. The implications of continuous reactor operation with regard to proliferation will be discussed later in this chapter. Those reactors typically operate at about 2,000 MWt, giving about 600 MWe.

Gas-Cooled, Graphite-Moderated Reactors

In the third form of nuclear reactor using thermal neutrons, graphite is used as the moderator. Because graphite is a less effective moderator than heavy water, the size of the moderator and of the total system needs to be even larger than for the CANDU. The graphite and the fuel rods can be cooled with helium or carbon dioxide; either gas can be used to supply heat to boilers for running the power turbines. In a variant of this design, the fuel (contained in small ceramic-encased seeds) can be spread throughout the graphite, and the whole cooled by gas. In a gas-cooled reactor it is possible to go to higher temperatures than it is with a water-cooled reactor. In the latter, pressure must be applied to keep the water from boiling when it comes into contact with the fuel rods, and this pressure must be much greater than that needed to contain a gas at the same temperature. Although the gas is not as effective as water in carrying off heat, the large size of the graphite reactor allows a large volume of gas to be used for the cooling. Graphite, like heavy water, does not absorb neutrons as much as light water does, and can operate with natural, unenriched uranium. In a graphite-moderated reactor, as in the CANDU, the fuel rods can be removed individually without shutting down the reactor. Commercial versions of these reactors operate in the 300–600 MWe region.

This reactor and the other "thermal" reactors described here are the common types used throughout the world to generate electric power. An accident in such reactors cannot produce a nuclear explosion because the interactions of the neutrons producing fission take place too slowly. To produce a nuclear explosion the fissioning material must stay together long enough for the neutrons released by the fission process to produce a continually increasing series of fissions until an appreciable part of the fissile material has fissioned. In nuclear weapons the typical interaction time of a neutron is 10^{-8} seconds, and the entire explosion takes place in a microsecond. The inertia of the bomb material holds it together long enough for the interactions to take place. With a thermal reactor, on the other hand, a typical neutron interaction requires 2×10^{-4} seconds; the interactions are twenty thousand times slower than those needed for a nuclear weapon. If one tried to make a nuclear explosion by removing the control rods instantaneously, a tremendous surge of power would take place and the heat generated would change the shape and activity of the reactor so that it would no longer function. The results would be catastrophic—the reactor would be destroyed and large amounts of radioactivity would be released—but would not involve a nuclear explosion.

The accident with the Chernobyl reactor is by far the worst such accident that has ever occurred, but no nuclear explosion took place there. An explosion blew the 1000-ton safety shield off the top of the reactor, but that explosion resulted from steam produced when the molten fuel rods came in contact with water. An additional explosion was caused by hydrogen gas formed by a reaction between the intensely hot fragmented protective surfaces of the fuel rods and the cooling water.[2] These were huge conventional explosions; the terrible effect of the Chernobyl disaster was the release of about 50 million curies of radioactivity into the air, which dangerously contaminated large areas of Belarus and Ukraine and spread a lower level of contamination to many parts of Europe and Russia.

TABLE 2

Characteristics of Thermal and High-Energy
Neutrons for Selected Isotopes

Isotope	Thermal Neutrons			High-Energy Neutrons		
	η	σ_f	σ_c	η	σ_f	σ_c
Th-232	—	0	7.6	2.3	0.01	0.35
U-233	2.29	527	54	2.5	2.8	0.3
U-235	2.07	579	100	2.5	2.0	0.5
U-238	—	0	2.7	2.75	0.05	0.3
Pu-239	2.11	741	267	2.9	1.9	0.6
Pu-241	2.15	1009	361	2.73	2.6	—

Fast Breeder Reactors

The word *fast* in the designation *fast breeder reactor* refers to the neutrons; *breeder* refers to the ability of such a reactor to produce more fissile material than it burns up. Thermal reactors rely on the large U-235 cross section for fission by low-energy neutrons, which allows such reactors to work with even less than 1% U-235 in the fuel. The reactors must be of large size to accommodate the moderator, which must be present to slow down the neutrons coming from the fissioning uranium. However, with sufficient U-235 in the fuel, it is possible for a reactor to operate without slowed-down neutrons. The fission caused by fast (high-energy) neutrons produces more new neutrons than that caused by slow (thermal) neutrons, as can be seen in table 2. The symbol η (*eta*) represents the number of neutrons produced per number of neutrons absorbed in fissile or fissionable material; σ_f and σ_c are, respectively, the cross sections (in barns) for fissioning and fissionless neutron capture.

Both the cross section for fission and the number of neutrons produced in each fission are important for keeping a chain reaction going in a reactor. In table 2, the superiority of Pu-239 over U-235 can be seen for both thermal and high-energy neutrons. For both of these elements the fission cross section is hundreds of times higher for thermal neutrons than for high-energy neutrons. Therefore, in order for a reactor to operate with fast neutrons, much more U-235 or Pu-239 must be present and must be very concentrated so that any neutrons produced by the fissile material will have a good chance of hitting other fissile material before leaking out of the reactor.

Mixed oxide fuels—for example, a mixture of 20% PuO_2 and 80% UO_2—are used in fast breeder reactors. Depleted uranium—uranium from which the U-235 has been removed—is also used. The dimensions (length, diameter) of the active fuel for high-power fast reactors are typically less than a meter, compared with a few meters for a light-water reactor and several meters for graphite-moderated reactors. It is essential that the materials used in a fast reactor do not slow down the neutrons and thus reduce the yield of neutrons from each fission. Because of the limited fuel dimensions, a special cooling medium that can carry large amounts of heat is needed. Liquid sodium is often used, both for its cooling properties and because it does not greatly slow down the neutrons.

Fast reactors can be used for breeding plutonium—that is, for making more plutonium than they use. If the chain reaction is to be kept up, one of the neutrons produced must be used to produce another fission. If an amount of plutonium is to be produced equal to the amount of U-235 or plutonium fissioned, at least one other neutron must be captured by U-238 to make Pu-239. Some neutrons will be absorbed by other elements in the reactor, so η, the number of neutrons produced per neutron absorbed, must be greater than 2.

The use of breeder reactors would make all uranium useful in power production, not just the 0.7% U-235 found in nature. Breeder reactors have been operated successfully in France. The United States decided to stop its breeder-reactor program, in part because a nuclear-energy program based on plutonium poses the danger of plutonium theft. The program shutdown was also induced in part by the availability of cheap uranium.

Thorium Reactors

Another look at table 2 shows the possibility of making a reactor that uses thorium and U-233, instead of using U-238 and either plutonium or U-235. If thorium 232 (Th-232), the naturally occuring isotope of thorium, absorbs a neutron to become Th-233, it decays by emitting a negative electron to become protactinium 233, and this in turn decays to produce stable U-233—in complete parallel to the production of plutonium through the capture of a neutron by U-238.

To start this reaction, however, one first must have some U-233, which does not occur naturally. The system can be bootstrapped by using U-235 (or plutonium) as the fissile material until the thorium reactor can breed its own U-233. Experimental work on this type of reactor has been done at the Oak Ridge National Laboratory; this work is of great interest to India, which has a plentiful supply of thorium ore but very little uranium.

REACTOR CONSTRUCTION BY LESS-DEVELOPED NATIONS

The design of a nuclear reactor can be greatly simplified if the reactor is not to be used for producing electric power. This is not just because the turbines and generators are no longer needed. Even more important is the fact that the reactor no longer needs to operate at a high temperature for reasonable efficiency.

If an underdeveloped nation wanted to build a reactor for plutonium production itself instead of having one built for it by a more developed country, it would probably choose to follow the design of the original reactor built by Enrico Fermi at the University of Chicago in 1942. This likelihood was pointed out by the late J. R. Lamarsh, of the Department of Nuclear Engineering at the Polytechnic Institute of New York, in testimony before the Joint Committee on Atomic Energy, in which he said that a reactor similar to the Brookhaven graphite research reactor (which is derived from the Fermi original) might be built in a few years' time by an underdeveloped nation.[3] The technology is by no means as complex as that of the commercial reactors now being built. Most of the construction materials are readily available. The reactor would not have to produce any power; radiation containment and safety standards would not have to be very effective. Complete and accurate descriptions of the Brookhaven reactor are available.

Lamarsh pointed out that it is necessary for a country working outside of IAEA constraints to use natural uranium to produce plutonium. Only two types of moderator are possible for a reactor that can use natural uranium: heavy water or graphite. Heavy water is under the control of the IAEA; building a plant to produce it would be very expensive and would also require a lot of technological assistance. Although the graphite used in reactors must be very pure (in particular, it must have no boron contamination), such graphite is manufactured from petroleum coke or coal-tar pitch and is similar to electrode graphite, which is manufactured in many parts of the world. Union Carbide, for example, has subsidiaries manufacturing electrode graphite in Brazil, Canada, Italy, Japan, Mexico, Puerto Rico, South Africa, Spain, and Sweden.

The Brookhaven reactor produced 30 megawatts of power and could make about 9 kilograms of plutonium a year.[4] It was air-cooled and consisted of a 25-foot cube of graphite, with 1,369 three-inch-diameter air channels penetrating it. Eleven-foot-long aluminum tubes, each containing thirty-three 4-inch-long, 1.1-inch-diameter uranium slugs, were placed in most of these channels. The graphite cube was split in two to allow air to be blown into the center and then out through the cooling tubes. The hot air produced was then vented to the atmosphere through a filter, using a 320-foot stack. Control was maintained by means of sixteen steel rods, 2-inch square by 16-foot, containing 1.75% boron. Emergency control was effected by dumping boron shot into holes at the top of the reactor.

Lamarsh also pointed out that because there is very little excess reactivity in a graphite reactor, control is not difficult. The speed of operation of control rods needed is not as high as that required for water-cooled power reactors. Air is also less corrosive than water at the temperature of operation, 300°F (although at very much higher temperatures air could support a huge fire in the graphite).

Although the Brookhaven reactor was elaborately controlled and instrumented, with impressive filtering to prevent the escape of any radioactive elements in the cooling air, an underdeveloped country might feel that such controls were not necessary for a reactor at a remote site.

The specifications of the Brookhaven reactor are as follows:

Power	30 MW
Plutonium	9 kg/year
Fuel (natural uranium)	60 tons
Moderator (graphite)	700 tons
Coolant (air)	300,000 cubic feet per minute
Fan power	5 MW
Exit air temperature	330°F
Control	steel rods containing boron
Reflector	4.5 feet of graphite
Shielding	iron plate plus 4.5 feet of concrete

Lamarsh estimates the professional engineering requirements for designing and constructing the reactor as follows: one civil-structural engineer
for structures and reactor building; one electrical engineer for control,
instrumentation, and circuitry; two mechanical engineers for heat transfer and mechanical devices; one metallurgist for uranium production;
and three nuclear engineers for design theory, nuclear measurements,
and reactor-heat transfer. Lamarsh felt that such a group of professionals
could supervise the design and construction of the reactor and uranium
mill in about three years.

His cost estimate (in 1976) was about $10 million plus labor. This
would be about $22 million now, plus some allowance for arrangements
for secrecy and the difficulty of getting materials. This estimate seems
low if one considers that the Brookhaven reactor cost $25.5 million in
1951 dollars; the cost breakdown was as follows:

Reactor	$9.3 million
Reactor building	3.0
Air-cooling system	3.8
Reactor laboratories	5.8
Site development	3.6
	———
Total	$25.5

In 1998 dollars, this would be about $275 million. This cost included
many facilities for research, and the design had to take into account the
location of the reactor near population centers on Long Island, but even
if we reduce the cost by a factor of two in order to take this into account,
we are left with a considerable discrepancy. A cross-sectional diagram of
the Brookhaven reactor is given in figure 13.

Such a reactor would be hard to keep hidden. Although the active
part of the reactor takes up a space about 25 by 25 by 25 feet, the
shielding and access needed would require that the building housing it
be much larger. The Brookhaven reactor itself had inside shielding 55
feet long, 37 feet 6 inches wide, and 33 feet 7 inches high. The dimensions of the reactor building were about three times this size; such a
structure would be impossible to conceal. During construction, the purchase of tons of uranium and graphite as well as large cooling fans would
be difficult to hide. In operation, the hot air ejected by the cooling fans

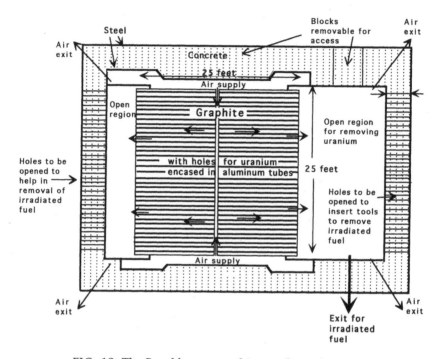

FIG. 13. The Brookhaven graphite-moderated reactor.
The reactor is much more complex than this diagram indicates.
A large fraction of the holes in the graphite are not occupied by
uranium fuel but are filled with additional graphite. After removal,
irradiated fuel is dropped into a water tank below.

would be detectable. Even the 5 MW of power needed for the fans would require input power lines or large motors or motor generators. So even though this type of reactor seems to offer a method of proliferation, the building of one could be undertaken only by a country that feels itself secure against any reprisal.

CHEMICAL REPROCESSING OF REACTOR FUEL

For a less-developed country, separating the plutonium produced in the fuel rods of a reactor from the uranium and fission products would be a difficult process. The actual chemical process is not in itself very difficult; the problem is with the high radioactivity of the products of fission. Every fission usually produces two unstable radioactive elements. Each may undergo two or three decays before evolving into a stable element. When a reactor is shut down, with the chain reaction stopped so that fissioning no longer takes place, these decays continue to generate heat—at first, at about 7 to 10% of the reactor's previous level.

When fuel rods are removed in order to be processed chemically to produce plutonium, about 150 days are usually allowed for the radioactivity to decay. At first the intense radioactivity of the fuel is due to the short-half-life isotopes. As they decay and disappear, the radioactivity decreases and isotopes with longer half-lives are dominant. Typical curves for this decay are shown in figure 14. After a few minutes, elements with half-lives of hours are the most radioactive; after a few hours, elements with half-lives of days are radioactively dominant. (Note that the curves are plotted on a logarithmic scale.) The radioactivity then continues to decrease, requiring about three years to be reduced by another 90% (to about 0.3% of its original value). Used fuel will usually be left to cool off for about 150 days before it is reprocessed; if it is left longer, a buildup of Pu-238 occurs because of decays from other heavy elements produced in the fuel rods.[5] Pu-238 is undesirable as part of a weapon because it fissions spontaneously at a very high rate, producing neutrons that can set off a nuclear explosion early when the weapon is detonated.

The problems of chemical separation will be described here from the point of view of a nation that has built a low-power graphite reactor such as the one just discussed. The amount of radioactivity of the fission products will be proportional to the amount of plutonium produced, and the fuel rods from this low-power reactor will be far less radioactive than those from a reactor of higher power. A reactor such as the one described earlier would use 60 metric tons of natural uranium and produce about 9 kilograms of plutonium a year. The amount of U-235 used during a year would be about 11 kilograms, and this would also be the weight of fission products produced.

According to estimates from higher-power reactors, operating this reactor for a year would cause a radioactivity of about 50 million curies. (A *curie* is a unit of radioactivity, producing 3.7×10^{10} radioactive disintegrations per second.) This figure does not in itself tell us how much radiation hazard there is. The radioactivity is spread over 60 metric tons of uranium fuel and about 1,370 fuel rods. Two-thirds of the radiation is

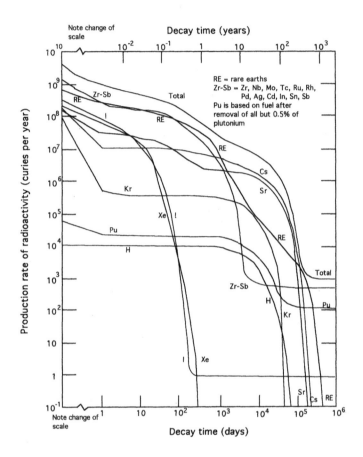

FIG. 14. Decay curves of fission products: RE = rare earths;
Zr−Sb = Zr, Nb, Mo, Tc, Ru, Rh, Pd, Ag, Cd, In, Sn, Sb;
Pu is based on fuel after removal of all but 0.5% of plutonium.

From T. H. Pigford, M. J. Keaton, B. J. Mann, P. M. Cukor, and G. I. Sessler,
"Fuel Cycles for Electric Power Generation," Report no. EEEP101, in
Comprehensive Standards: The Power Generation Case, EPA no. 69-01-0561
(Washington, D.C.: Office of Research and Development,
Environmental Protection Agency, March 1975), p. 50, fig. 2.2

in the form of electrons and α particles, and these are not able to penetrate even thin shields. A 1-MeV electron will be absorbed by a few millimeters of aluminum, and 5-MeV α particles would not even penetrate a piece of paper. During the handling of the fuel rods and the chemical processing, the dangerous radiation is the γ-rays, which may make up about a third of the total activity.

If a fuel rod was removed before it had a chance to cool, it would emit about 6,000 curies of γ-rays. Over half of these would be absorbed by the fuel itself. At a distance of one meter, the fuel rod would produce about 1,000 rem per hour. The radiation to which a human being is exposed is commonly expressed in a unit called a *rem* (from "roentgen equivalent man"). The *roentgen* unit, named after Wilhelm Conrad Roentgen, who discovered x-rays in 1895, is an amount of x-radiation that will produce 2.08×10^9 ion pairs per cubic centimeter of dry air at 0°C and 1 atmosphere of pressure. For materials other than air, and for any kind of radiation, the unit *rad* is used, which represents the deposition of 100 ergs, or 10^{-5} joules, of energy in a gram of material. For x-rays this represents almost the same amount of radiation as a roentgen. A rad of different kinds of radiation causes differing health effects on man, and to take this into account, the rem was devised. The important thing to know is that, on the average, half of the people exposed to 400 rem over a short time period will die if they don't receive special treatment. Radiation workers in the United States may receive up to 5 rem per year. A container with lead walls four inches thick would reduce a radiation of 1,000 rem per hour to about 0.4 rem per hour.

The fuel rods must be removed by using remote handling equipment and shielded containers; they are then placed in a water tank to cool. After a fuel rod has cooled for 150 days, its activity will be down to about 30 rem per hour at a distance of a meter. Processing 60 metric tons of reactor fuel a year and dealing with one day's worth at a time means working with about ten fuel rods at a time. If this processing is all done in one place, there will be a radiation level of about 300 rem per hour at one meter away. The persons working regularly on the processing must use great care; any radiation exposure is dangerous, but there would be a serious risk for anyone receiving 100 rem of radiation or more per year.

Very little of this radiation comes from the uranium and plutonium; its primary source is the fission products. The first chemical action in the processing is to separate the uranium and plutonium from these products. All of the first steps in the chemical processing must be done with remotely controlled equipment in heavily shielded rooms. The radioactive material must be shielded on all sides, not just on the side where workers may be, because the radiation can bounce from the air and the building walls to hit those nearby. Each of the fuel rods will generate about 1 to 2 kilowatts of energy just after the reactor is shut down, and even after 150 days each rod may be giving off about 50 watts of heat.

The operations in the shielded rooms can be surveyed by using television cameras or, more simply, mirrors; both keep the viewer out of a direct line of sight of the apparatus. Thick lead-glass windows can also be used if a direct view is desired. Maintenance of the system would be possible only after a great effort had been made to decontaminate the apparatus by flushing it with solvents.

To avoid the need for pumps for transferring liquids, the apparatus would probably be installed in a tall building, with the various vats and chemical containers connected by gravity flow. A motor-driven mixer could be turned on remotely, and valves allowing the flow of different chemicals and solvents could be connected to the region outside the shielding by long rods passing through the shielding and thus turned at a distance.

Major repairs of the apparatus would be almost impossible without the use of complex, expensive robotlike equipment that is difficult to obtain. Thus such repairs would probably not be done. If a serious breakdown occurred, the area would most likely be sealed off, and work started again elsewhere.

The reprocessing proceeds somewhat as follows. (Figure 15 shows the setup of a reprocessing plant. The process starts at the top of the building and proceeds downward.) First, fuel rods are cut open and the uranium, or uranium oxide, is removed and cut into small pieces; in some cases, whole fuel rods, both casing and uranium, are chopped up. The very radioactive fuel rods must be carried to the chopper in shielded containers, and removed and placed into the chopper by remotely controlled equipment. The remotely controlled chopper then delivers the finely chopped material by gravity into a mixing vat below.

The vat that receives this material is filled with nitric acid, which can dissolve the rod material. (After a year's operation, a small reactor such as the one described earlier, which used natural uranium, will

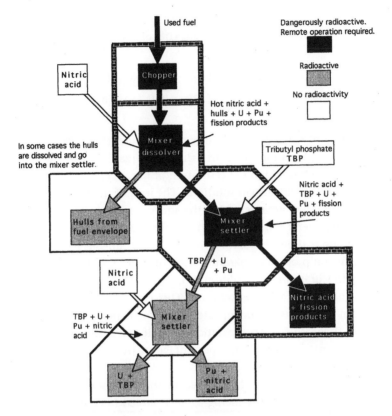

FIG. 15. Reprocessing plant. Dark shading indicates material that is dangerously radioactive (remote operation required); light shading indicates radioactive material; no shading indicates no radioactivity.

contain used fuel, 99.3% of which is uranium 238, with the remainder consisting of plutonium [0.015%], uranium 235 [0.68%], and fission products [0.02%].) The containers of the fuel elements might be dissolved as well, depending on the material. The dissolving would be aided by continually stirring the mixture in the vat. The vat would have to be partly sealed to contain any vapor; the eventual venting of the highly radioactive vapor would be controlled by using filters and a tall stack. After the fuel rods have been dissolved, the solid residues are drained off and the aqueous nitric-acid solution containing the dissolved fuel rods is transferred to another container.

Next a solution of tributyl phosphate (or TBP), n-$(C_4H_9)_3PO_4$, in a hydrocarbon solvent like kerosene is added. The following reactions occur:

$$UO_2^{++} + 2NO_3^- + 2TBP \leftrightarrow UO_2(NO_3)_2(TBP)_2$$
$$Pu^{+4} + 4NO_3^- + 2TBP \leftrightarrow Pu(NO_3)_4(TBP)_2$$

These reactions reach an equilibrium that encourages the transfer of the uranium and plutonium ions into the light organic solvent when the aqueous phase has a high concentration of nitrate ion, as is the case in the concentrated nitric-acid solutions. The ions of the fission products, on the other hand, are retained in the aqueous nitric-acid phase.

In actual operation, the two phases are mixed by stirring, and the mixed liquid is allowed to settle, with the heavy aqueous phase containing the fission products separating from the lighter organic phase containing the uranium and plutonium. The fission products are then drained off in the aqueous solution. This type of mixing-and-settling operation might have to be repeated, with the fission products drained off each time. With each separation a small percentage of the fission products remains, and a small percentage of the uranium and plutonium is lost.

Aqueous nitric acid is then added to the plutonium and uranium component. A chemical reducing agent is added to convert the plutonium ions from a tetravalent to a trivalent state. The trivalent plutonium ions separate into the aqueous phase and can be drained off with the aqueous solution. The separation process may have to be repeated several times to obtain a sufficiently pure product.

Once the fission products have been separated off, chemical operations can be performed on the remaining uranium and plutonium with very much less radiation hazard. The plutonium and uranium produce some gamma radiation, but most of it is of low energy and readily absorbed. The plutonium itself, though not dangerously radioactive, is still very hazardous to handle. The inhalation of even microgram quantities can be lethal.

Added to the other complications is the problem of cooling the mixing, dissolving, and settling vats. There are significant amounts of radioactivity in the vapor emitted by the vats—particularly in the gases produced either by the fissioning of uranium or by the general neutron-induced activity of the reactor. Several such gases would be released, either in the reprocessing itself or as a result of leaking from the unreprocessed fuel rods. Tritium, carbon (as CO_2), iodine, krypton, and xenon would be among these. Those that have short half-lives will soon decay, but tritium, C-14, I-129, and Kr-85 will survive. For a small-scale reprocessing plant such as the one discussed here, the use of fans and a vent stack could reduce the hazard involved in the release of such gases.

Concealment

If the reprocessing plant were concealed, the radioactivity of the gases released could reveal its location. All except Kr-85 can be removed by filtering, but krypton, a noble gas, will not combine readily with anything. The only way to prevent its release would be to use a complicated process of storage. About three krypton-85 atoms are formed for every one thousand fissions,[6] yielding about 0.4 curies of krypton per gram of uranium fissioned. Assuming that reprocessing goes on for three hundred days a year, resulting in 9 kilograms of plutonium, and that 1.2 kilograms of uranium are fissioned for every kilogram of plutonium produced, about 15 curies of Kr-85 would be produced and released into the atmosphere per day. Given the data collected in the vicinity of the U.S. Savannah River reprocessing plant, one might expect to find detectable quantities of krypton 85 at distances of a few kilometers from any reprocessing plant that produces 9 kilograms of plutonium a year.[7] The minimum amount that would signal plutonium production is probably about 20 picocuries of decay per second in a cubic meter of air, corresponding to about 0.7 decays per second—a figure only slightly higher than that for normal background. This measurement, requiring as it does the examination of a large volume of air, would be difficult to make.

The radioactive wastes from the reprocessing activity may also provide a means of locating the plant. The primitive reactor described earlier used 60 tons of fuel to produce 9 kilograms of plutonium, and the waste materials must be disposed of. The approximately 9 kilograms of fission products cannot be disposed of in a simple manner because of the heat they continue to develop for decades. If the wastes are not carefully controlled, there will be leakage into the groundwater that might reveal the "upstream" location of a reprocessing plant. Any crude-waste pit would be readily visible from the air.

Conclusion

Reprocessing reactor fuel to obtain enough plutonium for one bomb a year does not appear to be beyond the capability of a developing country, if it has some technical help. The facility would fit into a small building, and the acids and other materials required are readily available. Its operation might be detected by the presence of radioactive releases, but such detection would require access to areas close to the plant.

PROLIFERATION IMPLICATIONS

The high-power reactors described here are technologically very complex; only a highly developed country could build any of them. The designs for such reactors and the solutions to their problems have been worked on over a period of fifty years, and even a highly developed country would not now want to start this work by itself. A less-developed country wanting to acquire such a reactor would need to buy it from a nation experienced in the technology; and according to the requirements of the Nuclear Non-proliferation Treaty, the purchase would fall under International Atomic Energy Agency (IAEA) safeguards.

The use of light-water reactors, which require 3–4%-enriched uranium, provides a way of preventing proliferation. Ideally, the fuel is supplied by a producer under the supervision of the IAEA and is removed under IAEA supervision, which prevents it from being processed to extract the plutonium that has been produced. Once a year, about a quarter of the fuel is removed (that which is most depleted of U-235) and replaced in a time-consuming, multistep operation. First, the chain reaction is stopped by inserting neutron absorbers into the reactor; cooling water is still supplied, because the fuel rods continue to give off heat from the residual activity of the fission products (initially at about 7–10% of the normal operating heat) for a considerable time. After the reactor has cooled down, the large pressure vessel containing the fuel rods must be opened and the fuel rods removed. They are of such diameter and spacing that they are handled in bundles.

Because the fuel removal is an annual operation, it is possible for IAEA inspectors to schedule an inspection when removal occurs to make sure that the fuel rods are not taken to a processing plant where

TABLE 3

Presence of Various Plutonium Isotopes in Reactor Fuel

	Percent of Total Plutonium in Fuel	
Isotope	Power Reactor	Weapon-Grade Reactor
Pu-238*	1.3	0.012
Pu-239	60	93.8
Pu-240	24	6
Pu-241	9	0.35
Pu-242	5	0.022

Source: Data from J. Carson Mark, "Explosive Properties of Reactor-Grade Plutonium," *Science and Global Security* 4 (1993): 113.

*Although the Pu-238 is present in very small quantities, it emits so many neutrons by spontaneous fission that it contributes appreciably to the difficulty of using reactor plutonium for weapons material. It is produced by several complex routes, a prolific one being the following:

$$U\text{-}235 + n \rightarrow U\text{-}236, U\text{-}236 + n \rightarrow U\text{-}237, U\text{-}237 \rightarrow Np\text{-}237 + \beta^-,$$
$$Np\text{-}237 + n \rightarrow Np\text{-}238, Np\text{-}238 \rightarrow Pu\text{-}238 + \beta^-.$$

It is evident why a long exposure of reactor fuel to neutron flux is needed.

the plutonium that has been produced might be removed for use in weapons. If reprocessing is to be done, the fuel rods must be sent to processing plants that operate subject to IAEA inspection.

With heavy-water and graphite-moderated reactors, it is much more difficult to safeguard against the diversion of plutonium for weapon use. These reactors can use natural uranium, which is widely available and the supply of which is therefore difficult to control. In addition, the possibility of removing individual fuel bundles without shutting down the reactor makes it necessary to monitor fuel removal either with cameras or with inspectors who are present at all times.

When reactor fuel is processed for its plutonium, plutonium isotopes are typically found in the percentages given in table 3.

Although all of the plutonium isotopes will fission, only Pu-241 is comparable to Pu-239 in its effectiveness. The total amount of plutonium in the spent fuel rods is comparable to the residual U-235. In the case of light-water reactors, this is somewhat more than a quarter of the original 3–5% U-235 in the fuel.

The original "Atoms for Peace" proposals, in which nuclear know-how was exchanged for some form of control, was made by President

TABLE 4
Some Properties of Isotopes in Old Reactor Fuel

Isotope	Bare Critical Mass, α Phase (kg)	Spontaneous-Fission Neutrons ([gm-sec]$^{-1}$)	Decay Heat (watts/kg)
Pu-238	10	2.6×10^3	560
Pu-239	10	22×10^{-3}	1.9
Pu-240	40	0.91×10^3	6.8
Pu-241	10	49×10^{-3}	4.2
Pu-242	100	1.7×10^3	0.1
Am-241[a]	100	1.2	114

Source: Data from J. Carson Mark, "Explosive Properties of Reactor-Grade Plutonium, Science & Global Security, 1993, vol. 4, p. 115.
[a]Americium is present in old reactor fuel as a result of the β decay of Pu-241.

Dwight Eisenhower in 1953. At that time it was generally believed that a nuclear weapon could not be made from reactor-grade plutonium because of the large number of neutrons emitted by Pu-240 and Pu-238. Most physicists thought that these neutrons would set off any nuclear explosion prematurely, thus causing a "fizzle." Now it is known that although these isotopes do complicate the process of making a strong explosion, they do not prevent it. In fact, in a recent paper, the late J. Carson Mark, director of the Theoretical Division of Los Alamos National Laboratory from 1947 to 1972, points out that each of the plutonium isotopes can sustain a chain reaction.[8] He lists the properties of the various isotopes; some of these are shown in table 4.

Although Pu-238 is present as only 1% of reactor fuel, it contributes a large number of neutrons. Figure 16 shows the amount of the various plutonium isotopes as a function of the total neutron irradiation the uranium fuel has been exposed to, in terms of the power output of the reactor in gigawatt (1,000 megawatt) days per ton of fuel. Weapon-grade plutonium is exposed to reactor operation for only a short time. The original plutonium weapons of World War II were made with plutonium produced with an even shorter exposure.

It is unlikely that a developed nation, except under extreme time pressure, would use reactor-grade plutonium for weapons. A less-developed nation, however, unable because of surveillance or other reasons to oper-

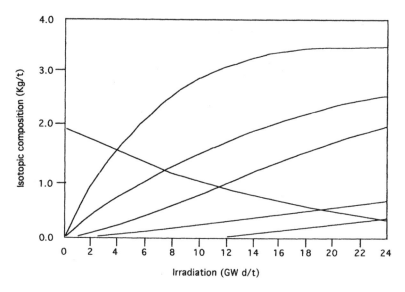

FIG. 16. Accumulation of plutonium isotopes in reactor fuel
as a function of irradiation. Irradiation is given
in gigawatt-days per ton (GWD/t).

From J. R. Askew, C. G. Campbell, and J. G. Tyror, "Reactor Physics,"
in W. Marshall, ed., *Nuclear Power Technology*, vol. 1, *Reactor Technology*
(Oxford: Oxford University Press, 1983), p. 69, fig. 2.11.
Reprinted by permission of Oxford University Press.

ate its reactors in an optimum way for the production of weapon-grade
plutonium, or a nation using plutonium stolen from the reprocessing
cycle, might find the use of reactor-grade material the only feasible way
of producing a weapon. The presence of Pu-240, Pu-238, and Pu-241
complicates the handling of reactor-grade plutonium, because in combination they raise the radioactivity to over fifteen times that of the
weapon-grade material. Most of the radiation consists of 5-MeV α particles and 20-keV electrons. Because these particles penetrate less than 15
microns of flesh, workers can be shielded against them; a glove box and
equipment to prevent the inhaling of any powder would be sufficient.
There is also neutron radiation of about 400 neutrons per gram per
second, but this can be attenuated somewhat by a thick plastic window;
And if the worker remains at least a foot away from the radioactive

material, distance alone will reduce the radiation to a safe level—about 0.04 neutrons per square centimeter per second.

The primary radiation hazard occurs in the process of separating the plutonium from the fission products in the spent reactor fuel, and it is probable that the principal source of the radiation coming from the separated plutonium will be the small contaminations of those fission products that have remained in it.

Another problem associated with reactor-grade plutonium is the heat it generates. For the reactor-grade plutonium used for table 3, there would be more than 10.5 watts generated per kilogram, compared with about a quarter as much for weapon-grade material.[9] Weapon-grade plutonium would be warm to the touch, whereas reactor grade would be hot. This complicates the design of a weapon, because some method of cooling the plutonium must be included.

Although neither uranium nor plutonium emits penetrating gamma rays, there is a problem associated with reactor-grade plutonium that has been stored for a long time: the Pu-241 in it decays with a 13.2-year half-life, emitting an electron and becoming Am-241; Am-241, in turn, with a 458-year half-life, suffers α decay and in the process emits a penetrating gamma ray. These gamma rays make it possible to detect old reactor plutonium that may have been hidden. They also complicate the use of the plutonium in the production of a weapon. The americium can be separated from the plutonium chemically, but this requires an extra step.

THE THREAT OF PLUTONIUM THEFT

The possible theft or diversion of the pure plutonium or plutonium compounds used in the fuel cycles of power reactors is a cause of concern. Reactor-grade plutonium can be made into an effective nuclear weapon, although the expected yield is lower than that from weapon-grade plutonium. Weapons made from reactor-grade plutonium will probably require the use of more fissile material than those made with the weapon-grade material.

The most efficient use of the fissile fuel in nuclear reactors (usually U-235) requires reprocessing the used fuel to get rid of the fission products that contaminate it and reduce its effectiveness. If the gaseous fission products are not removed, their pressure will eventually rupture the fuel rods' surface and expose the fuel to the cooling water. The used fuel has had most of its U-235 burned up, but, if it started as 3–4%-enriched uranium (the fuel typically used in light-water-moderated reactors), it will contain a larger fraction of U-235 than does natural uranium. More significantly, the used fuel, once it has been reprocessed, also yields an appreciable amount of plutonium. A light-water-moderated reactor loaded with fuel enriched to about 3.3% will produce a used fuel with about 0.8% U-235 and 0.65% plutonium. By combining this plutonium and the reprocessed uranium with new fuel and using it in reactors, the demand for new uranium fuel is reduced to about 65% for light-water-moderated reactors and to about 50% for heavy-water-moderated (CANDU) reactors. Breeder reactors are extreme examples of this ability of reactors to generate plutonium; in operation, such a reactor might generate 10–20% more plutonium than it burns up, doing so by converting the U-238 in its fuel to plutonium. If uranium ore were in short supply, these savings would be very important.

But there is no shortage of uranium; in addition, the cost of using reprocessed plutonium is much greater than the cost of using new, slightly enriched uranium for fuel. Even if plutonium were free, using it would be more expensive. This fact has been substantiated by a National Academy of Sciences study directed at finding ways of disposing of the plutonium from dismantled U.S. and Russian nuclear weapons.[10]

The Once-Through Cycle and the Reprocessing Cycles

An examination of the "once-through" fuel cycle (see fig. 17) shows that nowhere in this cycle is there much exposure to theft or diversion. The uranium, as it enters the reactor, has been enriched to about 3% U-235. Three-quarters of a ton of this fuel would have to be stolen to make a single uranium weapon, and an enrichment facility would also be needed. At the next step in the cycle, the used fuel removed from the reactor has about a third as much U-235 as it originally had and about 8 tenths as much plutonium as uranium 235, but the U-235 and plutonium are mixed in with highly radioactive fission products. Over a half ton of this radioactive material would have to be stolen or diverted to get enough plutonium for a weapon, and a complex reprocessing plant would have to be built.

On the other hand, the reprocessing fuel cycle (see fig. 18) has five places where plutonium can be stolen or diverted. Plutonium, uncon-

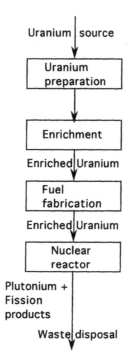

FIG. 17. Once-through fuel cycle. The plutonium produced is disposed of together with the radioactive fission products.

taminated by fission products, can be found in the reprocessing plant, in transport from the reprocessing plant to storage, in the storage location, in transport from storage to fuel fabrication, and in transport to the reactor. Plutonium, separated from fission products by reprocessing, is not highly radioactive. Most of its radiation is in the form of alpha particles, which will not penetrate even the surface of skin. Gamma rays are also produced, and are present in greater numbers from reactor plutonium than from weapon-grade, but shielding from them is not difficult.

The danger of this diversion led President Jimmy Carter in 1977 to defer indefinitely the commercial reprocessing and recycling of the plutonium produced in the U.S. nuclear power programs. The United States also discontinued its construction of a breeder reactor. However, it has not been very successful in persuading other countries to do the same: both Great Britain and France invested in expensive nuclear-reprocessing

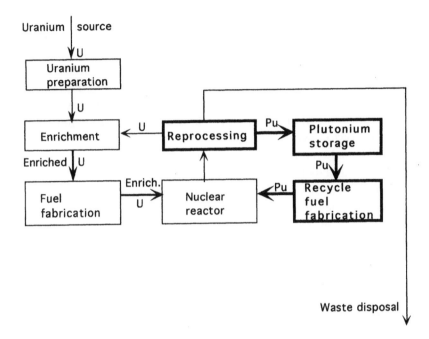

FIG. 18. Reprocessing fuel cycle. The plutonium produced
is separated from the radioactive fission products
and reintroduced to the reactor along with new fuel.

facilities, and many other countries signed long-term contracts for the reprocessing of their used fuel. These reprocessing facilities continue to operate.

Arguments can be made that the present glut of uranium will not persist very far into the next century and that within a few decades the cost of uranium will make reprocessing necessary. This argument is based on predictions of future increases in the use of nuclear power, and on predictions of the cost of developing other sources of uranium. There is a lot of uranium in the earth. The questions are: Will new, large, and easily developed sources be found? and, Will new and inexpensive methods be found for using the marginal sources already located? That these questions are unanswerable makes economic predictions inaccurate at best.

Besides the fact that it conserves uranium, the other justification for reprocessing is that it increases the self-sufficiency of a nation with no good source of uranium. This is the argument made by Japan, which now owns 14 tons of reprocessed plutonium, 6 tons of it in Japan and 8 tons still in France, where much of the fuel was reprocessed.[11] But in order to thus increase self-sufficiency, breeder reactors are necessary. By using these, U-238 (over one hundred times more plentiful than U-235) can be converted to plutonium, and so only a relatively small amount of natural uranium needs to be stored in order to provide a long-term source of reactor fuel.

Still, it would not require all that much space to store enough natural uranium fuel to fuel reactors for the once-through cycle. Twenty metric tons of uranium metal occupy 1 cubic meter. To fuel a 1-gigawatt electric reactor for one year, about 160 tons of natural uranium would be needed. As an example, in 1990 Japan used about 90 gigawatt-years of electric power. (About 28% was made by nuclear power.) If one assumes that all of Japan's future electricity will be made by nuclear power, and that its power use will increase linearly fivefold in fifty years, the total uranium requirement would be less than 2 million tons. This much uranium would occupy 90,000 cubic meters—or, if arranged in stacks 10 meters high, about two and a half football fields. The main problem would be to buy the uranium without causing a shortage and pushing up the price.

There may be ways of making the use of uranium resources more efficient without the risk of plutonium theft. One suggested method is to continuously reprocess fuel rods at reactor sites, with the plutonium being immediately used in the reactors. In this way no supply of plutonium would build up, and the amount transported at any one time would be small and confined to the reactor site. Another method that is now being examined involves combining the operation of a light-water-moderated reactor with that of a CANDU reactor. The light-water-moderated reactor starts out with slightly enriched uranium, possibly 3.3%. At the end of its normal use cycle, the amount of U-235 will have been reduced to 0.8% of the total fuel and the plutonium produced to about 0.65%. This percentage of fissile material although too low for a light-water-moderated reactor, is higher than that in natural uranium, the fuel normally used in a CANDU reactor. (See chapter 2.) The fuel in the rods is rich enough that the contaminants it contains are not sufficient to prevent operation. The main problem is that the gases that have built up in the fuel rods must be removed—a process that involves getting the casing off the old fuel rods, releasing the gases, repackaging the highly radioactive material, and inserting it into the CANDU reactor. If this can be done, the usefulness of the uranium will have been doubled without incurring any additional risk of theft.

Potential Thieves

At present, reactors worldwide are producing about 330 gigawatts of power per year. Using the production rate of light-water reactors, and assuming operation 75% of the time, about 250 metric tons of plutonium are being produced each year, of which about 60 to 70 tons are being separated from used fuel rods as pure plutonium or plutonium compounds. In Russia's disorganized custody of nuclear material, there may now be sources of weapon-grade plutonium. There are three groups that might want to steal or divert this plutonium: terrorists, maverick nations, and other non-nuclear-weapon states.

Even if it could steal the plutonium, a terrorist group would need a secure base of operations to manage the construction of an effective nuclear weapon. Even a country like Libya would have second thoughts about allowing a terrorist group to use its territory for this purpose. The terrorist group, without a secure base, might be able to build a bomb loaded with plutonium for dispersal and use this as a threat, claiming to have a plutonium weapon. (This weapon might use a conventional explosive to disperse plutonium. Plutonium in a finely divided aerosol can be lethal if inhaled in microgram quantities.) If it was known that a terrorist group had stolen plutonium, the threat might be effective, even if a weapon had not been built.

A maverick nation that would itself direct the theft of plutonium for its own purposes is a likely perpetrator. If the international community was foolish enough to allow such a nation to build a reactor and reprocessing equipment, this nation might, even under IAEA supervision, devise methods of diverting enough plutonium from the normal cycle to build a weapon.

The Virtual Nuclear-Weapon States

The third group—those non-nuclear-weapon states not considered to be maverick nations—currently have security arrangements that allow them to feel safer without nuclear weapons than with them. As the general technological development of the world increases, the number of these non-nuclear-weapon states that could quickly get nuclear weapons becomes increasingly larger.

The chance that any of these nations will now try to get such weapons is very small. This can be attributed to the successful nonproliferation policy that has been developed by the world community. Security arrangements made by the nuclear powers provide safety for most of the world.

However, a failure of these arrangements could radically change this attitude. If, for example, a nation such as Libya were to obtain and use a nuclear weapon, and if the nuclear powers did not punish Libya effectively, many nations might have second thoughts about going without the deterrence provided by such weapons. If North Korea was allowed to develop and market nuclear weapons, reaction might be extreme.

It is unlikely that any nation would develop nuclear weapons under any other circumstances, because doing so would upset its present security arrangements and greatly affect its economic treatment by the rest of the world. On the other hand, as they consider any change in policy, particularly toward any of the maverick nations, the world powers should keep in mind the possible effects of such change on the non-nuclear-weapon nations.

Many nations that use nuclear power have a supply of separated reactor-grade plutonium from used reactor fuel. Either they have reprocessed the fuel themselves to get the plutonium for use in their reactors, or they have received the plutonium from those nations that did the reprocessing for them. Both the United Kingdom and France are major marketers of chemical-reprocessing services, and both return the separated plutonium to the country that sent the fuel to them. Technologically well-developed countries, with plutonium in hand, would require only a short time, less than a year, to produce nuclear weapons.

Japan and Germany are so technologically developed that, if their international situation changed and they felt it desirable to obtain nuclear weapons, they would probably arrange to make weapon-grade plutonium rather than use the available reactor-grade material; the Japanese and possibly the Germans already have a small supply of plutonium that is almost the equivalent of weapon-grade.[12] On the other hand, nations for which the technical effort of obtaining weapons would be extreme, or those that felt the need for very rapid development, might instead choose to make use of available reactor-grade material.

The Nuclear Non-proliferation Treaty (NPT) prohibits the construction of the nonnuclear parts of a nuclear weapon, but a very good approximation of the results of explosive compression of reactor-grade plutonium can be obtained from complex computer simulation, which is allowed by the NPT.[13] It is reasonable to expect that governments, with no intention of violating the NPT, might commission studies leading to the design of nuclear weapons. Beyond computer simulation, the limits of what may be done have been well defined by George Bunn and Roland Timerbaev, former Soviet arms-control negotiator and Soviet and Russian ambassador to the International Atomic Energy Agency:

> The NPT text and negotiating history show that when a non-nuclear-weapon state party makes, tests or procures a component useful only for a nuclear explosive device, that party has violated its NPT undertaking not to "manufacture or otherwise acquire" such devices even though the activity occurs before final assembly. Second, if a component or equipment or material is useful for other purposes as well as nuclear explosives, but the party's purpose is to make a nuclear explosive, then the action can also constitute a violation of the NPT.[14]

Under these terms, an experimental study of the explosive compression of uranium or plutonium is prohibited by the NPT, but an academic research study might be made on a large group of metals. However, the configuration used for the tests would have to be very different from that of a nuclear weapon. It would also be possible, under NPT terms, to gain experience in the handling and machining of radioactive and poisonous metals, as well as experience with focused explosive charges, detonators, and the entire electronic basis for setting off an implosion, as long as the tests were ostensibly directed to other military and industrial uses.

Although there are no present indications that work of this sort has taken place in technologically advanced countries that do not have nuclear weapons, such an undertaking would not be considered a violation of international ethics. Several of these nations may in fact already have sophisticated nuclear-weapon designs, some taking into account the problems of using reactor-grade plutonium. A nation such as Germany or Japan, now without nuclear weapons, could have detailed plans for an entire crash program, including delivery systems, which might require only a few months to put into operation.

The plutonium produced by power reactors that might be used for weapons is under safeguards: a major international contretemps would occur if any nation used this material. Fortunately, the countries now in a position to produce weapons quickly are democracies that would find any rejection of safeguards on their part politically difficult because of the strong opposition in their societies that would probably result. Yet such opposition would most likely disappear if the nations involved were threatened in what seemed to be a calamitous way. If a technologically advanced nation under a dictatorship were to gain control of separated plutonium, public opposition would not be as effective, and the risk of virtual proliferation's becoming real would rise considerably.

It is a major success of the NPT that most nations have come to rely on that treaty and on IAEA safeguards systems for the assurance that their neighbors are not secretly developing nuclear weapons. If the NPT had not been indefinitely extended in 1995, the short-term extension that would most certainly have been agreed upon would have produced a far weaker nonproliferation environment for those nuclear developments, such as reactor construction, that proceed on very long schedules.

4

Uranium Enrichment

One way to make a nuclear weapon is, as we have seen, to use plutonium; the other is to use almost pure U-235.[1] This is not as effective a fissile material as Pu-239, but it is easier to make into a weapon. However, U-235 occurs only as a part (0.72%) of natural uranium, which must be enriched to be useful. Although plutonium was the bomb material of choice for the first weapons of the United States, the Soviet Union, Great Britain, France, and India, as well as for the untested weapon of Israel and the hypothesized one of North Korea, China's first weapon was made of highly enriched uranium, and the first four nuclear powers just mentioned have tested uranium weapons. Also, Pakistan's untested weapons are of highly enriched uranium; South Africa's now-discarded weapons were of uranium; and Iraq's broad-ranging program emphasized uranium.

There are a large number of ways of increasing the concentration of U-235 in uranium. To pursue any of them, most less-developed countries would need some outside assistance. Therefore, the development of nuclear weapons by the more volatile third-world countries can be delayed by keeping such assistance from them.

Some methods of isotope separation exploit the fact that the atoms or molecules being separated have the same energy whatever their mass. The relation holds whether the particles are in a gaseous state (for separation by diffusion) or in a particle beam (for enrichment by electromagnetic methods). All molecules in a gas mixture have the same average energy regardless of their mass. Because momentum is proportional to the velocity of the atom or molecule, whereas energy is proportional to the velocity squared, gas atoms of different masses but the same energy will have different average values of velocity and momentum. The lighter gas molecules have the larger velocity. The difference in velocity is proportional to the difference in the square roots of the masses.[2]

Singly charged atoms or molecules accelerated by the same electric field have the same energy. If these particles have different masses, they will have different momenta and therefore different radii of curvature when passing through a magnetic field; the heavier particles will have the greater momenta and hence the greater radii. Electromagnetic enrichment methods are based on these principles.

I will here summarize the chief methods of uranium enrichment before considering each in detail.[3]

ELECTROMAGNETIC SEPARATION. The first uranium bomb was made with uranium enriched in U-235 by separation in a mass spectrograph. This method was developed by Ernest Lawrence's group at the University of California, and the separation unit his group used was called a calutron. The United States stopped using this technique because it was inefficient. It was not considered to be a possible method for underdeveloped countries until an installation using electromagnetic separation was discovered in Iraq in 1991.

GASEOUS DIFFUSION. Gas will move through a porous wall from a region of higher pressure to one of lower pressure, with the lighter isotope moving preferentially. Gaseous diffusion is the principal separation method used by the United States. Thermal diffusion, a variant technique in which the lighter isotope moves to the hotter region, was tried briefly at Oak Ridge during World War II and abandoned.

CENTRIFUGE. Pressure-gradient diffusion by centrifuge, the most efficient method of separation in present use, was developed independently by the United States and the U.S.S.R to replace gaseous diffusion. It has not been adopted as a production technique by the United States because the capital investment required could not be justified in view of the already existing gaseous-diffusion plants. It is being used in Russia, the United Kingdom, the Netherlands, Germany, and Pakistan.

AERODYNAMIC ENRICHMENT. Only two of the several methods of aerodynamic enrichment have been attempted on a large scale, both of them related to centrifuge enrichment. Vortex-tube enrichment has been used by South Africa, and jet-diffusion enrichment was at one time being developed by Brazil.

CHEMICAL SEPARATION. Chemical separation methods are based on the tendency, in an equilibrium mixture of two uranium compounds, for U-235 to be in slightly larger concentration in the molecules of the more loosely bound compound than it is in the molecules of the other.

LASER SEPARATION. Different isotopes of the same element have slightly different energy levels. Laser-light frequencies can be so accurately tuned that they excite atoms of only one isotope by resonance to a higher state.

The excited atom can then be removed by electrical, chemical, or other means. This method has been developed by U.S. weapons laboratories and is nearly at a pilot-plant stage.

COMBINED TECHNIQUES. Combinations of two of the above methods described here may have some advantages for a less-developed country.

In the detailed discussion that follows, I shall compare the success of the methods. A less-developed country would be likely to pursue a proven method, and although the amount of electric power needed to enrich uranium is an important criterion, it represents only one of the costs of enrichment. Even with the very power-consuming gaseous-diffusion method used by the United States, power represents less than half of the total cost. A developing country trying to build nuclear weapons surreptitiously would place a higher premium on other criteria, such as the availability of materials and technology. Furthermore, I will emphasize the electromagnetic (calutron) method and laser-separation method, the former because of its surprising appearance in Iraq's nuclear-weapons effort and the latter because it is the most effective of the new technologies.

SEPARATIVE WORK UNIT

In discussions of methods of enriching the amount of the uranium-235 isotope relative to that of uranium 238, the term *separative work unit* (SWU) is regularly used, even in nontechnical discussions of proliferation.[4]

The SWU of a separation device describes its effectiveness in producing a small amount of enhancement as part of a "cascade" of separation units that, in combination, produce a large enhancement. It has little application for such batch-processing techniques as electromagnetic and laser separation, although an equivalent SWU value is used in comparing these techniques with others. The SWU is not a measure of the amount of *work* required to separate isotopes. The units used in expressing SWU are not those of work, but of mass—the mass of the material processed (generally in kilograms). An SWU of a little over 200 kilograms is required to produce 1 kilogram of 90%-enriched U-235 from natural uranium containing 0.72% U-235, with a residue of 0.25% U-235.

The separative work unit is commonly used in comparing various ways of enhancing U-235. A factory can be described in terms of the number of kilograms SWU it can produce in a year, or its efficiency can be described in terms of how many kilowatt-hours of electricity are required to produce 1 kilogram SWU.

Different enrichment techniques require very different amounts of energy to produce the same amount of separative work; these techniques will be discussed later. The unit is particularly useful in designing enrichment systems requiring many stages and similar components. Ideal (and unachievable) systems can be designed and evaluated in terms of SWU, and practical systems designed and compared with them.

In the separation system for which the SWU is applicable, a cascade of separation stages is used, each producing a small amount of separation. A large amount of unenriched uranium is introduced into the system at a low point in the cascade of separation stages, and this proceeds up the cascade, being enriched a small amount at each step and (as some of the unwanted isotope is removed) having its volume reduced slightly. At the same time, in the cascade below the feed point, the waste moves down, becoming of lower enrichment at each step. The result is a small amount of flow out of the top of the cascade, and the remainder, generally almost equal to the amount introduced, going into the waste stream. In each step of the cascade, a large amount of the less-enriched material is sent back to a previous stage for reenrichment. The actual flow up is very much greater than the net flow up, which is always equal to the product out. Similarly, the net flow down in the lower part of the cascade is always equal to the waste. If the separation system is composed of a number of small units working in parallel at each stage, that number will be reduced the more one proceeds up or down the cascade. Figure 19 shows a diagram of a very small cascade. Note the recirculation of the waste from each stage to an earlier stage. In an ideal cascade, this waste would be at the same level of enrichment as the feed it joins when it reaches the stage below.

Figure 20 shows a graph of an ideal cascade to produce 3%-enriched uranium, using 0.72% feed and leaving 0.25% waste. The vertical scale represents the number of stages; the horizontal, the upward (not net) gas flow. The downward flow at each point is almost equal to the upward flow. (Above the feed point, the difference between the upward and downward flow is the product; below the feed point, it is the waste.)

The SWU can be used to indicate the amount of separation at each

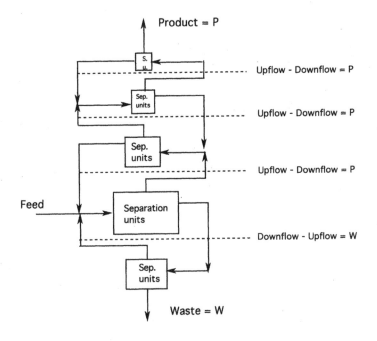

FIG. 19. Small cascade

stage and the relative number of separation units that are required at that stage. It can also be used to show the effect of different fractions of U-235 in the uranium feed, the waste, and the product. It is possible to list the number of kilograms SWU a small piece of apparatus will perform in a year; the number of such separation units required for a given application can then be determined. The horizontal axis of the graph in figure 21 shows the enrichment of U-235 desired, listed as a fraction. The maximum is 1 (100%). The vertical axis shows the number of kilograms SWU required to get to the desired enrichment. This graph applies only to a system starting with natural uranium, with its 0.72% portion of U-235. From the graph one can see that, starting with natural uranium, it takes about 200 kilograms SWU to obtain 1 kilogram of 90%-enriched uranium. To obtain 1 kilogram of 3%-enriched (0.03) uranium, 3.9 kilograms SWU would be needed (the graph would need to be enlarged to show this clearly). It is impossible to ever get to 100% enrichment; the SWU required would be infinite.

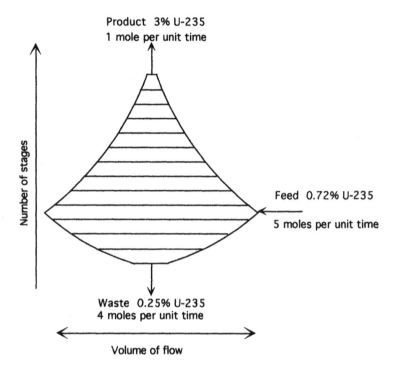

Product 3% U-235
1 mole per unit time

Number of stages

Feed 0.72% U-235

5 moles per unit time

Waste 0.25% U-235
4 moles per unit time

Volume of flow

FIG. 20. Ideal separation cascade.
Note that total flow is much greater than net flow.

From J. Shalter, E. Von Halle, and R. L. Hoglund, "Diffusion Separation
Methods," in *Encyclopedia of Chemical Technology*, 2d ed. (New York:
Wiley Interscience, 1965), vol. 7, p. 104.

The availability of partially enriched uranium, such as that used for
a reactor, can reduce the remaining effort needed to go to weapon-
grade. With reactor-grade (3–4% enriched) fuel as a feed, almost two-
thirds of the separative work has been done. This enriched feed can be
very useful to a developing country attempting to make weapon-grade
uranium.

The SWU required to obtain 1 kilogram of 3% enrichment (reactor
grade) is 3.9 kilograms. To obtain 1 kilogram of 90%-enriched uranium
with 0.25%-enriched waste, 32.6 kg of 3%-enriched uranium would be
required. Multiplying 3.9 by 32.6 gives approximately 127 kilograms
SWU. See figure 22.

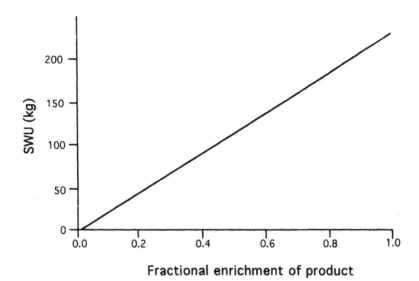

FIG. 21. SWU required to produce 1 kilogram of product
as a function of the enrichment fraction of the product.
$N_F = 0.72\%$, $N_W = 0.25\%$.

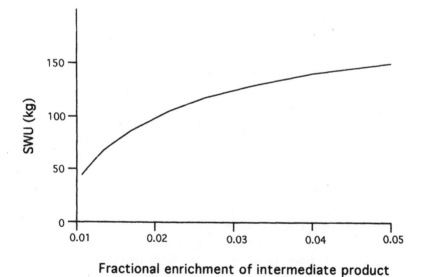

FIG. 22. SWU required to produce enough feed for 1 kilogram
of 90%-enriched uranium. The values for SWU are plotted as
a function of the enrichment of the intermediate level.
Waste enrichment is assumed to be 0.25%.

(A more detailed discussion of the separative work unit is given in appendix A.)

ELECTROMAGNETIC SEPARATION

Of the various separation methods involving the movement of ions in a magnetic field under the stimulus of an electric field, I shall discuss only one: electromagnetic separation accomplished by means of a calutron, an extension of the mass spectrograph. The latter is an instrument that can determine the masses of atoms by causing microgram quantities of different isotopes to move in separate trajectories through a magnetic field.

Enrichment by electromagnetic separation played an important role in the production of the first atomic bombs. It was the first enrichment method in effective operation in the United States and, together with the diffusion process, provided the means for producing the uranium used in the bomb dropped at Hiroshima. It was also the first method of enriching uranium used by the Soviet Union, which had trouble, initially, in getting a diffusion plant into operation. The first two Soviet atomic bombs were made of plutonium; the third used a mixture of plutonium and uranium, the uranium produced by both the electromagnetic and the diffusion methods. The Iraqis attempted to use the electromagnetic method in producing a uranium weapon, a fact that became known only after the Gulf War.

During World War II, physicists at the University of California devised a means of increasing the current in a mass spectrograph more than a thousandfold. When the United States entered the war, the Berkeley group was building a very big cyclotron, one that could reach an energy of more than 100 MeV. The technology of that time required a magnet with a wide gap between its pole tips to achieve such levels of energy. The new cyclotron was thus to have a big vacuum chamber and magnetic-field gap. (The magnet was later used for the 184-inch Berkeley cyclotron.) When the idea of using a high-current mass spectrograph for separating U-235 from U-238 was proposed, the new cyclotron magnet made possible a rapid method of testing the concept.

All operations involving particle beams must take place in a good vacuum (about one-billionth of an atmosphere) so that the particles will not collide with air molecules. The principle upon which a mass spectrograph works is that ionized atoms (in this discussion, I will assume that

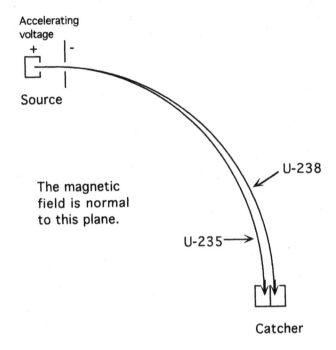

Accelerating voltage

+ | -

Source

The magnetic
field is normal
to this plane.

U-238

U-235 →

Catcher

FIG. 23. Orbits in a magnetic field.
Field is perpendicular to plane of paper.

each has lost a single electron and therefore has a single positive charge), having been given the same energy by acceleration through a static electric field (in the case of the original calutron, about 35 kilovolts), will have different momenta if their masses are different. Those atoms with different momenta will move with different radii of curvature in a magnetic field, and in a properly designed spectrograph they can be made to arrive at different destinations.

The radius of the circular path of each atom will be proportional to its momentum and inversely proportional to the magnetic field. If all atoms have been subjected to the same acceleration, those of the same mass will have the same velocity, and will move in circular paths of the same radius. The U-238 atoms will move in a path of larger radius than the U-235 atoms, as illustrated in figure 23. (In the magnets I shall discuss here, the ions move in a circular trajectory with a radius of about 1.4 meters, requiring a magnet with a pole diameter of about 3.2 meters.)

Ions emitted from a source will, generally, be moving in a broad range of directions, but an aperture placed a distance away from the source can restrict this range. In order to avoid the need to impose too much restriction, one can focus the trajectories of the atoms so that those with the same radius of curvature end up at the same place. Properly designed magnets can act as lenses for charged particles: for example, in a uniform magnetic field, trajectories starting from one place are focused to another after curving 180°, as can be seen in figure 24. The magnets considered here must be about 3 meters in diameter, and in this discussion a 30-centimeter gap between the pole tips is assumed rather than a gap of 60 centimeters, as was used in World War II. (This design is not as conservative but will save a lot of magnet power.)

Note that in figure 24 the magnetic-field lines are shown correctly only in the regions where they are used to bend the particle trajectories. Magnetic flux is produced by an electric current and can be thought of as being in a continuous loop closing on itself around the current causing it. (If the current is in a single wire, the flux will be in circles around the wire.) Current-carrying coils and electric power are required to produce the magnetic field; the current required to produce a field over a given length is more than one hundred times greater if the field is in a vacuum or air than if it is in iron. In magnets operating at the strength of field considered here, iron is always provided to carry the magnetic flux in those regions where a vacuum is not needed for the particle beams.

If the field is uniform, many trajectories originating at the same place at slightly different angles in a plane will, after curving through 180°, gather together again in what is called 180° focusing. If the focusing is in the horizontal plane, the field will have no effect in the perpendicular direction along the field lines; there will be no vertical focusing. For particles emitted at a range of angles from a point source, focusing will take place not to another point but to a line.

If the magnetic field is not completely uniform but becomes weaker in proportion to the radius of the central trajectory, focusing in the vertical plane can be introduced. (See figure 25.) With the proper rate of decrease, focusing in both vertical and horizontal planes will occur at the same point. This will not be at 180°, however, but at 255°. The designers of the first calutron used iron shims to modify the magnetic-field distribution and produce partial focusing in two planes (double-focusing) in an approximately 180° configuration.

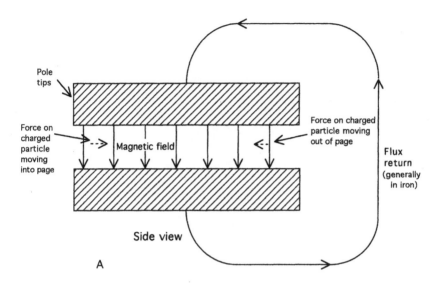

Side view

A

Particle trajectories in a uniform field

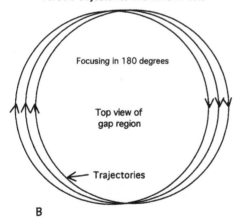

Focusing in 180 degrees

Top view of
gap region

Trajectories

B

FIG. 24. Uniform field magnet. The lower diagram
represents particle trajectories in a uniform field.

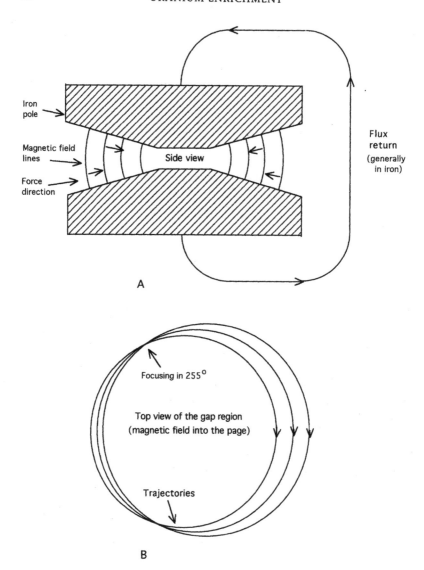

FIG. 25. Double-focusing magnet:
(A) double-focusing magnetic field;
(B) particle trajectories in a double-focusing field

The source of the uranium ions to be separated must be an ionized gas. It is difficult to produce ions from pure uranium, because it is very corrosive at the temperature at which molten uranium produces vapor that might be ionized (2,500°C). Therefore, uranium tetrachloride (UCl_4), which becomes gaseous at a temperature of about 600°C, is used. This can be ionized by running an electric discharge through it, which breaks it up into U^+ and Cl^- ions. Calutrons operate with the uranium atom primarily in a single ionized state (i.e., with one of its atomic electrons removed, changing the neutral atom to one with a single positive charge of one electron), but other ionized states may be present and will have different radius trajectories. A doubly ionized ion will, for example, have a trajectory with a radius smaller by a factor of the square root of 2 than a singly ionized one. The presence of these other ions will not cause a contamination, because the doubly ionized atoms will end up far from the singly ionized ones, but it will reduce the amount of U-235 separated.

The source will use electrodes to produce an electric field shaped to focus a beam. The gas must be contained to prevent its spreading out into the vacuum at which the calutron must operate. Calutrons operate at a vacuum of about 10^{-5} torr, or about 10^{-8} atmosphere. It is merely necessary to reduce the amount of gas in the calutron enough to make collisions of ions with gas atoms infrequent. This vacuum is readily achieved by an oil-diffusion pump backed up by standard mechanical pumps. To avoid contamination of the vacuum chamber by oil from the diffusion pump, and to help in removing any condensable vapor, a cold trap is placed between the diffusion pump and the calutron. The trap is cooled with either solid CO_2 or liquid nitrogen.

A calutron with two separate sources and collectors is shown in figure 26. This design allows two calutron units to be mounted in the same magnetic field. Each of the beams of these two independent separators consists of separate subbeams of U-235 and U-238. Calutrons with four primary beams were also used during World War II. The vacuum chamber must be large enough to house large ion sources and collectors for both units. The vacuum chambers used in the original calutrons were about 60 centimeters (2 feet) deep. The deeper the chamber is, the greater the amount of power needed to produce a magnetic field in the region. A smaller depth, one of 30 centimeters, is assumed for this discussion. (This was, apparently, the depth of the chamber used in the Iraqi design.)

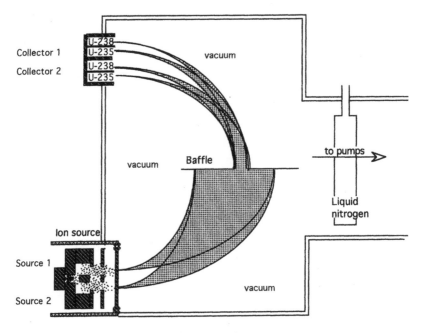

FIG. 26. Calutron with two sources

Effectiveness of the System

The discussion that follows is based on the World War II experiences of U.S. scientists and engineers, described in books published in the National Nuclear Energy Series. The list of contributors to the books on the Electromagnetic Separation Project, the Gaseous Diffusion Project, the Plutonium Project, the Los Alamos Project, and many others reads like a *Who's Who* of the scientific world. In the Electromagnetic Separation Project books,[5] for example, one finds writings by W. M. Brobeck, later the premier mechanical engineer in the design of particle accelerators; H. York, later director of Lawrence Livermore National Laboratory; E. J. Lofgren, later one of the great accelerator physicists; R. S. Livingston, the coinventor, with E. O. Lawrence, of the cyclotron; and a host of physicists who later became professors at the outstanding research universities of the United States.

It is assumed here that any less-developed country would experience the same types of problems in operating electromagnetic separation devices that the United States had during World War II. It is also assumed that a 35-kilovolt accelerating field, similar to that in the original calutrons, is being used, and that the magnetic field is about 4,000 gauss. On the other hand, a smaller gap between the magnet poles, 30 centimeters rather than 60 centimeters, is assumed. This would halve the power required for the magnetic field, though it would also complicate somewhat the designs of the ion source and the collector.

In World War II, two types of separator units were built: alpha units, for processing natural uranium to a U-235 content level of about 15%; and beta units, to raise this level to about 90%. Because the alpha units got rid of a large part of the U-238, the amount of material processed by the beta units was relatively small, so fewer beta units than alpha units were required.

The problems that faced the Oak Ridge scientists were daunting. It took two years for them to bring the operating ion current up to approximately a 0.1-ampere level. As attempts were made to raise the current, hot spots would develop at the uranium receivers, and critical parts would be destroyed. Unwanted uranium products would accumulate on insulators and short out the high voltage, or the accumulations would be so large that they blocked apertures.

The ion beam could be increased 1 milliampere for every kilovolt of voltage on the source. But that does not imply that the voltage could be raised to improve performance, because the additional energy of the beam might burn through other structures, or sparking might start, bringing the operation to an end.

The effectiveness of the system depends on the current of singly charged ions that can be produced as a clean beam to be deposited on the collector. Although a current of 0.1 ampere is considered attainable, this small value limits the effectiveness of electromagnetic separation. At this rate, 6.25×10^{17} singly charged ions can be transmitted per second. A gram mole, or 238 grams, of U-238 can be transmitted in 267 hours. Because U-235 accounts for only 0.007 of the total uranium, 38,140 hours (4.35 years) are required to produce 235 grams of U-235; this works out to about 54 grams per year. These calculations assume that the calutron is operating at full beam intensity without interruption. The experience of U.S. scientists during World War II suggests that obtaining a 0.1-ampere current would not be easy. (A more detailed description of the problems involved is given in appendix B.)

A large part of the U-235 can be lost between the ion source and the collector. (Even after two years of calutron operation during World War II, 85% of the U-235 ended up deposited, together with the U-238, all over the calutron.) This must be cleaned out after every batch run, and since the beta units separate uranium that has already been partially enriched, the material deposited in those units is very valuable.

Taking into account actual beam currents and operating time plus collection losses, the amount collected will probably be about 35% of what could be obtained with no losses and a beam current of 0.1 amperes. And this is after about two years of work. For a less-developed country, it would be reasonable to assume less than 25% effectiveness. If four beams are used, the result per four-beam unit would be about 54 grams of U-235 per year. At 90% enrichment, this would give about 60 grams of weapon-grade uranium. Assuming that a nuclear weapon uses about 25 kilograms of highly enriched uranium; and taking into account the approximately thirty beta units needed, it would take about 450 four-beam calutrons to produce uranium for one bomb a year.

Difficulties

The design and construction of the magnets required for a calutron appears to be a straightforward project that requires machine tools to shape the large pieces of iron, and copper or aluminum hollow wire for the coils. The design of an ion source and collectors, however, appears to be somewhat problematic. Because the source of the uranium, uranium tetrachloride, is solid at room temperature, becoming a gas at about 600°C, it must be heated. Then an electrical discharge must be put through the gas to produce the ionized uranium. The uranium ions must be in a strong electric field and accelerated in such a way as to form a beam, which is then injected into the calutron chamber to be separated into U-235 and U-238. To produce this acceleration, the ion source itself must be at a high positive voltage (35,000 volts) to repel and accelerate the positive ions.

This is a batch-processing system, the calutron being loaded with uranium and run until the charge is exhausted. The apparatus must then be shut down, the collection boxes removed, the apparatus cleaned out, and the charge and collection boxes replaced. This is by no means a simple procedure. The UCl_4 itself is very corrosive. Acid washes and even intense flame were used at Oak Ridge to remove the deposited uranium. Many of the parts were badly corroded, and accurate reassembly after cleaning was difficult. The receivers, heated to a high temperature by the ion beams, were badly eroded.

Insulators presented a major difficulty. The heat of operation and the treatment they had to undergo in the cleaning process made it necessary to use special insulating materials, such as zircon. The words of one Oak Ridge scientist express the magnitude of the problem: "The extent of the damage caused by these conditions was painfully revealed during August 1944 when 75 percent of the Alpha II M bushings put into operation failed. Especially at times like this, the calutron seemed truly a device for producing insulator failures."[6] Though improvements in insulators have taken place during the past fifty years, an underdeveloped country would have to buy special insulators from more-developed nations.

Power Requirements

A calutron has two principal power requirements: electric current is needed to power the electromagnetic, and power is needed for the ion beams. These power requirements are somewhat comparable in size. The early calutrons were mounted in large groups, effectively in a ring, so that the magnetic flux (which must close on itself) would not have to be conducted by large amounts of iron but would be used by other calutrons, as shown in figure 27.

The power required to produce the 4,000-gauss magnetic field we are discussing here depends on the size of coil used. Rather arbitrarily, we will assume a coil cross section of about 30 by 30 centimeters. With a coil of this size, about 60 kilowatts of electric power would be required for each magnet.[7] Were the cross-sectional area larger, the power requirement could be reduced.

It takes 3.5 kilowatts of power to produce a 35,000-volt ion beam of 0.1 ampere. But the U.S. experience with calutrons during World War II showed that about ten times that much power was needed (in part because of the acceleration of other ions, but primarily because of leakage currents from the ion source over the insulators supporting it, and small sparks from the source to other parts of the calutron). With four beams per unit, this gives a power requirement of 140 kilowatts per unit, or more than double that required for the magnetic field.

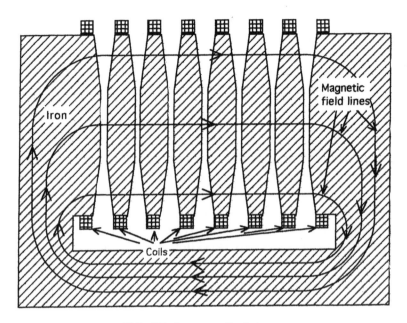

FIG. 27. A group of calutrons

The total power required for an installation with 450 magnets to produce 25 kilograms of U-235 a year would be about 90 megawatts. This amount would be used only while the apparatus was working, and thus, under my assumptions, only about half of the time. The power capability would, however, have to be of this size. Though this is a large amount of power, it is commensurate with power use at some industrial installations in developed countries.

The direct current used for the magnet coils requires transformers and power supplies. The latter could be in the form of either motor generators or solid-state rectifiers; both are commonly used in industry. The current from the supplies would have to be stable to about one part in a thousand, a stability that is routinely available in commercial units.

It has been reported that the Iraqis were planning to use 140 calutrons at a total power of 200 to 400 megawatts to produce 30 kilograms of U-235 a year.[8] My earlier estimate of 450 calutrons as the number needed to produce 25 kilograms of U-235 was based on my assumption of a low efficiency for each calutron. The power level that I gave earlier, 90 megawatts, is about seven times lower for each calutron than that reportedly used by the Iraqis. This could imply their use of a coil with a very small cross section. A coil package of the size I discussed earlier would require iron poles greater than 30 centimeters thick, and there could be many reasons why the Iraqis would have sought an alternative to using this much iron, with the attendant problems of putting it in place.

Required Components

Following is a list of the components needed for a calutron that will separate enough U-235 to make one fission bomb per year. A less-developed country would have to import those items shown in italics.

30 metric tons of uranium per year
A processing plant to produce UCl_4
450 calutrons, and, for each calutron,
  16 metric tons of *iron*
  1.3 metric tons of *aluminum wire*
    or 4.3 metric tons of *copper wire*
  1 *stainless steel vacuum chamber* 3 × 3 × 0.3 meters
  1 *fore pump* (a mechanical pump capable of producing a vacuum of 10^{-5} atmosphere)
  1 *15-inch (or larger) diffusion pump* (a pump capable of producing a vacuum of 10^{-7} to 10^{-9} atmospheres in series with a fore pump) and *pump oil*
  1 cooling trap
  15-inch valve (this could be left out, but not without decreasing the efficiency)
  4 *ion sources of great complexity,* with *special ceramic insulators*
  4 ion catchers
A power supply (30 megawatts) for magnets. This can be either a motor generator or solid state. *Parts* can be assembled indigenously.
Power supplies (60 megawatts) for the ion source (35 kilovolts). *Parts* can be assembled indigenously.
Low-conductivity water for cooling magnet coils
A heat exchanger
A source of and storage for dry ice or liquid nitrogen
Machine tools to shape the iron for the magnets

The calutron would appear to be a possible choice of separation device for a less-developed country that wants to avoid the prohibition on using other, less costly methods. Most of the components can be either assembled indigenously or purchased outright because of their many nonmilitary uses. The ceramic insulators are of a special nature and would be difficult to purchase. The power level is high, and the installation must be disguised. Cooling at this power level would be very hard to conceal because the effluents would raise the temperature of even a large river. The entire installation could be hidden in a shipyard or an automobile-assembly plant. To detect such an enterprise, one would have to look in detail at the components purchased and, taking into consideration other uses, determine whether an unusually large demand for power supplies, aluminum, or vacuum pumps is evident.

The ion source is the item requiring the greatest technical expertise. The chemistry involved requires special talent, but this could probably be readily obtained. Many competent physicists and chemists would be needed to construct the system and bring it into operation. For the U.S. calutron installation, intelligent people without technical training were taught to operate the system under the supervision of physicists. In a developing country, comparable operation would be more difficult because the indigenous workers would have even less technological experience than the Americans.

The system appears at first glance to be relatively simple to design and build, but the experience of the United States shows that in practice this is far from being the case. As is true of the other enrichment techniques that I shall discuss, there is a tremendous advantage in having the help of a person with actual experience with this type of separator. There are several countries that have electromagnetic separators, but only the United States, Russia, and China have any operating in ranges above 1 milliampere. Many nations have separators operating at less than 1 milliampere that are used for providing a supply of separated isotopes of a large number of elements. Experience with these would not be as useful as would experience with higher-current separators.

The power efficiency for a less-developed country would be very low, about 75,000 kWh/SWU. This value is very much larger than the figure of 2,500 kWh/SWU sometimes quoted. The lower number comes from a calculation of the electric power in the beam currents that deposit the uranium. The practical, larger number contains the power for the electro-magnet and the beam. The latter includes the part that does not hit the collectors and the leakage current that, in sum, are ten times that in the beams. An additional factor of two comes from my estimates of the efficiency of the process.

If, on the other hand, a country such as the United States were to further develop this method, it could increase the efficiency by using superconducting coils to produce the magnetic field. It might also be able to reduce beam losses and leakage current to a very low level, so that the only power required would be that for the separated beams them-selves. These improvements could lead to a power efficiency of close to 2,500 kWh/SWU.

There is also a remote possibility of reducing the effective accelerating voltage of the beam particles by some very sophisticated beam-handling techniques; a reduction of almost an order of magnitude might be possi-ble. However, at this point none of these improvements is possible for a less-developed country.

GASEOUS-DIFFUSION ENRICHMENT

Of the several types of diffusion, the only one that has been successful is gaseous diffusion. No other would be selected by a less-developed coun-try as an optimal way to enhance the concentration of U-235. This is the method used by the United States for its uranium enrichment. It was chosen (together with calutrons) to enrich the material for its first ura-nium weapon, used over Hiroshima. It was used until 1964 for produc-ing weapon-grade uranium and after that for enriching uranium for use in reactors. It was not replaced by the less-expensive centrifuge method because of the latter's capital costs. The Soviet Union used gaseous diffu-sion for its first uranium weapons, but later replaced it with the centri-fuge method. Gaseous diffusion was also the method chosen by China for making material for its first nuclear weapon, and it was the method chosen by all the major nuclear powers for producing enriched uranium until the centrifuge technology was developed.

Gaseous-diffusion separation works on the principle that the energies of molecules of differing masses are the same in a gas. This means that lighter molecules move more rapidly than heavier ones. In the case of

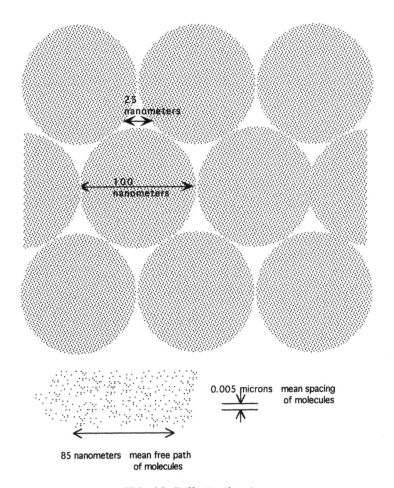

FIG. 28. Diffusion barrier

uranium hexafluoride (UF_6) the gas used in the process, the difference in velocities between molecules containing U-238 and those containing U-235 is very small, the ratio being 1 to 1.00429.

If the gas containing the uranium is enclosed by a porous wall, the more rapidly moving U-235 molecules will hit the wall more frequently than the U-238 ones and will more often pass through. In practice, the UF_6 gas is made to pass through the centers of cylinders with porous walls, the wall openings being about 25 nanometers (10^{-6} inch) in diameter (see fig. 28). A lower pressure is maintained outside. Because the lighter molecules hit the wall and its openings more often than the heavier ones, they go through in greater numbers, thus enriching the concentration of the lighter molecule outside. If the openings were much larger than the mean free path of the molecules (the average distance a molecule moves without hitting another molecule), a stream of gas would pass through carrying the light and heavy molecules equally. The amount of separation for each stage is very small. About twelve hundred stages are required to go from the 0.72% level of U-235 found in nature to a 4% enhancement. About three thousand stages are required to reach the 90% level.

It is of critical importance to the separation that the pores in the wall be very small. Fabrication of the porous wall is made more difficult by the fact that uranium hexafluoride, the only uranium compound suitable for this method, is very corrosive. Fluorine has the excellent property of occurring only as a single isotope, so the fluorine part of UF_6 is always of the same mass. Solid at room temperature, UF_6 is stable, but reacts with water to form UO_2F_2 (uranyl fluoride). At about half of atmospheric pressure, UF_6 becomes gaseous. It is corrosive to most common metals (although aluminum and nickel are not attacked) and reacts with organics such as lubricating oils. Silicon-based oil, now in general use in diffusion pumps, was developed partially because it would withstand uranium compounds. The cascade of diffusion stages through which the gas passes must be continuous and leak-tight. Cascades are complex structures; as explained earlier, in a separation cascade the amount of gas passing through the first stage must be many times greater than that passing through the last. Passing through a filter stage reduces the pressure of the gas, which must be restored by a compressor. A cooler for the gas is needed, because the compressor generates heat. Each stage has two outputs, one with higher enrichment than what was injected, and the other with lower enrichment. The reject gas, however, is of much greater enrichment than gas much earlier in the cascade and cannot be thrown away. It is reinjected into the cascade at a point where its enrichment is the same as the other gas—in general, with the incoming gas at the previous stage. All of this must take place in a continuous, sealed system.

Figure 29 presents a simplified diagram of a diffusion cascade. In practice, the cascade is more of a pyramid, with multiple parallel units at the bottom tapering to a few units at the top (see fig. 20). At an individual stage, the enhanced and rejected gas streams are at different pres-

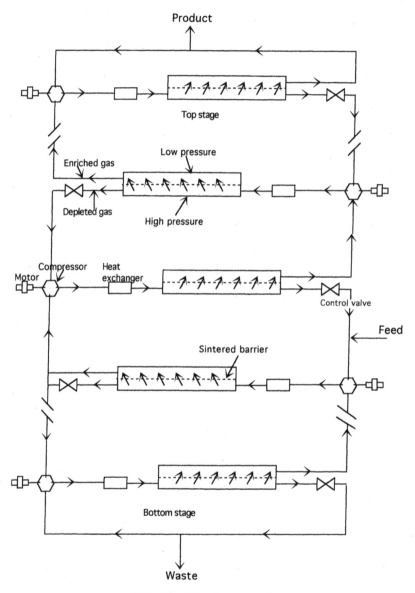

FIG. 29. Diffusion cascade

sures, but the gas flow up and down is about equal. If the flow streams are followed, it can be seen how individual stages are linked in a cascade. In each stage, the enriched stream from the bottom stage enters the central stage compressor and, after being partly compressed, is mixed with the depleted stream from the upper stage. The mixture is then compressed still further and fed to the diffuser in the central stage. The enriched stream from the central stage moves to the next compressor upstream, and the depleted stream is sent to the stage below for recycling. Groups of stages are coupled to make up operating units, and such groups make up the cascade.

Most plants operate at a pressure of about a third of an atmosphere, with about 85% of this pressure across the filter barrier. With the large pumps, valves, and piping involved, the elimination of in-leaking air becomes a major concern. The small pores can easily become clogged. A system capable of being evacuated to below 10^{-7} atmosphere is needed.[9] Per-stage losses need to be kept very small because of the large number of stages. A 0.1% loss per stage would result in a net loss of about 95% of the gas in three thousand stages.

Required Components

In an ideal system, the power required would be 900 kWh/SWU. A highly developed country can make a system that uses about 2,000 kWh/SWU, whereas a less-developed country would use at least 3,000 kWh/SWU. Small-scale production may make the use of a cascade much less efficient. For a less-developed country, this translates into an outlay of 600 megawatt-hours per kilogram of U-235, or 15,000 megawatt-hours for 25 kilograms. If the system is running at full capacity, it will use 1.7 megawatts for a year. Given a possible effective "on time" of 50%, this figure becomes 3.5 megawatts capacity to produce one bomb a year.

The equipment required for producing 25 kilograms of weapon-grade uranium per year using the gaseous-diffusion method is as follows. (Materials that must be imported are italicized).

1 acre of building
3.5 megawatts of power
At least thirty-five hundred stages (probably many more)

10,000 square meters of diffusion barrier with sub-micron-sized holes
At least thirty-five hundred of the following components
   pumps
   cooling units
   control valves
   flow meters
   monitors
   vacuum pumps

The installation would be hard to conceal in a country that did not have many large manufacturing plants. (Yet Argentina's secret gaseous-diffusion plant, which it started construction on in 1979, remained undiscovered until 1983.) Many parts of a diffusion system would be very difficult for an undeveloped country to produce or buy. In particular, making the diffusion barriers involves a complex technology, and the special pumps and flow meters also present problems. Special parts are needed, and the large-volume purchases that would be necessary are not easily concealed as part of a benign industrial project. Uranium hexafluoride, which is very corrosive, could cause leaks, and even very small per-stage losses would make it impossible to produce highly enriched uranium.

CENTRIFUGE ENRICHMENT

Most countries in the developed world choose to use the gas centrifuge for enrichment because its energy efficiency can be tens of times higher than that of gaseous diffusion.[10] A highly efficient centrifuge plant can produce 25 kilograms of weapon-grade uranium using 500,000 kilowatt-hours of electricity. The type of gas-centrifuge plant that a less-developed country could afford to build and operate might be ten to one hundred times less efficient.

The centrifugal forces used in the separation are in many ways indistinguishable from those of gravity, and a centrifuge produces a force on a molecule similar to that from a very strong gravitational field. A greater relative concentration of lighter gases is found in the atmosphere at high altitudes. In the centrifuge, this effect is exaggerated.

A centrifuge for uranium separation consists of a smooth cylinder that rotates on its axis at high speeds (see fig. 30). The material undergo-

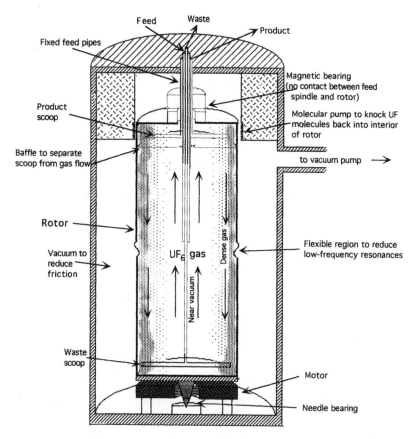

FIG. 30. Centrifuge

ing separation could be a gas or liquid, or separation could occur at a gas-liquid interface. Uranium, however, is used only in gaseous form, and only uranium hexafluoride is useful at easily manageable temperatures. UF_6 gas is injected into the rotating cylinder from a fixed tube introduced into the center of the centrifuge from above. The gas volume follows the cylinder, rotating at the same speed: the rotating outer wall gives its speed to the gas hitting it, and this gas, in turn, gives speed to the gas near it until all of the gas is rotating as if it were a single unit. Enriched gas and depleted gas are taken out by scoops at, respectively, the top and bottom of the centrifuge cylinder. The gas is made to circulate with a flow of gas down the periphery and back up nearer the axis.

The lighter gas is not taken off on the axis of the centrifuge, because the gas density there is too low. It is, instead, taken off by a scoop at a smaller radial distance from the axis than the depleted gas, which is taken off near the periphery.

Separation by centrifuge is much more effective than separation by gaseous diffusion. A single centrifuge stage can increase the U-235 fraction from natural uranium's 0.72% to 1.06%. An annual output of twenty-five kilograms of highly enriched uranium would require between twenty and two hundred stages of separation encompassing between one thousand and ten thousand individual centrifuge units. These units and the total power they require represent only a fraction of the needs of a gaseous-diffusion system. However, these figures are valid only for centrifuges of great speed and length, which are very difficult to build.

Ideally, the effectiveness of a centrifuge is proportional to the rotor's length and the fourth power of its peripheral velocity. (The enrichment of the gases containing different isotopes is proportional to the square of the velocity, but this separation also increases the amount of flow that is possible, leading to a fourth-power relationship.) However, practical considerations reduce the effectiveness to well below the fourth power.

One tends to think that the material inside a high-speed centrifuge produces a very great pressure on the cylinder wall, but this is not true with UF_6. Because UF_6 is solid at atmospheric pressure and room temperature, in order to keep it in a gaseous state it must be kept below atmospheric pressure unless temperatures are high. However, the supersonic rotor presents its own difficulties: at its high rotational speeds, the container undergoes very large outward forces. It must be made of material with a high strength-to-weight ratio, such as carbon fiber or a special steel called maraging steel, to counteract those forces. Also, very small deviations from axial symmetry can cause strong forces in supersonic rotors.

Resonances that occur in the structure at different rotational velocities present a severe problem as well. To understand a little about these resonances, imagine that a rotor is struck a blow with a hammer. It will ring at some group of "natural" frequencies; the longer the rotor, the lower the lowest frequency and the greater the number of frequencies excited. Although a blow will excite a group of frequencies, during rotation only one primary frequency is excited at a time. Imperfections in the rotor and its mounting cause an almost imperceptible blow to the rotor each time it turns. The frequency of this depends on the speed of rotation: the faster the rotation, the higher the frequency. If the timing of the repeated blow is at one of the "natural" frequencies of the rotor, a resonance occurs; the next time the rotor completes a rotation, the imperfection will give the same very small blow, and after thousands of blows a single resonance will be excited. This sequence is similar to the process of sitting in a swing and "pumping it up." These forces can be reduced by the use of self-adjusting damping bearings (invented by Gustave de Laval when he designed high-speed turbines at the end of the last century) that center the chamber's axis of rotation.

Low-speed rotors can avoid resonances, but are ineffective for enrichment. Long, high-speed rotors must pass through many resonances on the way up to speed. It is common for rotors to shake themselves to pieces as they are being turned on. The longer the rotor, the lower the speed at which a resonance occurs; but an effective centrifuge needs both speed and length. The more perfect the symmetry of rotor, the longer the resonance will take to be excited. If the rotor can be given sufficiently quick acceleration to high rotational speed, it can pass through the resonance before the amplitude of the vibration is sufficient to destroy the apparatus.

Another partial solution is to break up the length of the rotor by flexible bellows so that the rotor's resonant behavior resembles that of the shorter subsections. However, these cylindrical bellows must be thin, flexible, and strong—a combination that makes them very difficult to produce. An imperfectly made bellows section will itself cause a resonance that might destroy the centrifuge.

The rotors must be symmetrical and leakproof, and they must be protected from UF_6 corrosion by a layer of aluminum. It can be assumed that electron-beam welding is required to obtain the needed precision.

Following is a listing of the properties of a hypothetical moderate-size centrifuge.[11]

Radius	10 cm
Length	150 cm
Rotational frequency	800 rev/s
Peripheral speed	500 m/s
Separation factor	1.51

Separative power	15.2 kg SWU/yr
Inventory (material in centrifuge)	0.26 g U
Throughput	600 kg U/yr
Holdup time[12]	13.7 seconds

The United States has developed much larger units, but does not use them commercially. Over a period of twenty-five years, the U.S. program increased unit size from 38.1 centimeters long and 7.6 centimeters in diameter to 12.2 meters long and 61 centimeters in diameter, increasing the annual separative capacity per unit from 1 kilogram SWU to 200 kilograms SWU. The long centrifuges developed in the United States have not proved as effective in regular use as shorter ones developed by Russia and by Urenco, a British, Dutch, and German company formed to produce reactor-grade (3–4% enriched) uranium.[13]

The development of the modern centrifuge in the United States has an unusual history.[14] An Austrian physicist, Gernot Zippe, was captured by the Russians at the end of World War II and was set to work developing centrifuges for the Soviet nuclear-weapon program. Having succeeded, Zippe was allowed to return to Austria in 1956, and in 1958 he came to the United States. Here he joined the small centrifuge effort of Jesse Beams at the University of Virginia. Beams had separated uranium isotopes in 1940, but the technology had not been developed sufficiently during the war to compete with gaseous diffusion. In this poorly funded effort, the difficulties had not been overcome after the war. Zippe solved some crucial problems, however, and the U.S. centrifuge-development program started in 1960 (although without Zippe's participation). He introduced the idea of using bellows to break up the rotors into smaller lengths, and he introduced two ideas for the rotor bearings that allowed almost frictionless rotation. For the lower bearing, supporting the weight of the rotor, Zippe used a kind of needle bearing, allowing the rotor to rotate on a small, almost frictionless "point"—actually, a two-millimeter-diameter grooved ball revolving in an oil bath (the grooves cause the oil to circulate properly). The upper bearing was magnetic, with the rotor supported, floating without friction, in a magnetic field.

In 1960 Zippe returned to Europe, where his designs were used by Urenco. U.S. development continued, however, leading eventually to the immense centrifuges mentioned earlier, each capable of separating

200 kilograms SWU a year. The Soviets and Urenco continued with centrifuges that, though smaller and with less separative power, provided a better and less expensive method of separation. The smaller units probably operate at about 10 to 20 kilograms SWU per year.

Output in terms of kilograms per year is only one of several criteria that apply to centrifuges. Construction and maintenance costs can be of much greater importance. The United States stopped its centrifuge development in 1985. Although by then centrifuges were probably somewhat less costly to operate than gaseous-diffusion plants, the demand for enriched uranium had dropped, and no extra capacity was needed. The capital cost of switching over to centrifuges was too high to be justified.

In terms of the number of separation stages and centrifuges, and the power requirements, a gas centrifuge is over ten times more efficient than a gas-diffusion plant. A centrifuge plant could conceivably operate at about 50 kWh/SWU, although the hypothetical centrifuge described earlier would operate at about 200 kWh/SWU in a developed country and at about 600 kWh/SWU in a developing country.

None of the components of this technology would be available in a developing country. The maraging-steel or carbon-fiber rotors and the special bearings would need to be obtained from a developed country. Although less effective than long rotors, short rotors would most likely be built. (Pakistan used short rotors for enriching uranium to build its atomic weapons. Its use of this technology was made possible by the return to Pakistan of an engineer who had worked at Urenco.) It is possible that local industries would be able to assemble the system.

Required Components

To produce enough 90%-enriched U-235 for one bomb a year, a minimum of about 330 centrifuge units such as the one described earlier, in twenty stages, would be needed—assuming a completely efficient cascade; or a minimum of about 5,000 of the less complex, short centrifuge units, each having a separative power of about 1 kilogram SWU per year. A developing country, which would very likely use the shorter units, would need the following equipment. (Again, items that could not be produced indigenously and would not normally be purchased for another purpose are italicized.)

5,000 very high precision rotors of material of very high tensile strength
10,000 specially crafted bearings
5,000 damping systems
5,000 containers
5,000 motors
5,000 pumps
5,000 flow valves
Flow meters
High-vacuum pumps
400 kW of power
140,000 kWh/kg

The operation could be concealed in a large light-manufacturing plant. The centrifuge cylinders would have to be made with great accuracy, and be of very strong material. (The ones found in Iraq were made with German help.)[15] Assembly would require special techniques, such as electron-beam welding.

AERODYNAMIC ENRICHMENT

There are many methods of aerodynamic enrichment, but only two have been seriously developed, one using the vortex tube and the other the separation nozzle.[16] Both are similar to the centrifuge method in that a pressure gradient is set up by centrifugal forces. However, in these two aerodynamic-enrichment systems, the gas moves over a fixed curved surface to gain the acceleration necessary to produce the pressure gradient. A carrier gas, such as hydrogen, is mixed with UF_6, at a carrier-to-UF_6 ratio of about twenty to one. Hydrogen moves at the needed high velocities without becoming supersonic and producing shock waves, and the UF_6 is dragged along with it.

In vortex-tube enrichment (see fig. 31), a mixture of UF_6 and H_2 is injected tangentially to a tube's inner wall and spirals down the tube; at the end, the heavy and light fractions are separated by a skimmer. The light fraction is about one-twentieth of the total. Jet-nozzle enrichment (see fig. 32) operates without the spiraling effect, and the light fraction is about 25% of the total. Vortex tubes and jet nozzles are very small (with a radius of curvature of about 0.1 millimeter), and many of them are required.

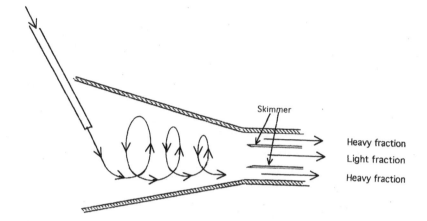

FIG. 31. Vortex-tube enrichment

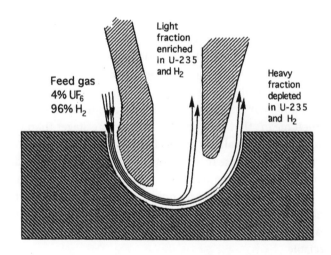

FIG. 32. Jet-nozzle enrichment

South Africa has used the vortex-tube method successfully, developing it with German help. An enrichment of 80% was reached for the first of six nuclear weapons that were built; presumably, a higher level was reached for the subsequent ones. Brazil tried the jet-nozzle method, but had more success with gas centrifuges. Any proliferation that might result from the use of these methods would most probably require the assistance of South Africa or Brazil—or of Germany, which also helped Brazil.

CHEMICAL ENRICHMENT

Chemical enrichment requires two chemical compounds of uranium, with the uranium tightly bound in one and loosely bound in the other. (Free uranium ions are the best example of the latter). If the two compounds can be mixed, the lighter isotope of uranium will be slightly more concentrated in the compound with the loosely bound molecule. The difference is greatest at low temperatures. The problem is in mixing the two compounds: they do not exchange ions readily, particularly at low temperatures.

Recently, the Japanese and French have discovered catalysts that make the ion exchange possible. In the Japanese system, ion exchange takes place between a liquid solution of uranium and a finely divided ion-exchange resin. The French method relies on an exchange between two liquid phases, one aqueous and the other organic. A third process, developed in the United States, also uses an exchange between two liquids, UF_6 and $NOUF_6$. The per-stage enrichment of these processes is small, which means that they require many more stages than does gaseous diffusion. Very detailed chemical knowledge and special chemical tools are necessary. If these techniques become more common, developing nations may be able to use them. The equipment is not large and could be housed in a relatively inconspicuous building. The techniques require about 50 kWh/SWU, somewhat less than is required for centrifuge separation. Other operating costs, such as those for chemicals, can be appreciable.

Chemical enrichment involves a large amount of uranium in liquid solution. Loading this material takes a long time. Indeed, the protracted start-up time of this method is a major disadvantage. It would take a little less than a month to begin producing 3%-enriched U-235 by the Japanese method; the French process reputedly would take fifteen months; for 90%-enriched material, the Japanese process would take five to eight years, the French twenty to thirty years. Although, clearly, chemical enrichment would be used primarily to produce 3%-enriched uranium for reactors, this material could, in turn, be further enriched by one of the other processes to reach 90% enrichment; this would require of the other process only about one-third the work it would take to bring raw uranium to 90% enrichment using only that process.

If chemical-enrichment processes are used to obtain the higher enrichment, they face a complication: as liquids with a high density of uranium approach high enrichment, enough U-235 may accumulate in a small part of the system to allow a chain reaction to start. Equipment design would have to take this into account.

LASER SEPARATION

Lasers provide a promising tool for the efficient enrichment of uranium because atoms and molecules of different isotopes of an element have slightly different excited energy levels, and a laser can be made to emit light with such well-defined energy that a mixture of two isotopes can be irradiated by it to raise one isotope, but not the other, to an excited state.

By itself, this accomplishes nothing; in a very short time, the excited isotope reverts to its original condition. However, if enough energy can be deposited by the laser to excite the isotope to ionization (thus ejecting an electron from the atom and making the atom positively charged), a more permanent condition is achieved, because the ionized atom can then be swept out of the mixture by an electric field. In order to effect a separation, an excitation energy to ionization must be made available to one isotope and not to the other. Normal ionization is not selective and requires over one hundred times as much intensity as excitation to one of the resonant, intermediate states. For atomic ionization, the photons must have an energy of over 6.2 electron volts and be in the very difficult ultraviolet region.[17] For these reasons, when separating U-235 and U-238 isotopes, a two- or three-step process is used (see fig. 33). The first step, from the ground state, must be very selective for U-235. Excitation of the second and third levels can be achieved with a laser beam of broader energy width if no U-238 has been moved into an excited level. In fact, some U-238 will be excited, and the use of a selective second and even third laser helps increase the purity of the product material.

The excitation of atoms by this method would most effectively be accomplished by means of four laser beams, each of approximately 2.0–2.1 eV. Two beams would be required for the first step (the material to be

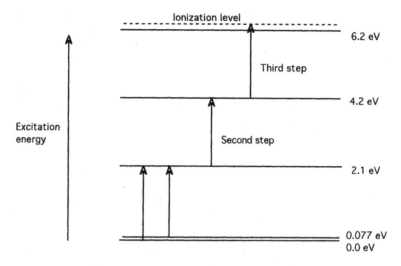

FIG. 33. Some atomic energy levels of U-235

separated must be in the form of hot vapor, which means in this case it will exist in two different ground states) and one each for the second and third steps. Suitable energy levels for these steps can be found in the uranium atom and in molecules of gases such as uranium hexafluoride. The first process I shall describe here is *atomic-vapor laser isotope separation,* or AVLIS.

In the following discussion, the assessments of the difficulties and efficiencies involved in laser separation are based on my own judgment, not on any practical experience on my part with this technique. Quite justifiably, most of the details of laser separation are shrouded in secrecy.

In principle, the separation of U-235 and U-238 isotopes from atomic vapor can be very efficient. If you merely calculate the energy that is needed to ionize the U-235 and not the U-238 of a mixture in a vapor form, only 6.2 eV are required for each atom. A simple calculation gives 0.7 kilowatt-hours to separate a kilogram of U-235. When the practical difficulties of performing this conceptually simple separation are taken into account, the power requirement will be shown as over a thousand times larger.

Figures 34 and 35 show diagrammatic views of a possible atomic-vapor laser isotope-separation (AVLIS) system. This entire system must operate in a region of high vacuum, with the laser light coming into the

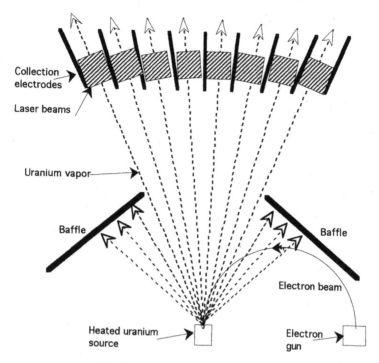

Collection electrodes

Laser beams

Uranium vapor

Baffle

Baffle

Electron beam

Heated uranium source

Electron gun

FIG. 34. Side view of AVLIS system

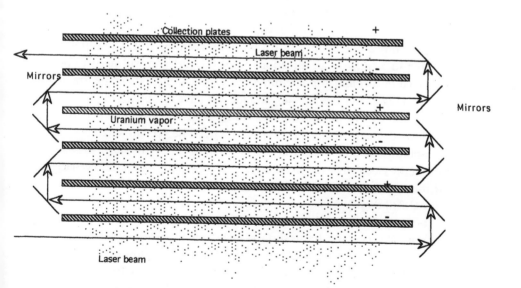

Collection plates +

Laser beam −

Mirrors

Uranium vapor +

Mirrors

−

+

−

Laser beam

FIG. 35. Top view of AVLIS system

region through windows. A vapor of natural uranium, containing a mixture of U-235 and U-238, is produced by using an electron beam to heat a crucible containing uranium. The path of the electron beam is curved by a weak magnetic field, so the source of electrons can stay out of the way of the uranium vapor. The uranium vapor is not generally ionized, and thus is not affected by the magnetic field. It drifts toward collector plates that, alternately positive and negative, are charged to a high voltage.

When the vapor is between the plates, the laser beams required to effect each of the transitions discussed earlier, united in a single beam, are passed through the vapor and selectively ionize the U-235, thus giving it a positive charge. The positive ions of U-235 are attracted to the negatively charged collection plates. The remainder of the uranium vapor drifts onto a large collection plate on the far side of the small U-235 collection plates.

Uranium Vapor

A vapor of atomic uranium is made by heating a uranium ingot in a crucible to above 2000°C—well above its 1130°C melting point. Molten uranium is very reactive, so the crucible must be made of special materials. It is not necessary to heat the uranium to the boiling point (3500°C) because only a small amount of vapor can be used. The uranium can be heated along a line by directing a beam of electrons at it. The vapor is emitted in a spray in all directions from the line and will need to be restricted by a collimator as it moves to a region where it can be irradiated by laser beams (see fig. 34). Shields will have to be used to prevent the uranium vapor from being sprayed to all parts of the chamber. The windows through which the laser light enters the vacuum chamber of the isotope separator must be kept clear, as must the high-voltage insulators for the electron beam. In addition, the vapor must not be allowed to hit the many plates used to collect U-235; otherwise they would catch more U-238 than U-235.

The long narrow surface of the molten uranium will radiate a large amount of heat energy. If this surface can be kept to a width of 1 centimeter, every meter of its length will radiate about 17 kilowatts of heat energy; there will be other heat losses as well. It will require as much power to compensate for the heat losses as is carried by the lasers themselves. (The efficiency of the laser method is so great, however, that the compensating power required is not very significant.) Uranium vapor will be moving in all directions from the heated source, so the collection plates need to cover all areas to which the vapor is emitted. Uranium vapor that does not pass through the collectors will be deposited on many other parts of the system and must be scraped off for recycling. Parts of the apparatus will have to be shielded from the heat or cooled. An electron beam of about 10 kilovolts will probably be needed; in the apparatus described here, this beam must develop a current of around 1.7 amperes per meter of its length and deposit the current in a uniform way on the surface of the uranium being heated.

Some of the atoms in the vapor will have been ionized by the heat, and these will be deflected out of the way by the magnetic field. Others will be in excited states that have a short lifetime, and the vapor beam must take long enough to reach the laser-interaction region that these excited states have time to decay to the ground state (or possibly to a very low level nearby).

Laser Beams

The windows through which laser beams are introduced into the vacuum must be kept very clean to prevent absorption of the light and damage to the windows. Lasers of four different frequencies will probably be used; their beams need to be combined into a single beam, and this must be done without much loss of intensity—in itself a difficult problem. In order to make efficient use of the lasers in a small apparatus, the beams must be reflected back and forth as shown in figure 35. Mirrors generally absorb some of the light; losses of this kind must be kept to a minimum.

Providing power to the lasers presents a major problem. The power needed to excite the laser material is about one thousand times that in the laser beam. The amount of power required could make it difficult to obtain a beam of well-defined shape and narrow energy spectrum. A solution to this problem is to excite or pump the ionizing lasers with other lasers. The issue of heat is thus pushed one step back, and the fact that the pumping laser will operate with a great deal of heat becomes of minor concern since its beam can be of less-well-defined shape and wider energy spectrum. The final laser used on the vapor will probably be of a dye type and be pumped by a copper-vapor laser. Dye lasers of the required power do not run at the high pulse rate necessary for this technique (possibly 50,000 pulses per second). As a result, multiple dye lasers must be used, with their outputs combined to reach the pulse rate needed. The laser installation required would need to be very large.

Other Technical Problems

The entire system operates in a high vacuum. A large roughing pump will be needed to get the vacuum down to about one-hundred-thousandth of an atmosphere, and a large diffusion pump to get it down to about 10^{-10} atmosphere. A freezing trap filled with liquid nitrogen will be needed between the separation apparatus and the diffusion pump.

Because this is a batch-processing system, the evacuated container holding the separation apparatus must be opened periodically for the removal of U-235 and the uranium residue, and for the addition of new uranium for separation. The entire apparatus must be cleaned. The delicately aligned collection plates and the laser beams must be realigned upon reassembly, and a good vacuum reestablished.

Some of the difficulties that must be overcome in laser separation are due to the fact that, as with the calutron, uranium will be deposited all over the interior of the apparatus and must be cleaned out after each run. Insulators must be cleaned regularly or they will become covered with evaporated uranium and experience electrical breakdown. The windows and mirrors needed for laser-beam operation must be completely shielded from uranium vapor—or, possibly, replaced after each run.

Efficiency of AVLIS

To estimate the efficiency of the AVLIS system, one must look at the component processes in more detail. If the atomic beam is too dense, charge-exchange scattering comes into play: an ionized U-235 atom drifting toward the attracting charged collection plates may hit one of the more copious U-238 atoms and take an electron from it. The newly ionized U-238 atom will then be collected, contaminating the U-235. If the average drift distance is about 1 centimeter, and if the chance of such a collision is to be less than 10%, for the cross section of about 10^{-14} square centimeters, the density of gas vapor must be such that there are less than 10^{13} atoms per cubic centimeter. The U-235 density would be less than 0.7% of this, or 7×10^{10} atoms per cubic centimeter. A vapor density of 10^{13} atoms per cubic centimeter is, in fact, a very good vacuum.

With this density of uranium vapor present in the interaction region, the interaction length of a laser beam will be about 15 meters, and the beam will interact with about 1.7×10^{-10} moles per pulse in a path 15 meters long. In fact, of the hot atoms moving in the beam, only about 40% will be at the lowest energy level and another 30% at a slightly higher level; two lasers of slightly different frequency will be used to excite these. After this first excitation, two others are needed, of equal or greater intensity.

In these estimates, I assume that the excitation would take place in a column 15 meters long, with a cross section of 1 square centimeter. The apparatus could actually be much shorter than 15 meters, and I shall postulate one that is 1 meter long, with fourteen mirror systems reflecting the laser light through the uranium vapor for a total of 15 meters. The four different laser beams would all be in the same place and of the same area. The collection plates would be a little more than 1 centimeter apart. The uranium vapor in the 1-square-centimeter region would be stripped of its U-235 in one laser pulse; it would be replaced very quickly with new vapor, and a new pulse would occur. If the vapor moves at 500 meters per second, a pulse rate of 5×10^4 per second is required.

In the scheme being discussed, the first excitation can be about 2 eV and the second can, in principle, be over 4.2 eV and move the electron to ionization (see fig. 33). Actually, because of the high optical frequency required to ionize in two steps, three steps may be used. The last stage of transition to ionization is critical. If the process used is normal ionization, the light used must be not just as strong as it was for the lower levels but many times more intense, because such a transition is normally over one hundred times less likely to occur than are the resonant transitions between the lower energy levels.

There are special ionization methods at selected frequencies that have larger resonant cross sections and allow the use of a light intensity comparable to that used for the lower energy levels. In making an estimate of the intensity of light needed, I have assumed that eight times as many photons must be present in each of the laser beams as would be required to nominally excite about two-thirds of the U-235 to each of the levels.[18] I have assumed that resonant excitation to ionization is possible, but that this might require sixteen times as many photons, rather than eight. Under these circumstances, the total light energy required for all stages would be about ten times greater than the minimum required to produce transitions from the lowest level. Note that 2-eV photons are used in this estimate, rather than the 6-eV ones used in the earlier one. If the lasers used in each stage do not have narrow energy spectra, the energy required at each stage can be very much greater, and the total laser energy required could be orders of magnitude greater.

There can be very large losses of beam intensity because of reflection from the mirrors, so special, low-loss mirrors must be used. In addition, there will be intensity losses from the vacuum-system windows through which the laser light must pass. To take these into account, an additional factor of two should be applied to the intensity estimated. This brings the total laser energy to twenty or more times greater than the first estimate. If contamination of the windows and mirrors occurs, this will limit the length of run possible in the batch process.

There are advantages of scale that make it easier to obtain the described performance in a large apparatus. With a longer apparatus, fewer reflections will be required, and the task of matching the four different lasers so that they will operate effectively will be easier. Furthermore, the vapor emitted from the crucible can be used more efficiently. So the power required for the crucible relative to the U-235 collected can be possibly ten times less.

Only about 70% of the U-235 in the vapor will be at energy levels that can be excited by the laser. The remaining 30% will not absorb energy from the laser, so although it makes no contribution to the output of the separator, neither does it affect the energy balance. As with the calutron, the wasted uranium must be recycled. If this comes from an intermediate step of a multistep process, it will be very valuable, and any losses would be expensive. Of the U-235 excited, only about 80–90% will be ionized at the intensities postulated, and at best 80–90% of the ionized U-235 will reach the collection plates. A great deal of unwanted U-238 will also reach the plates.

Among the many possible difficulties are the following: it is hard to produce a properly directed electron beam for heating the uranium in the crucible; the vapor density of the uranium will not be at an optimum level at all points; although it will be possible to shield the plates from the direct beam of vapor, this shielding will not be complete. For these reasons, in the first step of enrichment, the resulting U-235 will be enriched only to about a 5–7% level. However, most of the separative work will have been done. A second separation stage using 7%-enriched U-235 will have to operate on only 10% of the material that the first stage processed, and a third only on 1%. In considering the yield of weapon-grade U-235 from the system, I shall reduce the yield estimate by about 10% to take into account the two or three stages that would be required.

Output

Taking all of the factors just described into consideration, a yield of 4.4 grams of U-235 would be obtained per hour in the 1-meter-long laser isotope-separation apparatus, using a laser power of about 70 watts. The total power required for the laser will be about one thousand times greater, or about 70 kilowatts.

Power is also needed for heating the uranium. If we assume that the molten uranium is held in a crucible that does not transmit heat readily, the major heat loss will be by radiation from the surface of the molten metal. Radiation from a surface with a heat of 2000°C is about 1,700 kilowatts per square meter into a hemisphere. (It is assumed that that radiation can be prevented from radiating into the hemisphere below the crucible.) The region into which this radiation emanates can in principle be restricted by intermediate shields, but these would collect deposits of uranium from the vapor.

In this example, I assume that the molten area that is radiating heat is 1 centimeter wide. For the 1-meter-long crucible considered here, this would produce a total radiation of about 17 kilowatts. In this particular example, the area collecting the uranium vapor would not cover the entire hemisphere. For a larger-scale operation, it might cover it, and several times as much collection could be had from the same crucible.

In practice, the power required is not a major cost factor, so power losses are not important. The waste of uranium vapor, however, and the need to scrape off and collect all that is deposited, would be costly. The 1-meter apparatus is nominally capable of producing about 40 kilograms of U-235 a year. A more realistic estimate is about 25 kilograms—the amount needed for a single bomb.

For an efficient apparatus, this gives a figure of merit of somewhat less than 20,000 kWh/kg to produce 90%-enriched U-235; while with a small-scale apparatus, this figure might be a few times larger, possibly 60,000 kWh/kg. The corresponding figures for SWU would be 100 and 300 kWh/SWU, respectively. The power required is critically dependent on the efficiency of pumping the laser. For a technologically undeveloped country, the efficiency would be much less, and the power required much greater—if the laser could be made to work effectively. Still, the total power required is low enough to make it a relatively insignificant factor in deciding whether to build the apparatus. These power requirements for the laser isotope-separating apparatus can be compared with a figure of 100–600 kWh/SWU for centrifuge enrichment.

An additional factor making laser separation interesting to both developed and less-developed nations that want to build nuclear weapons is its potential for use for separating plutonium isotopes. A nation using nuclear power will have a large reserve of plutonium contaminated with Pu-240 that can be separated from the fuel rods of power reactors. Laser-isotope separation can be used to remove the Pu-240, leaving plutonium more suitable for weapons use.

Extrapolation from the method of U-235 separation described here would not be simple, in part because plutonium is immensely hazardous in comparison to uranium. The processes for handling the plutonium, and especially for removing it from the apparatus—both when collecting it and when cleaning the walls—would be difficult and dangerous.

A laser-separation apparatus would be very difficult for a less-developed country to build. The high-power laser required would probably not be available commercially and would have to be developed. Building a uranium-vapor source would be challenging. It seems, then, that this method would be feasible only in a technologically advanced country.

On the other hand, the scale of the apparatus is very much smaller than that of the apparatus for other methods, and its potential greater. Even though it would be necessary to import some technology, the total number of pieces of special equipment would be small. Moreover, the method does not have to work well in order to be useful to a country trying to construct a few nuclear weapons. In particular, an inefficient apparatus could be used as a second stage in conjunction with a centrifuge or some other first-stage apparatus.

If laser isotope separation were to be used in a developed country, it would have to compete successfully with the very effective centrifuge-separation methods. For an underdeveloped country, the method would merely have to produce some U-235. Developing nations that are trying to avoid restrictions on the production of nuclear weapons might find this method useful.

When the United States chose between centrifuge and laser separation in 1984, the cost of both systems was considered to be about equal.[19] A possible reason for the choice of AVLIS was the likelihood that further development (particularly with respect to powering the laser) would lead to a major improvement in efficiency.

Molecular Laser Isotope Separation (MLIS)

An alternative laser-separation method is *molecular laser isotope separation,* or MLIS. Here uranium isotopes combined with other elements in a molecular compound provide the raw material for the separation. The energy-level structure of a molecule is much more complex than that of an atom, and imparting energy selectively to U-235 compounds rather than to those containing U-238 is more difficult. Two basic methods are used: *photodissociative separation,* in which laser energy is used to break chemical bonds; and *photoreactive separation,* in which selectively excited molecules undergo a chemical reaction more readily than unexcited ones.

PHOTODISSOCIATIVE SEPARATION. This method has been used by a German group, Uranit. In this process, a laser is used to remove a fluorine atom from UF_6 to produce UF_5 + F. The UF_6 is first cooled by expansion through a nozzle and then irradiated with light from an infrared laser to excite vibrations in those UF_6 molecules containing U-235. Subsequent irradiation by another laser then dissociates the excited U-235 molecules into UF_5 + F. The UF_5 condenses into a powdered form that can be separated. As with the ionization stage in the atomic-separation technique, the final stage of dissociation may require a large amount of laser power.

PHOTOREACTIVE SEPARATION. The most interesting form of this method is *chemical reaction by isotope-selective laser activation,* or CRISLA. Molecules of UF_6 are exposed to a laser; those containing U-235 are selectively excited. Mixed with the UF_6 molecules is a commercial proprietary reagent. This supposedly reacts about ten thousand times more strongly with the selectively excited U-235 molecules than with those containing U-238, and the product of the reaction can then be separated by standard techniques. The advantage of this process is that very little laser power is needed. However, CRISLA has not been well tested.

These descriptions do not do justice to the difficulties inherent in the laser techniques required, which are so problematic that the U.S. government has chosen to put its major development effort into the AVLIS process instead.

Laser-Assisted Enrichment

There are other methods of using a laser to select U-235 for separation. In one of these that involves a diffusion process, the laser is used to heat selectively molecules containing U-235 rather than ones containing U-238, thereby increasing the average velocity of these molecules. In another, also involving diffusion, an infrared laser is used to excite UF_6 molecules containing U-235 to a high vibrational state. As these molecules collide with others in the gas, their vibrational energy can be converted into translational energy, which can then be used to enhance the diffusion of the $^{235}UF_6$ molecules. Laser-assisted enrichment has an advantage over straight laser isotope separation in that it does not require high laser power.

COMBINED TECHNIQUES

At first glance, it seems that the combined use of two or more techniques for enrichment would not be a useful option for a technologically underdeveloped country. An example from the Soviet Union, however, shows that this is not necessarily true.

At the end of World War II, the Soviets started a crash program to produce an atomic weapon. They built both a gas-diffusion plant and a calutron separator.[20] Though the calutron installation was very small in comparison with that of the United States in Oak Ridge, the gas-diffusion system was of considerable capacity.

Although the diffusion system went into operation, in its first development it never succeeded in producing weapon-grade material. The stage losses in the pumps were too great, and virtually nothing came out of the top end. It was possible, however, to get an appreciable yield at about 40% enrichment.

The partially enriched uranium from the diffusion separation underwent further separation in the small calutron, resulting in 90%-enriched material. The use of partially enriched uranium allowed for a reduced load on the electromagnetic system, enabling it to produce about 400 grams of highly enriched uranium—the first such uranium the Soviets were able to make.

A less-developed country attempting to build nuclear weapons might have difficulties with its separation techniques that would prevent it from obtaining weapon-grade uranium. A separation method requiring many stages, such as a gas-centrifuge or gas-diffusion system, can be very effective in producing 3–4%-enriched uranium, yet quite ineffective in producing highly enriched uranium. The effort, in terms of SWU, of enriching to the 3% region is greater than that required to go from 3% to 90%, but the number of stages required is very much smaller. It is the large amount of raw material needed to make the low-level enrichment worthwhile that makes it so costly in terms of SWU. If the uranium could be brought to 25% enrichment by one of the multistage methods, the load on a calutron or laser system would be reduced over thirty times. If a chemical method was attempted, the time required to bring a system into operation at 90% enrichment could be prohibitive, whereas operation at 3% enrichment might be possible. Again, in these circumstances, having available a small calutron or laser system would be useful, because with 3%-enriched material, the size of the second-stage system could be reduced by three-quarters.

For the same reason, small-scale calutron or laser-enrichment plants could also be of great use for a country that has access to a large quantity of reactor-grade uranium. Reactors use about a metric ton of 3%-enriched uranium per megawatt, or over 20 kilograms of U-235. Thus, the charge of a 40-megawatt (electric) reactor would provide enough U-235 for about forty nuclear weapons. If this fuel could be diverted before the reactor was activated, thus preventing its being made dangerously radioactive, weapons could be produced from it at a greatly reduced cost. The need for control of even very small installations of calutrons and laser separation units was pointed out several years ago by Paul J. Persiani of the Argonne National Laboratory.[21]

A COMPARISON OF TECHNOLOGIES

For a country that wants to avoid the restrictions of the Nuclear Non-proliferation Treaty (this treaty is discussed at length in chapter 6), the efficiency of a process, or the cost per kilogram of enriched uranium after the process is put into operation, is not the most important consideration. Rather, the availability of engineers, the supply of critical materials, and the ease of concealing the installation are its first concerns.

In terms of all these criteria, the gas-centrifuge method is the most likely choice; therefore, the greatest effort at control should be focused on this technology. The cost of operating a gas-centrifuge enrichment system is about half that for the gas-diffusion system used by the United States. Centrifuge technology is used by Russia and by the major European enrichment company, Urenco. It is the means by which a large part of the enriched uranium used in the world's reactors is produced. The laser-enrichment method AVLIS, a new technique, uses less power, but will most likely not be able to produce 3–4%-enriched uranium at a much lower cost in the near future.

3–4% enriched uranium, almost all of it produced by centrifuge plants, is treated as a commodity on the world market. There are primary, secondary, and spot markets. Many engineers have been trained in its production, and as a result, the technology has spread; it is to be found in Pakistan and has begun to be developed in Iraq.

The advantages of the centrifuge technology do not preclude a less-developed country's enriching uranium by any of the other methods that have been discussed (although the use of the gaseous-diffusion technique seems very unlikely because of its poor efficiency and large size requirements). The supply of technology relating to any of the methods described here should be rigidly controlled, because special circumstances such as the availability of engineers and technology may make one of the other techniques more appealing. In particular, the development of one of the batch-processing techniques, or of the calutron or AVLIS method, might be very useful in bringing partially enriched uranium up to weapon-grade.

Tables 5 and 6 compare some of the characteristics of the various technologies.

TABLE 5

Power Requirements of Enrichment Devices

Device	Approximate Power Requirements (kWh/SWU)		
	Ideal	Industrialized Country	Developing Country
Electromagnetic	600	2,500–7,500	25,000–75,000
Diffusion	900	2,000	3,000
Centrifuge	?[a]	50–200	600
Chemical	?	50	—[b]
Laser (AVLIS)	0.0035	100 (?)	600 (?)

[a]Depends on materials.
[b]Not suitable except in conjunction with another system.

TABLE 6

Difficulty of Construction and Concealment of Enrichment Devices

Device	Degree of Difficulty		
	Obtaining Parts	Technology	Concealment
Electromagnetic	Low	Moderate	High
Diffusion	High	High	High
Centrifuge	High	High	Moderate
Chemical[a]	High[b]	High	Low
Laser (AVLIS)	High	Very high	Low

[a]For enrichment to 3%.
[b]Requires proprietary technology.

5

Bomb Assembly

The following discussion applies to the type of weapons used by the United States and the Soviet Union early in their weapons programs. A less-advanced technology is required for this type of weapon than for the weapons to be found in modern stockpiles. (An excellent reference is *The Los Alamos Primer,* by Robert Serber [University of California Press, 1992], an expansion of the notes for lectures Serber gave to physicists who joined the work at Los Alamos during the war.)

The reaction that produces a nuclear explosion is different from the one that takes place in a nuclear reactor, particularly in the speed required for the reaction. In both, energy is produced by the fissioning of uranium (or plutonium) nuclei when they absorb a neutron. Each fission of U-235 (or Pu-239) will produce, on average, over two new neutrons. If all of these interact with other U-235 (or Pu-239) nuclei, they will produce two fissions, then four, and so on until, in the later stages of an explosion, a very large number of fissions—for example, after eighty generations, 2^{80}—might occur if all of the neutrons interact. The reaction will still take place, however, if, on the average, more neutrons are produced than are lost.

The reactor or bomb must be built of materials that do not readily absorb neutrons (the sole exception being the uranium that fissions); below a critical size, the neutrons escape the bomb too readily and no buildup of energy occurs.

An explosion must be prevented in a reactor, and reactor design takes advantage of the fact that very slow, low-energy neutrons interact very much more readily (with a larger cross section) with U-235 (or plutonium) than do fast ones. The slowness of the neutrons makes a nuclear explosion in a reactor impossible, even if control of the reactor is lost. The reactor would heat up rapidly and expand, but not with explosive force. The neutrons, which start with an average energy of over 1 MeV, are slowed down by collisions with atoms such as hydrogen, which do not usually absorb neutrons. When the neutrons are slow, they are able to interact easily with the U-235 to produce more neutrons. (Each fission produces about 200 MeV of total energy.) Because the slow neutrons have a very large cross section for causing fission, only a small concentration of U-235 is needed for a reactor. With sufficient uranium, and the use of heavy water or very pure graphite to slow the neutrons, the reactor can be made to work even with natural uranium, although most reactors at present use uranium enriched to about 3–4% U-235.

GUN-BARREL WEAPONS

For a weapon, a very fast reaction is needed. If the fission multiplication grows slowly, the uranium will heat up and expand before much of the material has had a chance to fission. When the uranium has expanded to a lower density, the neutrons will not have as good a chance of hitting the uranium nuclei because there will be more space between them. The neutrons will go farther before they interact, and will escape more readily from the uranium material, even though the physical size of the bomb has increased, because of its expansion. The bomb will expand beyond its critical size (the size at which more neutrons are produced than are lost) and the chain reaction will stop. The reaction must go fast enough that a reasonable fraction (5–30%) of the material can fission before the inertia of the bomb can no longer hold it together. In the first uranium weapon, the efficiency was a few percent. For the plutonium bomb, it was about 20%.

A fast reaction is necessary, and therefore no time is available for slowing down the neutrons. Fast neutron fissioning is needed. The cross section for this is much lower, and a much larger fraction of U-235 is needed; about 90% is used in most nuclear weapons. In this case, the whole chain reaction takes place in a few microseconds.

To increase the efficiency in the gun-barrel weapon, material is placed around the outside of the U-235 to reflect escaping neutrons back into the weapon. Heavy material is placed around the outside as a tamper so that its inertia can slow down the expansion. The strength of the tamper material is not pertinent. The tamper will be heated to a gaseous state before much expansion takes place. Only the mass of the tamper material is important. The material generally used is natural uranium.

Because a minimum (critical) amount of uranium is needed for the chain reaction to take place, any amount of material less than the critical amount can be assembled without an explosion. An explosion is pro-

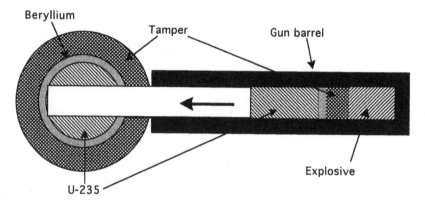

FIG. 36. Gun-barrel weapon

duced by bringing together two or more subcritical masses to make a critical mass. A subcritical mass can also be made critical by compressing it to increase its density. If, for example, the density is doubled, the chance of an interaction by a neutron in any given distance is doubled. Because the volume of a sphere changes as the cube of its radius, the escape distance to the exterior of the mass is reduced only by about 20%. In modern weapons, plutonium is compressed to several times its normal density.

The weapon is fired by bringing together or compressing subcritical masses so rapidly that they are not set off before they are assembled. Neutrons are always present from cosmic rays or from the nuclear materials to start the chain reaction. The U-235 itself does not produce many neutrons from spontaneous fission, but if U-238 is used as a tamper, one might expect about 15,000 neutrons per second from it. Not all of these will interact to set off a chain reaction. The subcritical pieces must be brought together at a rate of about 1,000 meters per second. This can be done using conventional explosives (see fig. 36). The mass of the uranium projectile being accelerated requires a large explosive force and a very strong gun barrel; the gun has to be used only once, so this problem is alleviated. A pulse of neutrons is injected at the instant of assembly.

IMPLOSION WEAPONS

For plutonium, the situation is very much different because of its Pu-240 content. Spontaneous fission, which produces neutrons, occurs 3 mil-

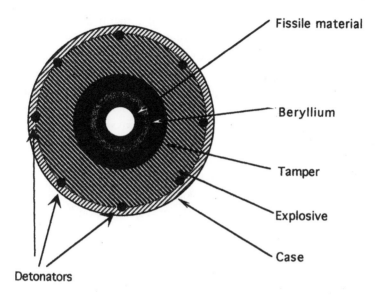

Fissile material

Beryllium

Tamper

Explosive

Case

Detonators

FIG. 37. Implosion weapon

lion times as often with Pu-240 as with U-235, and 65,000 times as often with Pu-240 as with U-238. The velocity of assembly by a gun-barrel device is not high enough. The interaction would be set off prematurely, and the Pu-239 material would expand too soon, making it subcritical before the explosion developed. A "fizzle" would occur, with a few tons of energy being released. It is the contaminating Pu-240, not the Pu-239, that causes the difficulty.

Assembly must be faster for a plutonium weapon. This can be achieved by using shaped charges to bring many subcritical parts together rapidly from all directions, causing an implosion that compresses a thin spherical shell or a subcritical sphere of Pu-239 to a higher density by a spherical shock wave (see fig. 37).

The manufacturer must have a shop in which uranium or plutonium can be machined accurately. Although uranium's physical properties do not make machining the metal difficult, it tarnishes rapidly in air and may have to be worked under an oil film. Plutonium, on the other hand, is very hazardous to work with. Even a few micrograms, if inhaled, can be deadly. If beryllium is used as a reflector, it causes its own difficulties: it is not a metal commonly used in industry, and metal of high purity must be obtained. Machining beryllium is difficult because it is very brittle; it fractures almost as readily as glass. It is also extremely toxic to many people, and machinists must use protection when working with it. An oil film was considered to offer sufficient protection from beryllium in the United States during and shortly after World War II, but this is no longer the case under the strict safety standards currently in effect. The older method might today be considered satisfactory in a less-developed country.

Work with shaped charges, explosives designed so that the shock wave of the explosion has a desired shape, could probably be done in many less-developed countries but would require extensive experimentation. Firing the explosives, particularly for the implosion device itself, is a special problem. About one hundred detonators must be placed around the periphery of the shaped charges. These send an electric current through the explosive to start the explosion; they must be triggered within a fraction of a microsecond of each other. A considerable amount of energy is needed to set off an explosive rapidly, and it is no easy task to design a switch that will do this for each of the detonators. In a laboratory, many standard power tubes are available that could be used to operate such a switch, but these require a lot of auxiliary apparatus, such as sources of filament power and of cooling. Something more compact is needed. The United States uses switches called *krytrons*.

Countries making weapons have to get krytrons or their equivalents from manufacturers, or embark on a program to build them. The technology does not appear to be very difficult. One method, described in unclassified literature, is to use a small enclosed spark gap with the gas sulfur hexafluoride, SF_6, surrounding the electrodes. A very small unit can be designed to hold off a large voltage. To fire the gap, light from a krypton fluoride laser with a 248-nanometer wavelength is injected into the region of the spark gap to ionize the SF_6 and fire the gap. A large number of spark gaps need to be fired, and a single laser, connected to each gap by a separate optical fiber, can accomplish this.

In order for them to operate, these firing units must have a source of high-voltage current available in condensers. Many types of condensers are available commercially that can hold a large amount of charge at high voltages. On the other hand, it is very difficult to design a condenser from which the charge can be made to drain in a fraction of a microsecond: wires connecting such condensers to the switches and to the explosive have a quality called inductance that prevents the rapid buildup of current. To minimize the inductance, the conductors must be of large area and very short. The design of the condenser must be such that its contribution to the inductance is low. A less-developed country may have to purchase such condensers from abroad. Even if the specifications mentioned here are not well met, an effective weapon can be produced, but its yield will be low and unpredictable.

A final hurdle for this method as well as for the gun-barrel design is to obtain the pulse of neutrons needed to trigger the bomb. The act of compressing uranium or plutonium into a very small sphere will allow the neutrons naturally emitted by these elements to start the chain reaction of the explosion. The timing of the start, however, is very critical in obtaining maximum yield, and in order to control this, a source of neutrons is introduced.

One method of obtaining neutrons involves the use of polonium 210 and beryllium to produce an alpha-neutron reaction. In this reaction, an alpha particle from polonium 210 hits a beryllium nucleus and produces a neutron plus a carbon nucleus ($\alpha + Be^9 \rightarrow n + C^{12}$). (The polonium emits only alpha particles, no gamma rays or electrons; alpha particles, or helium nuclei, have a very short range in materials.) A neutron source of this type contains polonium and beryllium close together, separated only by a thin foil to prevent the alpha particles from hitting the beryllium. The source can be placed in the center of the bomb so that, when the parts of the bomb collapse on themselves as the weapon is fired, the source will be crushed. This mixes the polonium and beryllium, producing neutrons. All of this is straightforward. The problem is that polonium 210 has a half-life of 138 days (that is, after 138 days only half of it will be present, after 276 days only a quarter, and so forth), and a country using such a trigger must be able to regularly replenish the polonium 210 in its stored weapons. A research reactor can provide the polonium 210 needed.

A better method, but one more technologically challenging, makes use of a compact accelerator shooting either a beam of deuterium (hydrogen 2) nuclei into deuterium to produce helium 3 plus a neutron, or a beam of tritium (hydrogen 3) into deuterium (or vice versa) to produce helium 4 plus a neutron. Both of these reactions produce copious neutrons. Such

TABLE 7

Yields Using Two Different Firing Systems,
as a Function of Spontaneous Neutrons

Relative Intensity of Spontaneous Neutrons (multiple of Trinity)	Yield			
	Nominal (20 kt)	Above 5 kt	Above 1 kt	1 kt to Fizzle
	Using the Trinity Firing System			
1	0.88	0.94	0.98	0.02
10	0.28	0.54	0.82	0.18
20	0.08	0.29	0.67	0.33
30	0.02	0.16	0.55	0.45
40	0.006	0.08	0.45	0.55
	Using a System Twice as Fast as Trinity's			
1	0.94	0.97	0.99	0.01
10	0.54	0.74	0.90	0.10
20	0.28	0.54	0.82	0.18
30	0.16	0.40	0.74	0.26
40	0.08	0.30	0.67	0.33

Source: Mark, "Explosive Properties of Reactor-Grade Plutonium," p. 121.
Note: The numbers in the "Yield" columns represent the average fraction of times the yield of the weapon would be larger than the column heading. Yields are in kilotons of TNT equivalent. The numbers in the left-hand column represent the relative neutron intensity in the weapon material compared with the intensity for the Trinity weapon.

compact accelerators are now made commercially in very small sizes for use by oil geologists. (The accelerators can be introduced into oil wells to help study the earth through which the well is being drilled.)

WEAPONS USING REACTOR-GRADE PLUTONIUM

Reputedly, the United States has successfully fired a weapon made with plutonium containing the fractional amount of Pu-240 that would be found in fuel from nuclear reactors. One method of firing such a weapon would be to use a larger amount of plutonium and tamper than that used in a uranium weapon. The inertia of the extra mass would slow down the expansion of the plutonium when unwanted neutrons trigger it prematurely and allow the development of the chain reaction. The weapon tests that have taken place over the past forty years or so have, among other things, allowed the development of faster and more forceful firing systems that improve the yield from plutonium weapons. A new nuclear-weapon state would have difficulty in getting a large yield. J. Carson Mark has estimated the yields that would be obtained by firing a weapon using the same firing system as that used in the original "Trinity" test and one twice as fast; his estimates are presented in table 7.

The worst reactor plutonium would probably produce fewer neutrons than forty times the number produced by Trinity. Even the "fizzle" yield of a properly fired weapon using reactor plutonium would be about 500 tons equivalent. Weapons made with reactor plutonium must be considered in most ways equivalent to those made with weapon-grade plutonium. Had even a fizzle-yield weapon been used for the World Trade Center it would have produced an even more terrible outcome. Had Iraq possessed a fizzle-yield weapon during the Gulf War, the strategy of the United States would have had to be very different.

6

Efforts to Prevent
Nuclear Proliferation

E ver since the United State dropped atomic bombs on Hiroshima and
Nagasaki, it has had a policy of preventing nuclear proliferation. The
Baruch Plan, a proposal for international control of atomic energy made
in 1946, was the first attempt at non-proliferation. After the USSR rejected the Baruch Plan, the United States maintained the policy of secrecy prescribed by the Atomic Energy Act of 1946 (the McMahon Act).
Senator Brian McMahon, in introducing this legislation, described it as
being designed

> to conserve and restrict the use of atomic energy for the national
> defense, to prohibit its private exploitation, and to preserve the
> secret and confidential character of information concerning the
> use and application of atomic energy.[1]

In addition to this policy of secrecy, the United States tried, for a
while, to gain control of the earth's richest uranium resources, hoping
to slow other nations' efforts to develop nuclear energy. This monopo-
listic policy was abandoned when the wide distribution of good uranium ore became known. With the explosion of the first Soviet atomic
bomb in 1949, and the successful test of Great Britain's in 1952, a
different policy was needed to restrain the development of atomic
weapons. Also, other European nations were then starting programs for
the development of power reactors. It was felt that the technology they
developed for this would soon give them a good base from which to
build atomic weapons.

ATOMS FOR PEACE

In 1953, realizing that its secrecy policy was not effective, the United
States decided on a policy of control by cooperation. President Dwight

Eisenhower made his "Atoms for Peace" speech, offering U.S. cooperation to all countries that wanted to develop nuclear energy for peaceful
purposes. The Atomic Energy Act of 1946 was replaced by the Atomic
Energy Act of 1954, which permitted, under suitable controls, the transfer of nuclear equipment, materials, and technical understanding from
the United States to other nations. These controls were to be ensured by
applying U.S. safeguards, which included an inspection system.

Because nuclear weapons can be made either from plutonium or from
uranium enriched in uranium 235, it was necessary to have safeguards
verifying that any plutonium produced in nuclear reactors was not diverted to nuclear weapons.

Some people believe that the Atoms for Peace policy is the source of
much of our present problem of proliferation. This policy let the technology for the production of atomic power be given to other nations, while
the United States retained control of any material that would be useful
for producing atomic weapons. At that time it was thought, generally,
that the plutonium produced in reactors operating to produce nuclear
power would not be suitable for bomb construction. As I explained in
chapter 3, Pu-240 is produced during reactor operation by the exposure
of the Pu-239 already produced by the reactor to more neutrons from
the reactor. Many scientists believed then that Pu-240 emits so many
neutrons that if it were present in large quantities in a nuclear weapon, it
would make the weapon explode prematurely when it was fired, causing
a fizzle. (The plutonium used for weapons is made from uranium exposed to reactor neutrons for only a short time, and therefore has only a
small degree of Pu-240 contamination.) If inspectors were present when
the reactor fuel rods were changed, they could determine whether the
fuel was indeed contaminated. Later, it was shown that effective weapons can be made from plutonium contaminated with a large amount of
Pu-240. Although the explosion may be weaker than that from a weapon
made with uncontaminated plutonium, it may still be equivalent to
several thousand tons of TNT (see chap. 5). Gerard Smith, the chief U.S.
negotiator in many U.S.-Soviet arms-control talks, tells of V. M. Molotov, Soviet foreign minister, protesting to John Foster Dulles, U.S. secretary of state, that the Atoms for Peace proposal would lead to a worldwide spread of stockpiles of weapons material. Smith had to explain to
Dulles that Molotov was better informed about the technology than was
the secretary of state himself.[2]

Although the assistance in the design of nuclear reactors that the United States gave to other nations potentially allowed them to start nuclear-weapon programs, the controls then in force being insufficient for preventing weapons production, few nations have used this assistance. Argentina and Brazil were helped in their now-terminated programs. India used help in its program from both Canada and the United States.

The major contribution by the United States to the spread of nuclear weapons was, possibly, the education in nuclear processes and nuclear power it provided to scientific students from all nations. In the 1950s, nuclear power was believed to be the cheap, new source of energy that was going to power the postwar world's development. All nations wanted it; scientists and students came to the United States to learn about it. Foreign scientists, trained in the United States, would be most likely to advocate the use of reactors designed and built by U.S. companies. As it turned out, these reactors are less useful for producing plutonium than competing European and Canadian designs. It is hard to believe, however, that even the most stringent secrecy on the part of the United States could have done more than delay for a few years the construction of nuclear reactors by the developed nations.

The United States also tried to keep enrichment technology secret, knowing that any country that mastered it would be able to produce weapon-grade uranium. The Soviet Union had a similar policy toward its allies, but made an exception for China when it was closely tied to the Soviet bloc. The Chinese program resulted in the explosion of that nation's first nuclear weapon in 1964. France, searching for partners in its enrichment efforts, looked to the European Economic Community (EEC). But the United States, with its offer of inexpensive, partially enriched uranium for use in reactors, persuaded the other EEC nations that such an enrichment plant was unnecessary. The French, who wanted to be independent of the United States, then decided to construct a gaseous-diffusion plant on their own.

A number of international agencies have been created to control nuclear materials and to prevent proliferation. They have slightly different functions (although these overlap considerably), largely because each of these agencies originated from different international political pressures. I shall now describe the principal agencies.

EURATOM

European cooperation on atomic energy resulted in the establishment of the European Atomic Energy Community (Euratom) by Belgium, France, the Federal Republic of Germany, Italy, Luxembourg, and the Netherlands.[3] Euratom was established in 1957, at the same time as the European Economic Community, but by a different treaty. Euratom's purpose was to coordinate, promote, and control the development and use of nuclear power in Western Europe, and to provide an organizational structure for obtaining help from the United States. The nations of Europe wanted to share the costs of developing nuclear power, which they felt essential to the development of the European economy. Euratom was to provide a common market for the flow of goods, labor, and investment for nuclear development. It was to help guarantee access to nuclear materials, and to promote pertinent research. It did not have as a purpose the prevention of the development of nuclear weapons. A major member, France, was embarking on a program of producing a nuclear force; as a result, Euratom is vested with the ownership of all special fissile material *except that destined for military purposes.* France has interpreted this policy to mean that all of its plutonium-producing facilities are exempt from inspection.

When Euratom came into existence, the United States and to a lesser extent the United Kingdom were the source of almost all nuclear-related materials and technology. Their supply contracts required that their inspectors have access to installations making use of the materials they exported in order to verify that the materials were not being diverted from the purpose for which they had been supplied. Euratom's control system, which was accepted by the United States and the United Kingdom, made it possible for the Europeans to avoid direct foreign control.

THE INTERNATIONAL ATOMIC ENERGY AGENCY

In his "Atoms for Peace" speech before the United Nations in 1953, President Eisenhower expressed the shift in U.S. policy away from secrecy and denial. He proposed that those governments involved in nuclear research and development make contributions from their stockpiles of fissionable materials to an organization, the International Atomic Energy Agency

(IAEA), which would be responsible for the storage and protection of the contributed fissionable materials.[4] The IAEA would also be responsible for distributing fissionable materials for peaceful purposes, especially for energy production. Part of the U.S. plan, apparently, was to reduce the stockpiles of weapons material by diverting it to peaceful purposes. In this, as it turned out, the United States was not successful.

Before the IAEA could be set up, changes had to made in the U.S. Atomic Energy Act of 1946, and these were incorporated into the Atomic Energy Act of 1954. These changes included removing most controls on the secrecy of nuclear research, approving ownership of nuclear facilities and fissionable material by private industry, and enabling the government to enter into agreements for cooperation with other nations on peaceful uses of nuclear energy.

Secretary of State John Foster Dulles had begun bilateral negotiations with the Soviet Union on the formation of the IAEA in January 1954. The Soviets first tried to link the IAEA plan to a general disarmament plan, a response similar to the one they had earlier made to the proposed Baruch Plan for international control, when they were also far behind in the development of nuclear armaments. By September 1954, they had changed their position. It had become clear that the United States would have its own peaceful international programs, and that any influence the Soviets might have on these would be through an agency like the IAEA. Furthermore, the United States had obtained a draft agreement regarding the formation of the agency from the nations that were the major suppliers of uranium: Great Britain, Canada, Belgium, France, South Africa, Australia, and Portugal. By the time the U.N. General Assembly met that autumn, the Soviets had acquiesced; over two more years were required to produce the completed treaty.

The International Atomic Energy Agency was to have some nuclear material of its own, and its own bureaucracy and control system. It differed from the agency proposed in the rejected Baruch Plan in that it did not have a monopoly on the ownership of nuclear materials and those activities classified by that plan as "dangerous." An important decision in preparing the treaty was that the obligation of a state to submit to safeguards was not a condition of membership in the IAEA, but arose from the state's application for and receipt of agency assistance. This meant that the United States, the United Kingdom, and the Soviet Union, none of which needed assistance from the IAEA, would not be required to have any safeguards on their own nuclear activities, although safeguards would be required on work they performed for states without nuclear weapons. Originally, nuclear materials were to be given to the IAEA from many countries, but such donations never really occurred. Assistance from the agency has to be paid for.

Safeguards were set up by the IAEA against the diversion of nuclear materials for military uses. In 1957, when the IAEA came into existence, the United States had some forty bilateral agreements regarding nuclear-research reactors. These agreements allowed the United States to inspect the reactors to assure that they were being used for peaceful purposes. The United States was very supportive of the creation of an IAEA inspection force. (Countries can also initiate bilateral arrangements for inspection.) By 1968, the agency had expanded its safeguards to reactors of all sizes, and to reprocessing and fuel fabrication. These safeguards apply only to those nations receiving assistance, not to the nuclear-weapon powers that provide the assistance.

Although the agency's statute provides for it to "conduct its activities in accordance with the purposes and principles of the United Nations to promote peace and international cooperation," and although its director general submits an annual report to the U.N. General Assembly, the IAEA is not an agency of the United Nations. It operates with a board of governors, who are selected in such a way as to have representatives not just from the technically advanced nations, but also from a broad geographical spectrum. Under the board is the director general, who oversees the secretariat and staff. A large and representative general conference takes place once a year, at which the director general dispenses information and delegates make recommendations. It serves, primarily, as a forum. The IAEA staff reflects the organization's international character, although the technically advanced nations are better represented among the technical staff and inspectors than are the less-developed ones.

The IAEA has two basic functions: to promote peaceful and safe uses of nuclear energy, and to apply safeguards against its assistance being used to "further any military purpose." The role the agency assumed was to monitor the flow of fissile material; it has no enforcement power. IAEA safeguards verify actions that are taking place or that have been taken. If an inspection team finds that there is a possibility that fissile material is being diverted, it can inform the IAEA board, which would first call upon the government concerned to make changes in its operations. If the government refused, the IAEA could raise a public alarm; there are no effective sanctions it could apply. Its relationship with the United Nations allows it to refer violations to the U.N. Security Council. As an international agency, it must regard all nations—including maverick states such as Iraq—with the same degree of trust or suspicion.

SAFEGUARDS

The IAEA statute does not require members to accept safeguards unless they have sought and received assistance from the IAEA in some peaceful nuclear activity. The IAEA does not require member states to enforce safeguards when they give nuclear assistance to other states. Obligations to use safeguards are to be found in treaties such as the Nuclear Nonproliferation Treaty (NPT), discussed in detail later, and the Nuclear-Free-Zone Treaties; in bilateral agreements between nuclear suppliers and their recipients; and in multilateral arrangements such as the Nuclear Suppliers Group guidelines.[5] In the first few years after the IAEA was started there was no general agreement on its use of safeguards, but in recent years its safeguarding role has become increasingly important with regard to problems of nuclear proliferation.

In 1963 the United States started to use the IAEA to supervise the safeguards required by its bilateral agreements on nuclear plant and material transfers. Its agreements with the European countries were usually supervised by Euratom, whereas its transfers to the rest of the world were supervised by the IAEA. Other nations followed suit: the Soviet Union, which had earlier opposed safeguards, started changing its policy in 1963. By 1966, a document outlining an IAEA safeguards policy had been agreed upon. Called INFCIRC/66, it detailed provisions that remained in effect until the Nuclear Non-proliferation Treaty entered into force in 1970. They still apply with regard to nations that are not party to the NPT.

The basic safeguards procedures of the IAEA emphasize auditing, accounting, and verification. The precise arrangements are negotiated between the state and the agency. The agency examines the design of any facility to ensure that it will not serve any military purpose and that it permits effective safeguarding. Routine inspections, scheduled on the basis of annual usage of nuclear materials or their maximum potential production, are required—as are special inspections.

Safeguards agreements can be of two types: they can apply only to some material or apparatus being transferred to a country; or they can be "full scope," applying not just to some specific material but to all nuclear activity in a country. The latter type of agreement is most often made in relation to safeguards under the Nuclear Non-proliferation Treaty.

Safeguards under the NPT differ in some respects from those specified in INFCIRC/66. NPT safeguards conform to the somewhat different conditions of INFCIRC/153, called the Blue Book.[6] Because INFCIRC/153 specifies that all of the nuclear facilities of a state are to be under full-scope safeguards, the system used (describe by INFCIRC/153) is designed to reduce the burden of safeguards on legitimate nuclear activity of the nations receiving assistance. It is a less flexible agreement than that of INFCIRC/66 and emphasizes material flow rather than facilities as the principal place to apply safeguards. Under INFCIRC/153, the IAEA has no right to preliminary information on any new facility. According to former IAEA officials David Fischer and Paul Szasz, under these safeguards "an entire reprocessing or enrichment plant could be exported to an NPT country (such as Iraq) without any notification to the IAEA."[7] Monitoring the supply of both equipment and material comes about primarily through export controls (which I shall discuss later). INFCIRC/66, which still applies to dealings with nations not party to the NPT, or those who signed the document before the NPT came into effect, is in many ways a broader document. The sale of uranium- or plutonium-processing equipment to a non-nuclear-weapon state that is *not party to the NPT* triggers the application of safeguards.

The restrictions limiting the effectiveness of the IAEA in safeguarding against nuclear proliferation are not a part of the IAEA statute itself, but result from interpretations of the statute and from pressures exerted by the nations that are subject to safeguards. The discovery of Iraq's secret nuclear-weapon program and more recent difficulties in North Korea are causing a reevaluation of the IAEA's safeguarding methods.

IAEA inspections should not be confused with those of UNSCOM, the United Nations Special Commission on Iraq. This commission operates under special rules agreed to by Iraq to end the Gulf war, and reports directly to the Security Council. UNSCOM has its own personnel, representing a broad range of nations, although the technological specialists are largely from the developed ones. It has been given broad powers of inspection and the mandate to destroy weapons of mass destruction, or tools for their production. In the case of dual-purpose equipment that can be used for peaceful purposes as well as for weapons, it installs surveillance equipment, such as cameras, to monitor the use of the equipment. The commission has been remarkably effective in these special circumstances.

THE NUCLEAR NON-PROLIFERATION TREATY

Further progress toward prevention of proliferation came as a result of the efforts of the Irish government in the U.N. General assembly.[8] In 1958, Ireland's foreign minister, Frank Aiken, introduced a draft resolution calling on nations involved in the test-ban negotiations under way at the time not to "supply other states with nuclear weapons while these negotiations are taking place." Although supported by the Soviets, the resolution was opposed by the United States because it had deployed weapons on the territories of its NATO allies. In 1959, the Irish resolution was modified to require that nuclear powers "refrain from handing over control of such weapons to any nation not possessing them." This ban was "subject to inspection." The resolution was adopted by the General Assembly with U.S. support; France and the USSR abstained. The resolution was amended in 1960, with the phrase "subject to inspection" removed and a prohibition added on the transmittal of information necessary for the manufacture of nuclear weapons, and adopted by the General Assembly. The Soviets supported it, but the United States abstained because the resolution did not require verification of the new ban. Finally, an Irish resolution put forward in 1961 was adopted unanimously. It required that the nuclear powers "undertake to refrain from relinquishing control of nuclear weapons and from transmitting the information for their manufacture to states not possessing such weapons." There was also a stipulation that states without nuclear weapons would not receive or manufacture such weapons.

The Soviet Union opposed any non-proliferation agreement that would permit a multilateral nuclear force (MLF) in Europe. As contemplated by its proponents, such a force would consist of ships or submarines, manned by crews from all NATO nations, that would carry nuclear weapons under some sort of NATO control. For the Soviet Union, the proposed MLF appeared to be a means of giving the Federal Republic of Germany some form of control over nuclear weapons, and this the Soviets violently opposed. Negotiations between the United States and the Soviet Union in the period up to the end of 1965 reflected this Soviet stance.

For the United States, it was a choice between a nuclear nonproliferation treaty and the multilateral force, and the government was itself divided. The State Department, probably because of NATO desires, supported the MLF, whereas the Arms Control Agency, with support from the Defense Department, favored a treaty. With waning support for the MLF by some of the NATO member nations, and difficulties anticipated in getting congressional agreement, President Lyndon Johnson and Secretary of State Dean Rusk abandoned the MLF and were prepared to take the crucial step of signing a treaty by which the United States agreed that nuclear weapons should not be transferred to nonnuclear states directly or indirectly. The U.S. Senate also supported the idea of a treaty, and the way seemed open for an agreement with the Soviets.

There were other obstacles, however. Many of the nonnuclear nations demanded that an agreement place more obligations on the nuclear nations than the requirement that they not transfer nuclear weapons to the nonnuclear nations. It became apparent that three overlapping sets of negotiations were needed: negotiations between the United States and the Soviet Union; between the United States and its allies; and between the United States and the USSR on one hand and the nonaligned nonnuclear states on the other.

Some of the difficulties encountered in reaching an agreement are reflected in Articles I and II of the Nuclear Non-proliferation Treaty itself.[9]

Article I
Each nuclear-weapon State Party to the Treaty undertakes not to transfer to any recipient whatsoever nuclear weapons or other nuclear explosive devices or control over such weapons or explosive devices directly, or indirectly; and not in any way to assist, encourage, or induce any non-nuclear-weapon State to manufacture or otherwise acquire nuclear weapons or other nuclear explosive devices, or control over such weapons or explosive devices.

Article II
Each non-nuclear-weapon State Party to the Treaty undertakes not to receive the transfer from any transferor whatsoever of nuclear

weapons or other nuclear explosive devices or of control over such weapons or explosive devices directly, or indirectly; not to manufacture or otherwise acquire nuclear weapons or other nuclear explosive devices; and not to seek or receive any assistance in the manufacture of nuclear weapons or other nuclear explosive devices.

Articles I and II reflect the concern of the Soviet Union at that time that the nuclear nations of Western Europe might create a future federation and turn their nuclear weapons over to that group, thus in effect giving some control over nuclear weapons to West Germany. Some analysts now seem to have found ways in which nuclear weapons could be transferred to a united Europe that do not violate the restrictions in these articles.

Article III of the treaty implies the use of "full-scope safeguards" by the IAEA and also deals with Euratom. The use of such safeguards is spelled out in the IAEA's INFCIRC/153 statement. Originally, the IAEA's safeguards system usually applied only to nuclear facilities and materials that were being transferred. Article III, section 1, of the NPT states, in its second and third sentences:

Procedures for the safeguards required by this article shall be followed with respect to source or special fissionable material[10] whether it is being produced, processed or used in any principal nuclear facility or is outside any such facility. The safeguards required by this article shall be applied to all source or special fissionable material in all peaceful nuclear activities within the territory of such State, under its jurisdiction, or carried out under its control anywhere.

These two sentences mean that the IAEA is authorized to monitor the flow of all nuclear material in a country, not just the material that had been declared by the country subject to safeguards. In a legal analysis of the NPT and its model agreement (INFCIRC/153), George Bunn, first general counsel of the U.S. Arms Control and Disarmament Agency and one of the U.S. negotiators of the provisions of the Nuclear Nonproliferation Treaty, states:

The model agreement confirms that, by signing the NPT, non-nuclear-weapon parties consented to inspection of places where nuclear material might one day be present, whether or not the places or the material had been declared and whether or not nuclear material was yet present.[11]

At the time the NPT was being negotiated, the European Atomic Energy Community had provisions for safeguarding nuclear materials and installations used for civil purposes. The European community wanted to use the Euratom safeguards system for NPT inspections in Euratom countries. The Soviets were concerned that this was really a form of self-inspection; the Europeans, striving toward European integration, felt it necessary to bolster Euratom because it was part of that effort. The issue was finally resolved with Euratom non-nuclear-weapon states being allowed to jointly negotiate safeguards agreements with the IAEA. When put into effect, the NPT provided that both agencies would apply safeguards, as can be seen in section 4 of Article III:

Non-nuclear-weapon States Party to the Treaty shall conclude agreements with the International Atomic Energy Agency to meet the requirements of this article either individually or together with other States in accordance with the Statute of the International Atomic Energy Agency.

The non-nuclear-weapon states were worried that they might be placed at a commercial disadvantage by rules that applied only to them. The United States and the United Kingdom tried to allay these fears by volunteering to have the IAEA safeguards applied to all of their own nuclear activities except those relating to national security. However, the Soviet Union opposed the U.S.-U.K. suggestion, and India and many other countries felt it had little value. Article IV, section 2, of the treaty did support assistance to nonnuclear nations in peaceful uses of nuclear energy.

All the Parties to the Treaty undertake to facilitate, and have the right to participate in, the fullest possible exchange of equipment, materials and scientific and technological information for the peaceful uses of nuclear energy. Parties to the Treaty in a position to do so shall also cooperate in contributing alone or together with other States or international organizations to the further development of the applications of nuclear energy for peaceful purposes, especially in the territories of non-nuclear-weapon States Party to the Treaty, with due consideration for the needs of the developing areas of the world.

When the treaty was being negotiated, nuclear explosions were still being used for peaceful purposes in the Soviet Union and were being contemplated by others (the use of nuclear explosions for large excavations in construction projects in the United States had been proposed by Edward Teller, among others); this is reflected in Article V. (Such explosions were eventually found to be of little use, and the radioactive contamination from them to be very dangerous.)

Significantly, the non-nuclear powers also insisted that the superpowers promise both to negotiate in good faith an end to the arms race and to work toward a treaty on general disarmament, as expressed in Article VI:

Each of the Parties to the Treaty undertakes to pursue negotiations in good faith on effective measures relating to cessation of the nuclear arms race at an early date and to nuclear disarmament, and on a treaty on general and complete disarmament under strict and effective international control.

These articles are reinforced by declarations in the preamble that also urge a test ban. In this section the signatories characterize themselves as, among other things,

Declaring their intention to achieve at the earliest possible date the cessation of the nuclear arms race and to undertake effective measures in the direction of nuclear disarmament,

Urging the cooperation of all States in the attainment of this objective,

Recalling the determination expressed by the Parties to the 1963 Treaty banning nuclear weapons tests in the atmosphere, in outer space and under water in its Preamble to seek to achieve the discontinuance of all test explosions of nuclear weapons for all time and to continue negotiations to this end.

A review of the treaty in five years, and possible subsequent reviews, are provided for in Article VII. In Article X, a twenty-five-year period is set for reconsideration of the treaty. (Reconsideration took place in April and May of 1995 and resulted in an extension of the treaty for an indefinite period.)

A further problem raised by the nonnuclear nations was that of security assurances for those nations that were being asked to give up the right to have nuclear weapons. A suggested clause forbidding nuclear-weapon states from using or threatening to use nuclear weapons against parties to the treaty could not be adopted because the United States had been allowed to place nuclear weapons in West Germany, a party to the treaty (but not the owner of the weapons), and the Soviets argued that this clause would prevent their retaliating against West Germany for a nuclear attack by U.S. forces there. To solve this problem, the United States, the United Kingdom, and the Soviet Union made parallel declarations recognizing that the threat or use of nuclear weapons would put at risk the peace and security of all states. They pledged, as members of the Security Council, to assist the threatened states and to counter any threat to use nuclear weapons. This resolution was approved by the Security Council on June 19, 1968.

The Nuclear Non-proliferation Treaty was signed in Washington, Moscow, and London on July 1, 1968. It went into effect on March 5, 1970; ninety-seven nations had signed it, and forty-seven ratified it. Neither France nor China signed the treaty, although France assured other nations that it would abide by its provisions.

Many nonnuclear nations greeted the treaty with little enthusiasm. West Germany felt that the Soviet interest in non-proliferation was directed primarily against it. In addition, the proposed multilateral force, which Germany favored, had been dropped by the United States in favor of the NPT. France, suspicious of U.S. motives, believed that that treaty would be used to give America commercial and political advantage; for the French, the basic issue was one of national security and independence. Similar motives can be attributed to China, another nuclear nation that did not sign. India, which would soon explode its first nuclear weapon, also did not sign; it, too, was distrustful of American policy.

The NPT is now the basic treaty constraining the spread of nuclear-weapon technologies to the less-developed world. Its initial purposes, however, were to prevent Japan and the developed European nations (other than Great Britain and France) from feeling the need to build up their own nuclear arsenals, and to assure the USSR and some other nations that Germany and Japan were not diverting nuclear materials to nuclear weapons. To this end, the NPT controlled the entire fuel cycle of power reactors except for uranium mining and milling. With this control, it was felt, each nation would be assured that other nations were not secretly starting the construction of nuclear weapons. Under the conditions of the treaty, information about and assistance in developing nuclear power would be provided to a state only in exchange for that state's agreeing to the controls.

The NPT is not explicit in its restrictions. The most important restriction for the purpose of preventing proliferation to the less-developed nations is specified in section 2 of Article III.

> Each State Party to the Treaty undertakes not to provide: (a) source or special fissionable material, (b) equipment or material especially designed or prepared for the processing, use or production of special fissionable material, to any non-nuclear-weapon State for peaceful purposes, unless the source or special fissionable material shall be subject to the safeguards required by this article.

Extension of the Nuclear Non-proliferation Treaty

In 1995, when the treaty had been in effect for twenty-five years, a conference was convened to consider its extension.[12] Of the five acknowledged nuclear powers, four of them—the United States, Russia, the United Kingdom, and France—wanted the treaty extended for an indefinite period; the fifth, China, found acceptable either an indefinite extension or multiple fixed extensions of no less than twenty-five years each. A group of fourteen nonaligned states, led by Indonesia, wanted the treaty extended for a series of twenty-five-year periods, subject to certain goals being reached in each period. The Arab states refused to approve any extension of the NPT that did not include pressure on Israel to accept the NPT, including full-scope safeguards. All of the non-nuclear states wanted a comprehensive test-ban treaty; binding assurances by the nuclear powers that they would not use nuclear weapons; a cutoff in the production of, and the eventual elimination of stockpiles of weapons-usable fissile material; and the elimination of nuclear weapons and other weapons of mass destruction.

Major support for an indefinite extension came, as expected, from the developed nations, and also, crucially, from a large group of Third World states (forty to fifty)—nations whose insufficient resources made it impossible for them to obtain nuclear weapons and who were concerned that more powerful neighbors might obtain them.

For a treaty like the NPT to be effective, it is important that there be a consensus among the signatories; a lack of cooperation would make the treaty useless. A vote on the treaty's extension might have led to the perception of such a lack: it would have put on record the votes of many nations that, although wanting an extension, would have found voting for it politically difficult. Canada led the effort to obtain instead a consensus for an indefinite extension. It tried to get unconditional agreement to the extension, but later called for commitment to accountability (see condition 2 below) and implementation of the treaty. The president of the conference, Jayantha Dhanapala of Sri Lanka, together with the twenty most active delegations (which included the nuclear powers) formulated three draft conditions based on the Canadian proposal and on suggestions by other nations—among them, particularly, South Africa:

1. A "strengthening of the review process." This would provide for a review conference every five years, as in the past, but would assure more systematic preparation for the conferences and would assure that they focus on substantive issues. A preparatory committee would meet for two weeks in each of the three years prior to a conference to choose the specific issues.

2. A statement of principles and objectives for nuclear nonproliferation and disarmament. This would affirm the treaty's goals of the complete elimination of nuclear weapons and the formulation of a treaty on general and complete disarmament. It would also set forth twenty principles and objectives dealing with its universal application, nonproliferation, nuclear disarmament, nuclear-weapon-free zones, security assurances, safeguards, and peaceful uses of nuclear energy.

3. An extension of the treaty. This, in effect, would make it possible to finesse the problem of a vote by noting that because a majority favored an extension, the treaty would be extended indefinitely.

On May 11, Dhanapala got the consent of the active delegations to adopt the three draft conditions without a vote (as is sometimes done in the United Nations under similar circumstances). It was clear that a majority favored these conditions and that a form of consensus could be obtained in the absence of any protest. This was what happened: the participants simply agreed by their silence to accept Dhanapala's compromise.

The issue of Israel's nuclear weapons was resolved, without specifically mentioning Israel, by a call for all states in the Middle East that had not yet done so to accede to the NPT as soon as possible.

The terms for the extension are of four types:

1. Those that required serious efforts by the nuclear powers to get rid of their nuclear weapons:

The nuclear-weapon states reaffirm that they will pursue negotiations on nuclear disarmament.

A universal and verifiable comprehensive nuclear-test-ban treaty should be negotiated no later than 1996.

Negotiations on a non-discriminatory and universal convention banning the production of fissile material for nuclear weapons or other nuclear-explosive devices should begin immediately and come to an early conclusion.

The nuclear-weapon states will engage in efforts to reduce the number of nuclear weapons with the goal of eliminating nuclear weapons completely.

2. Those that encouraged the establishment of nuclear-weapon-free zones and security assurances:

In addition to the terms that require participating nations in nuclear-weapon-free zones to refrain from developing nuclear weapons and to obey rules excluding nuclear weapons from the zone, protocols are included to be signed by the nuclear powers agreeing to obey the zone treaty restrictions. The extension treaty encourages the respect of the treaties by the nuclear powers and the signing of the protocols.

Further steps should be made to assure non-nuclear-weapon states party to the treaty against the use or threat of nuclear weapons.

3. Those that strengthened IAEA safeguards:

Effort should be made to give the IAEA the resources, both financial and human, to carry out its responsibilities.

The IAEA's ability to detect undeclared nuclear activities should be increased.

States not signatories of the NPT should be urged to enter into comprehensive safeguards agreements with the IAEA.

Full-scope safeguards and binding commitments not to acquire nuclear weapons should be required by supplier states before entering into arrangements to supply fissionable material or reprocessing equipment to a non-nuclear-weapon state.

Fissile material transferred from military to peaceful uses should be placed under IAEA safeguards.

4. Those that encouraged the peaceful use of nuclear energy in the non-nuclear-weapon states:

Research into, and the production and use of, nuclear energy for peaceful purposes is a right of all parties to the treaty.

There should be the fullest possible exchange of equipment, materials and scientific and technological information for the peaceful uses of nuclear energy.

Preferential treatment should be given to the non-nuclear-weapon states party to the treaty, particularly developing countries, in activities promoting the peaceful uses of nuclear energy.

ENFORCEMENT OF THE NUCLEAR NON-PROLIFERATION TREATY

No international agency enforces the provisions of the Nuclear Non-proliferation Treaty. Each nation has its own export policy and is guided by its own interpretation of the provisions of the treaty. In an attempt to make the actions of the nuclear-supplier nations more uniform, special committees have been set up to clarify the meaning of Articles I and II, and to provide "trigger lists" of materials that should be exported only under safeguarded conditions. The safeguards involved would be effected through the IAEA.

The Zangger Committee

The Zangger Committee was set up in 1970 by parties to the NPT to put together a detailed list of what could not be sold, transferred, or received by adherents of the treaty without triggering the application of IAEA safeguards. This list would allow a common understanding of the rules regarding safeguards required for companies or nations attempting to supply material or equipment to other nations. The committee, representing over a dozen industrialized states (now thirty members), met regularly, but only after four years—in June 1974, a month after India's first nuclear explosion—did it adopt a trigger list. This list specified items whose export would trigger the application of IAEA safeguards to the facility for which the items were intended, and whose export to a nation that did not accept the application of the safeguards should be forbidden. The Zangger Committee produced and keeps up-to-date its list of material and equipment, as well as definitions of technology, major critical components, and the criteria needed to interpret the trigger list. The list's effectiveness has been limited because dual-use items, those that can be used both in normal commerce and in building nuclear weapons, are not included.

The Nuclear Suppliers Group

The United States had reservations about the completeness of the Zangger list and also about the absence from the formulating committee of some nations, such as France, which could not be represented because they did not sign the NPT. India's success in producing an atomic explosion in 1974 showed that a developing country could produce a nuclear weapon,[13] which gave further impetus to the effort of finding a more effective group to extend the trigger list.

Representatives of the nations able to provide nuclear technology met in London in 1974 to see what additional restrictions could be agreed upon to retard further proliferation. Because of French president Valery Giscard d'Estaing's concerns about proliferation, France joined the group from the outset, finding it possible to do so because the group that was meeting was not directly connected to the NPT.

In 1977 the group, which called itself the Nuclear Suppliers Group, added to the Zangger list a more comprehensive list of trigger items whose export would require safeguards. The group had seven members: the United States, France, West Germany, the United Kingdom, Canada, Japan, and the USSR. (At this writing, it includes thirty-four states.) No general agreement was reached on applying full-scope IAEA safeguards. A gentleman's agreement rather than a treaty, the trigger list that the group produced was in effect until 1992, when the group developed a more detailed list. The group's original list can be summarized as follows:

1. Uranium (numerical quotas)
2. Reactors, etc.
   Nuclear reactors
   Reactor pressure vessels
   Reactor fuel-charging and -discharging machines
   Reactor control rods
   Reactor pressure tubes
   Zirconium tubes
   Primary coolant pumps
3. Nonnuclear materials for reactors
   Deuterium and heavy water
   Nuclear-grade graphite
   Reprocessing plants
   Fuel-element fabrication plants
   Equipment for the separation of isotopes of uranium
   Plants for the production of heavy water, etc.
4. Technology transfer; that is, the transfer of technical data important to the design, construction, operation, or maintenance of enrichment, reprocessing, or heavy-water-production facilities or major critical components thereof. Major critical components include
   Diffusion barriers
   Gas-centrifuge assemblies, corrosion resistant to UF_6
   Nozzle units
   Vortex units

Many suppliers avoided the intent of this list by operating on the assumption that anything not listed could be supplied. As we have seen in the case of Iraq, parts for centrifuges and for reprocessing plants have been sold without the application of safeguards.

Measures to prevent the proliferation of nuclear weapons are now focused primarily on preventing access to the technology required to build a weapon rather than on IAEA safeguards. New rules regarding the transfer of technology have been set up; if followed, these controls of supply could be very effective. The Nuclear Suppliers Group reached a new agreement in March 1992. In a document titled "Guidelines for Transfers of Nuclear-Related Dual-Use Equipment, Material and Related Technology," the group stated that suppliers should not authorize transfers of equipment, material, or related technology identified in an annex to the original list, either for use in a non-nuclear-weapon state in a nuclear explosive activity or an unsafeguarded nuclear fuel cycle activity; or in general, when there is an unacceptable risk of diversion to such an activity, or when the transfers are contrary to the objective of averting the proliferation of nuclear weapons.

A long list is given in the annex. Its major components include:

Industrial equipment (over 22 subheadings)
Materials (30 subheadings)
Equipment and components for uranium-isotope separation (46 subheadings)
Equipment related to heavy-water production (10 subheadings in addition to trigger-list items)
Equipment for implosion-systems development (13 subheadings)
Explosives and related equipment (28 subheadings)
Nuclear-testing equipment and components (7 subheadings)
Other (11 subheadings)

The items listed here are further described in detail. The list is quite comprehensive with respect to laser separation, and is particularly comprehensive for centrifuges. Some restrictions apply to calutrons: for example, there are restrictions on high-vacuum pumps, machine tools, and power supplies, and there is a direct ban on electromagnetic isotope separators with a current of over 50 milliamperes.

Had this list been in place ten years ago, and had it been enforced, it would have curbed proliferation, but the number of potential suppliers is much greater now. To the original seven members of the Nuclear Suppliers Group have been added Argentina, Australia, Austria, Belgium, Brazil, Bulgaria, the Czech Republic, Denmark, Finland, Greece, Hungary, Ireland, Italy, Luxembourg, The Netherlands, New Zealand, Norway, Poland, Portugal, Romania, Slovakia, South Africa, South Korea, Spain, Sweden, Switzerland, and Ukraine. In addition are such countries as India and Taiwan. Most of the countries outside the group, such as China, India, Israel, and Taiwan, may act responsibly, but the number of potential suppliers is now so large that it may be possible for any nation determined to have nuclear weapons to find help in getting them.

COCOM and the Wassenaar Arrangement

Other methods of coordinating export policy have existed. The one of greatest importance to the Western alliance was COCOM. In 1949, officials from the United States and the countries of Western Europe met to consider how to prevent the Soviet Union from strengthening its military capabilities through trade with the West. A uniform policy about what should and should not be exported to the Soviet bloc was needed. This was accomplished through a coordinating committee that became known as COCOM. Its decisions were effected as gentleman's agreements. In fact, it was often desirable that there be no formal structure; political parties in some of the European countries did not share the view of the United States or even the views of their own governments regarding the dangers of a powerful Soviet bloc. A formal agreement would have initiated much political flak.

COCOM did not control the exports of the nations involved; it suggested a common policy. In the 1950s, when the United States dominated the decisions of this group, it was the source of almost all of the new technology that might flow to Europe, Japan, or the Soviet Union. No member of the Western alliance could afford to be cut off from this new technology. As Europe developed its own resources, the American dominance of COCOM lessened, although it was still strong.

The United States used COCOM to control the flow of technical information and materials to the Soviet bloc. COCOM was also useful in regulating the transfer of technology to the problem nations of the Third World. COCOM's origins in the coordination of East-West trade made it difficult for it to assume a role in the regulation of technology transfer between any other nations, and with the collapse of the Soviet Union, its existence came to an end.

Its place has been taken by the Wassenaar Arrangement Regarding Export Controls for Conventional Arms and Dual-Use Goods and Technology, the aim of which is to prevent destabilizing accumulations of conventional weapons and the transfer of arms and sensitive technologies "for military end uses" in maverick states. All of the NATO nations except Iceland are members of this group, plus Australia, Austria, the

Czech Republic, Finland, Hungary, Ireland, Japan, New Zealand, Poland, Russia, Slovakia, Sweden, and Switzerland. The United States has identified the maverick states as Iran, Iraq, Libya, and North Korea.

Effectiveness of Control

An examination of the technical complexity of all of the processes I have described in earlier chapters shows that a country trying to build a nuclear weapon would put a high premium on obtaining both detailed design information for the method it had chosen and the assistance of engineers, physicists, and chemists who had experience with these technologies. Urenco, an international consortium for uranium enrichment, trains engineers in centrifuge-enrichment technology; it cannot completely control the future activities of the people it trains. As a result, Urenco has become a source of engineering and technical assistance for developing nations trying to build centrifuges. Furthermore, most of the scientists in the less-developed countries received their training at European, American, and Soviet schools and laboratories. It is nearly impossible for schools to give students an education in the modern physical sciences that does not increase their knowledge of how to build nuclear weapons.

7

The World's
Nuclear Development

The following discussion describes the present political and technological situation regarding nuclear weapons and their development
in those nations that own them, in those that desire them, and in those
that are capable of supplying the technology for building them.[1] The
discussion is organized in terms of the various regions of the world,
because local interactions generally determine the desire or the perceived need for these weapons. Figure 38 charts the growth since 1945 in
the number of nations that have nuclear weapons.

I shall begin my discussion with those nations that first possessed
nuclear weapons: the United States, the Soviet Union, the United Kingdom, and France.

THE ORIGINAL NUCLEAR-WEAPON STATES

The United States

The United States is a major source of all the components of nuclear-
weapon technology. As a result of the START I treaty, the U.S. reduced
the number of its deployed strategic nuclear warheads by mid-1996 to
about 8,402, in addition to 950 tactical weapons. It has a stockpile of
about 1,000 metric tons of weapon-grade plutonium in addition to the
intact nuclear cores of the thousands of nuclear warheads it has dismantled. Since 1945, it has consistently tried to prevent proliferation, although there have been two lapses, one with regard to Israel and the
other with regard to Pakistan (discussed later). It is firm in its support of
the Nuclear Non-proliferation Treaty and the Nuclear Suppliers Group.

As the world's first nuclear power and as its scientific leader after
World War II, the United States became the training ground for scientists throughout the world. The training they received here provided a
basis for the development of nuclear technology by most U.S. allies
during the Cold War and for the development of much of the world's

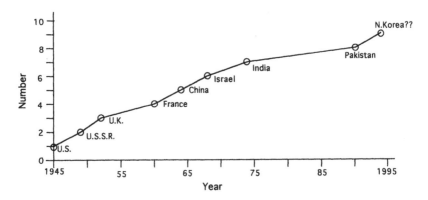

FIG. 38. Change since 1945 in the number of nations
owning nuclear weapons

nuclear industry as well. About 22% of U.S. electrical power is generated
by nuclear reactors—110 in all.

The Soviet Union

The USSR started research on nuclear weapons before the end of World
War II. At the end of the war it developed the technology, to a large
extent on its own; it made its first weapon in 1949. The Soviet Union
had help in the form of information from spies such as the British
scientist Klaus Fuchs, which let the Soviets know which technologies the
United States was using. (Even the "Smythe Report,"[2] with its general
information about some methods that had been used successfully, could
have been of assistance to the Soviets.) Their first weapon was made
from plutonium. Later weapons also used uranium; the uranium was
enriched primarily by gaseous diffusion, with some of it being fed, at a
low enrichment level, to calutrons for final enrichment.

The Soviet Union supported the NPT, joined the Nuclear Suppliers
Group, and helped in the final setting up of the IAEA. It was usually
consistent in trying to prevent nuclear proliferation, although it did
help China develop nuclear weapons until 1959. The demise of the
Soviet Union put the START I treaty in limbo and reduced the effectiveness of the NPT.[3] Russia was left with most, but not all, of the Soviet
Union's nuclear weapons and nuclear-production facilities. Russia also

retained the nuclear command structure needed to fire the strategic missiles and activate the weapons. Tactical nuclear weapons were also controlled by Russian personnel.

The policy of the United States has been to get the non-Russian successor states to the Soviet Union to join the NPT as non-nuclear-weapon states, turning their weapons over to Russia, thus leaving the United States only one nuclear power to deal with. This policy had been successful: on May 23, 1992, Russia, along with Belarus, Kazakhstan, and Ukraine—the three other successor states with nuclear weapons on their territory—signed a protocol by which they agreed to participate jointly in the START I treaty. In addition, Belarus, Kazakhstan, and Ukraine agreed to adhere to the NPT and to the elimination of all nuclear weapons, both strategic and tactical, on their territories within the seven-year START I elimination period. By the end of 1996, all three states had removed all tactical and strategic weapons to Russia.

But the ratification of the START I and NPT treaties had proved contentious, in part because of a dispute between Ukraine and Russia regarding primarily the ownership of the Black Sea fleet. Finally, at a meeting on December 5, 1994, the United Kingdom, the United States, and Russia had provided the requested security guarantees to Ukraine (and also to Belarus and Kazakhstan)—an action that allowed the START I treaty and the NPT to be brought into force at the same meeting.

Russia

Under the START I treaty, the United States and Russia must reduce their strategic nuclear forces to 6,000 warheads deployed on 1,600 delivery systems. Both had begun the deactivation of their nuclear forces before START I was in force, and by mid-1996 Russia had reduced the number of its deployed nuclear warheads to 6,669 and had destroyed over 1,200 launchers and bombers.

The dismantling of Russian tactical weapons is going forward at a rate of about 2,000 a year. The United States is providing help in this effort with funds from the Nunn-Lugar program, authorized by the U.S. congress to help the former Soviet Union denuclearize and demilitarize. Both Russia and the United States are separating their warheads from the delivery systems. They may also be dismantling the warheads to the extent of removing the nuclear cores from the explosive detonating systems and securely storing them.

On January 14, 1995, Russia and the United States agreed that they would no longer target strategic missiles at one another; the United Kingdom joined this agreement on February 15. Russia and China had signed a similar agreement on September 2, 1994. (Retargeting, however, can be done in a few minutes.)

The START II treaty for further joint reductions of the numbers of nuclear weapons was signed between the United States and Russia on January 3, 1993. If ratified by both nations, this agreement would lead, by January 1, 2003, to each having a total of between 3,000 and 3,500 warheads. The United States ratified the treaty in January 1996 but ratification by Russia is very problematical. The majority of the Russian parliament finds the treaty discriminatory against Russia because it requires Russia's deactivation of multiple-warhead and mobile missiles, of which it has a large number, and their replacement by submarine-launched missiles, of which it has very few. The United States, on the other hand, has no mobile missiles and a large and effective submarine force. Recent U.S. efforts to expand NATO are contributing to this resistance.

Russia is a major nuclear supplier, marketing nuclear reactors, enriched uranium, and a full range of other equipment. It is a major uranium producer, with about eight large mining and primary processing centers. It has used a wide range of methods for uranium enrichment (starting with gaseous diffusion and then shifting to centrifuge enrichment), for which it has developed very efficient plants. Its commercial centrifuge enrichment plants are reportedly capable of producing more than 14 million kilograms SWU per year. Russia used calutrons to enrich some of the material for its first uranium bomb and is now experimenting with laser separation.

At present Russia has twenty-eight power reactors in operation, which produce a little over 10% of its electric power. Three reactors are still being used to produce weapon-grade plutonium. There are major chemical-reprocessing plants for plutonium separation at Chelyabinsk, Tomsk, and Krasnoyarsk. In addition to a stock of about 200 metric tons of military plutonium, Russia has about 40 metric tons of plutonium in its power-reactor fuel rods and many tons of reprocessed reactor plutonium. As is true in the United States, the nuclear cores of the thousands of warheads Russia has dismantled are being stored intact.

The Theft of Nuclear Material from Russia

The chaotic political and economic conditions of the past few years have weakened Russia's control of its nuclear weapons and nuclear-weapon materials. During the Soviet period, the rigid state security system made the selling of any nuclear material very difficult, even if it could be stolen. As a result, controls were not as stringent as they are in the United States.

Although Russia has continued the Soviet Union's adherence to the NPT and support of the IAEA, stories repeatedly arise of nuclear-weapon material, apparently stolen from Russian nuclear installations, being for sale on the streets of Europe. It must be kept in mind, however, that many of these reported interceptions of stolen material were the result of sting operations by the German police, in which the total amount intercepted was usually a couple of kilograms; there is no way of determining how much may have been otherwise disposed of. (The possibility of theft is discussed in more detail in chapter 8.)

Belarus

By the end of 1996, all of the strategic nuclear weapons that had been left in Belarus on the breakup of the Soviet Union had been returned to Russia. Belarus has no nuclear reactors, plans for the construction of two of them having been canceled after the Chernobyl accident in 1986. The only nuclear facility in Belarus is the Institute of Power Engineering in Minsk, which has enough highly enriched uranium to make one or two nuclear bombs. Belarus is not a member of the Nuclear Suppliers Group; although it does not market much in the way of nuclear technology, its lack of strong controls makes it a route for the export of material stolen from Russia.

Kazakhstan

In 1991, upon the dissolution of the Soviet Union, Kazakhstan held about 1,400 strategic nuclear weapons, a number of tactical weapons, and a test site at Semipalatinsk. By the beginning of 1996, it had re-turned all tactical and strategic nuclear warheads to Russia. In November 1994, about 60 kilograms of highly enriched uranium, originally desig-nated for use in Soviet naval reactors, was discovered by the United

States to be in badly monitored storage. This uranium has now been bought by the United States and is stored here.

Kazakhstan has one power reactor and three (possibly four) research reactors operating. It mines uranium and exports yellowcake uranium and uranium hexafluoride. It produces beryllium and possibly zirconium. The Semipalatinsk nuclear-test site, which Kazakhstan was left with after the dissolution of the Soviet Union, presents the country with the serious problem of decontaminating the area, which was made extremely radioactive by nuclear-weapon tests.

Ukraine

Upon the breakup of the Soviet Union, Ukraine held over 1,500 strategic nuclear weapons, and between 2,600 and 4,200 tactical ones. These were under Russian control, but Ukraine was reluctant to let them leave its soil. A controversy between Russia and Ukraine with regard to the Crimea and the Black Sea fleet was one of the factors delaying the return of these weapons and also Ukraine's ratification of the START I treaty.

Had Ukraine taken control of the Russian weapons in its territory, it would not only have stirred up a quarrel, but, because it did not have the command-and-control system essential for using the weapons, also have acquired weapons that it could not launch or even maintain. Security guarantees by Russia, the United States, and the United Kingdom persuaded Ukraine's parliament to vote in November 1994 to accede to the NPT as a non-nuclear-weapon state, and subsequently to ratify the START I treaty, which has now entered into force. By June 1996 Ukraine had transferred all of the nuclear weapons to Russia.

Ukraine has no reprocessing or uranium-enrichment plants, but it does own about 75 kilograms of highly enriched uranium that is now under safeguards. It has fourteen operating nuclear reactors capable of generating 12,000 megawatts, or about 25% of its electric power. It has about 30 tons of reactor-grade plutonium in reactor fuel being used or stored. Ukraine has two major mining areas; it exports yellowcake uranium and uranium hexafluoride. It is planning more uranium exploration and mining. It also exports hafnium, zirconium, and heavy water and sells automatic equipment for nuclear-power plants.

The other nations of the former Soviet Union have no nuclear weapons and only minor nuclear-related facilities, such as mines and small nuclear reactors.

The United Kingdom

The British participated fully in the initial nuclear-weapon development during World War II, and supplied much of the early support for building the first bombs. They exploded their first nuclear weapon, made of plutonium, in the Monte Bello Islands (120 kilometers off the northwest coast of Australia) in 1952. They now have about 260 nuclear weapons.

Great Britain put the world's first commercial power reactor into operation in 1956; it now has 25 power reactors producing about a fifth of its electricity (9,000 MWe). It reprocesses all of its fuel and by 1995 had accumulated about 44 tons of reactor-grade plutonium. It also has marketed reprocessing services, reprocessing fuel from Germany, Italy, Japan, the Netherlands, Spain, Sweden, and Switzerland.

As a nuclear-weapon state, Great Britain is proficient in the whole range of nuclear technology. It has used both the diffusion and the centrifuge methods of enrichment and is a member of Urenco, the uranium-enrichment consortium. Although Great Britain is active in the sale of research reactors, the graphite-moderated power reactor it developed has not attracted many customers. Great Britain is a party to the NPT and, as a member of the Nuclear Suppliers Group, works with safeguard agreements and has been careful in its observance of the group's guidelines.

France

Although some of the initial discoveries leading to the understanding of fission were made by French physicists, the French did not play much of a role in the development of the first atomic bomb. Hitler defeated France in 1940, before serious work on the bomb project began. Frédéric Joliot-Curie, Hans von Halban, and Lew Kowarski had been among the French pioneers working on understanding fission; von Halban and Kowarski joined the British effort after the fall of France. Bertrand Goldschmidt, a French theoretical physicist, worked for a few months with Enrico Fermi in Chicago at the beginning of the Manhattan Project.

After the war, the French developed nuclear capabilities on their own. On February 13, 1960, France exploded its first nuclear weapon, of plutonium (with an energy equivalent to about 70 kilotons of conventional explosive), at the Reggane test center in Algeria. Although Algeria gained its independence from France in 1962, France continued to perform regular tests there until 1966, when it moved to its present test site on the Muruoa and Fangatofu atolls in Polynesia. It now has 450 nuclear warheads.

About 75% of France's electric power is produced by its fifty-seven nuclear reactors. It is the world's major supplier of reprocessing services, providing reprocessing to Belgium, Germany, Japan, the Netherlands, Sweden, and Switzerland. France currently has over 40 metric tons of reprocessed plutonium.

France has uranium mines and the capability of gaseous-diffusion enrichment. It sells nuclear reactors. It has operated a prototype breeder reactor since 1993, but the full-scale reactor, in operation since 1985, has experienced trouble and may be shut down.[4] In the past, France has been cavalier about providing assistance to nations bent on obtaining nuclear weapons: it has exported reprocessing technology to nations as varied in their political orientations as Israel and Pakistan.

OTHER WESTERN NATIONS

Canada and the remaining European nations, except Albania and the former Yugoslavia, sell nuclear components. With the same exceptions, all have joined the Nuclear Suppliers Group and ratified the NPT. In the following discussion I shall describe the most active of these nations.

Canada

Canadian scientists helped in the initial development of atomic weapons during World War II, and Canada was among the first countries in the world to build a reactor—an experimental one, completed in 1945. A 40-megawatt reactor was completed in 1947. Both reactors used heavy water for cooling and moderating, and both were fueled with natural uranium. Canada has concentrated on the development of this kind of reactor; its CANDU (Canadian deuterium uranium) reactor, a very efficient producer of plutonium, has attracted about 5% of the world market. Canada's reactors produce about 20% of its electric power. Canada has large deposits of uranium, which it sells worldwide.

Germany

Germany started using nuclear power to generate electricity in 1968; it now has twenty-one nuclear-power reactors generating about 30% of its electrical power. It has small deposits of uranium and operates a centrifuge-type uranium-enrichment plant with a capacity of about 500,000 kilograms SWU per year. Germany at one time had a small pilot reprocessing plant; plans for a larger, commercial operation were dropped in the late 1980s because of public opposition. Most of the reprocessing of German reactor fuel is done in France. Also as a result of the public opposition, Germany has decided to let the plutonium from the reprocessing that has no immediate practical use accumulate in France. Ten of Germany's reactors are now licensed to burn plutonium (used with uranium in a mixed oxide fuel, or MOX). About 1.8 metric tons of plutonium are stored in Germany, while a total of about 60 metric tons, under IAEA safeguards, reside, unseparated, in stored reactor fuel.[5]

Germany has shown no interest in owning nuclear weapons as long as it has nuclear security guarantees, now provided by NATO. With its supply of reactor plutonium (some, possibly, of weapon grade), Germany would require little time to construct atomic weapons. For it to make a uranium weapon would take more time.

Germany is capable of supplying any of the technology required for nuclear-weapon production and has helped Argentina, Brazil, and South Africa in their nuclear development. When Iraq's nuclear program was discovered, it became clear that Germany had provided much of the material for Iraq's centrifuges, and that German nationals had helped design them. This German assistance was made possible by loopholes in the Nuclear Suppliers Group guidelines. Germany has since tightened up its controls, apparently as a result of the disclosures of its involvement in Iraq, and is expected to observe the NSG guidelines more closely.

Belgium

About 60% of Belgium's electricity is produced by nuclear power. Belgium is a major supplier of MOX for the rest of Europe. Until 1980, it also reprocessed reactor fuel. It now receives the plutonium used in MOX from reprocessing plants in France. At present, Belgium owns about 680 kilograms of separated plutonium, and it has another approximately 3,000 kilograms in its fuel-production plants. In addition to MOX, Belgium exports reactor components, some other types of nuclear equipment, and nuclear design.

Italy

Because of public opposition, Italy abandoned its use of nuclear power in 1990; earlier, it had four operating nuclear reactors. It owns about a ton of separated reactor plutonium from fuel that was reprocessed in Great Britain. This now may have been returned to Italy. It also has in storage about 5 metric tons of plutonium in used fuel. Italy is a supplier of reactor components and has good capabilities in fuel fabrication and reprocessing.

The Netherlands

The two reactors in this country produce about 6% of its electrical power. It has sent its fuel to Great Britain and France for reprocessing and may have received about 500 kilograms of separated reactor-grade plutonium from them. It also has about 2 metric tons of plutonium in reactor fuel. It supplies a broad range of nuclear technology—in particular, reactor components. It is a member of the Urenco centrifuge-enrichment consortium.

Sweden

Twelve nuclear reactors provide about 50% of Sweden's electrical power. Sweden does not itself reprocess used fuel, but before 1970 it sent its used fuel to France and Great Britain for reprocessing. Sweden no longer plans to do this, shifting instead to a once-through fuel cycle. Sweden has about 27 tons of plutonium in reactor fuel from previous years.

Sweden has the capability of exporting reactors, reactor components, and a broad range of technology, but has restrictions on the export of nuclear technology that are more conservative than those of the Nuclear Suppliers Group.

Switzerland

Switzerland's five nuclear reactors produce about 40% of the country's electrical power. Switzerland is committed to a fuel cycle that uses reprocessed plutonium in its reactors. Reprocessing is done in Great Britain and France, and the separated plutonium is delivered to Switzerland in the form of MOX made in Belgium and Germany. Possibly 1 metric ton of plutonium has been delivered to Switzerland in 20 metric tons of MOX. The Swiss utilities plan to discontinue the use of MOX after present reprocessing contracts expire. Switzerland exports a broad range of nuclear products—in particular, reactor components and heavy-water technology.

Romania

Romania at one time had a secret program for building atomic weapons.[6] Although it had signed the NPT in 1970, in 1989 Nicolae Ceausescu, then the president of Romania, declared that his country was technically competent to manufacture nuclear weapons. The democratic government that came to power later that year denied Ceausescu's statements. However, in 1992 the government reported that an unknown nuclear substance had been discovered at a nuclear-research institute, and invited the IAEA to conduct a special investigation. Later, IAEA Director General Hans Blix reported that the substance in question was nuclear waste from plutonium separation, and that Romania's previous Communist government had violated its safeguards agreement with the IAEA by separating about 100 milligrams of plutonium from irradiated uranium in a laboratory-scale experiment. It was later reported that during the Ceausescu regime secret plans had been developed for a medium-range missile with a nuclear warhead.

Romania has no operating nuclear-power reactors, although five are under construction, each with a power output of 700 MWe. It does have two operating research reactors, one of them supplied by the United States. Uranium is mined in Romania, and uranium oxide manufactured.

Romania also has a fuel-fabrication plant and a heavy-water production plant in operation.

CHINA AND NORTHEAST ASIA

Because the Korean War (1950–53) stimulated the development of nuclear weapons, it is useful to review some of the events of this war that have determined Chinese and Korean attitudes toward these weapons through the latter half of this century.

In 1945, at the end of World War II, the United States took over the southern part of the Korean peninsula from the Japanese army. The Soviets, similarly, occupied the northern portion; the split was at the 38th parallel. The two regimes that were set up under these auspices were united only in their hatred of the Japanese, who had occupied Korea from the turn of the century until the end of World War II.

North Korea is larger in area and has more natural resources than South Korea, yet its population is about half as large. After the split, South Korea emphasized economic development and recruited an army of about 100,000, equipped only with small arms. North Korea emphasized large construction projects and a large military, with an army of about 135,000 that included a tank brigade. When the United States withdrew its troops from South Korea early in 1950, North Korea took this act as signifying the end of U.S. concern with the region. North Korea invaded South Korea on June 25 of that year and within three days had seized Seoul, the capital. U.S. troops (under U.N. auspices) arrived in July, but by September North Korea had nevertheless overrun almost all of South Korea, whose troops by then occupied only a small area around the southern port city of Pusan.

General Douglas MacArthur, the U.S. and U.N. commander, counter-attacked with an amphibious landing at Inchon, on the northwest coast near Seoul. This successful maneuver cut off the North Korean army, which made a disastrous retreat. The U.N. army advanced into North Korea, and by the end of October 1950 it had reached the northern border with China at the Yalu River.

China, after earlier warning the U.N. troops away from its border, entered the war in November with an overwhelming number of troops. (By the end of 1952 it had put 1.2 million troops into Korea.) The U.N. troops had retreated to about thirty miles south of Seoul by January 4,

1951. By the end of March, they had advanced again to the 38th parallel. MacArthur then publicly advocated expanding the war to China itself, and as a result was dismissed as commander by President Truman. From this time until the end of the war in 1953, the U.N. troops fought a holding action in the region north of Seoul. The Chinese had entered the war believing that massive manpower was more important than modern firepower. By the spring of 1951, they had changed their minds. In spite of considerable matériel aid from the Soviet Union, China had suffered almost 600,000 casualties.

Negotiations on an armistice were begun, but by July 1951 they had become deadlocked, and they remained so until the spring of 1953. Early in the war, the United States had threatened the use of atomic weapons. In a press conference held on November 29, 1950, President Harry Truman said that he would take "all necessary steps to meet the military situation," and that this would include "every weapon we have."[7] General Dwight Eisenhower, now president, was determined to end the impasse even if it meant a resumption of hostilities. Sherman Adams, assistant to President Eisenhower, recalled in his memoirs that in May 1953, Secretary of State John Foster Dulles informed Prime Minister Jawaharal Nehru of India that the United States "could not be held responsible for failing [*sic*] to use atomic weapons if a truce could not be arranged."[8] An armistice was signed on July 27, 1953.

In December 1953, when Washington announced that it would withdraw two army divisions from the peninsula, U.S. news reports stated that the government "would compensate for a planned reduction of ground forces in Korea by the increased firepower made possible by atomic cannon."[9]

Disputes over Taiwan, to which Chiang Kai-shek had retreated in 1949 when his Nationalist Chinese forces were defeated by the Communists, furthered the understanding that the United States was prepared to use atomic weapons if it got into a conflict with China. During the Korean War, the United States had given the Nationalists considerable support and encouraged their harassment of the Chinese coast. In 1954, a Chinese newspaper stated that more than seventy ships bound for China had been hijacked in the region near Taiwan. Even after the Korean armistice, this hostile situation continued to exist, culminating in the shelling by the Chinese of the Taiwanese islands of Quemoy and Matsu, a few miles off the mainland coast. Among other U.S. responses was a congressional resolution giving President Eisenhower the authority to use the armed forces of the United States "as he deems necessary for the specific purpose of securing Formosa [Taiwan] and the Pescadores against armed attack."[10] The United States, although indicating its readiness to fight a major war over Taiwan, did not send massive battle groups to the area. The U.S. stance, plus unofficial comments and previous threats, may have led Chinese leaders to the conclusion that the United States planned to use atomic weapons against any Chinese threat to Taiwan.

The Chinese might well have seen the need for the development of atomic weapons without the stimulus of their threatened use by the United States. A strong motivation might also have been supplied by their deteriorating relationship with the Soviet Union, but even so the Korean War and the crisis over the Taiwan Strait would have strengthened their resolve.

China

By the time China started to develop nuclear weapons, many of its scientists had received training in nuclear physics in Europe, the United States, and, especially, the Soviet Union. Nikita Krushchev said, "Before the rupture in our relations, we'd given the Chinese almost everything they asked for. We kept no secrets from them. Our nuclear experts cooperated with their engineers and designers who were busy building an atomic bomb. We trained their scientists in our own laboratories."[11] There was even a plan to give a prototype implosion weapon to the Chinese, but this was never carried out.

China made a two-pronged effort to build nuclear weapons: it used gaseous diffusion to enrich uranium, and it built a reactor to produce plutonium. As Krushchev said, the Chinese did have considerable Soviet assistance in both of these efforts. In 1960, an economic crisis and the anticipated withdrawal of Soviet assistance caused the Chinese to scale back their effort. They then gave priority to a uranium weapon, which they exploded in 1964. China now has about 380 warheads of both plutonium and uranium.

As a major nuclear power, China has mastered the whole range of nuclear technology. It markets heavy water, natural uranium, 20%-enriched uranium (using gaseous diffusion for the enrichment process), and nuclear reactors. In addition, China sells fuel assemblies, reprocessing services, and electronic equipment. Pakistan got engineering assistance from China in its nuclear-weapon program, particularly in developing the centrifuge cascade. China has two active reactors that are producing weapon-grade plutonium and two large power reactors. The country is estimated to have some 1.7 tons of separated weapon-grade plutonium in reserve.

China became a member of the IAEA in 1983 and has recently signed the NPT. Its selective enforcement of safeguards on its exports represents a major breach in the world's adherence to that treaty.

Japan

Japan has fifty nuclear-power reactors that supply about 28% of its electricity. It is committed to developing nuclear power for its electrical plants, and does some of its own reprocessing. It has been developing a fast breeder reactor for the production of plutonium, but a series of noncatastrophic accidents in 1995 has dampened the enthusiasm for this difficult project.[12] Japan is now estimated to have about 5 metric tons of separated reactor-grade plutonium in addition to about 80 metric tons present in used fuel. It also has some weapon-grade plutonium.

A major centrifuge plant for uranium enrichment is being developed, and chemical enrichment worked on experimentally. Japan is marketing an excellent high-power reactor and has become a major nuclear supplier. It also sells a variety of engineering services.

The destruction of Hiroshima and Nagasaki by nuclear bombs gave rise to indigenous political resistance to the development of nuclear weapons by Japan. However, recent disclosures show that government attitudes may not always reflect this reluctance. An article by Arjun Makhijani revealed that in August 1994 a Japanese newspaper, the *Mainichi shimbun,* leaked a 1969 document of the Japanese foreign ministry in which it was argued that the country did not need nuclear weapons "for the time being," but that it should "keep the economic and technical potential for the production of nuclear weapons while seeing to it that Japan will not be interfered with in this regard."[13] The country's technological development would probably enable it to produce a plutonium weapon in a few months; a uranium-based weapon would require a little longer.

South Korea

In 1992, South Korea had nine operating nuclear reactors generating about half of its electrical power, with three more under construction. It has 16 metric tons of plutonium in its used fuel rods. In the past it got most of its uranium and some of its technology from Canada, but it is now fabricating its own fuel components. South Korea's ability to export nuclear-power components is restricted largely because the country itself needs almost all it can produce. It is in the process of building an enrichment plant to supply partially enriched uranium for its own nuclear-power industry, and it will soon be able to export a broad range of products, such as enrichment services, reprocessing, reactors, and reactor components. By the end of the century, South Korea may be one of the world's major sources of nuclear-power equipment. It is a signatory of the NPT and has made a safeguards agreement.

Taiwan

Historically a province of China, off whose coast it lies about one hundred miles, Taiwan was ruled by Japan from 1895 until 1945. It was given back to China after Japan's defeat in World War II, and was the base to which the Nationalist Chinese Kuomintang government, headed by Chiang Kai-shek, retreated in 1949 after being defeated by the Communists. The island remained under the dictatorial rule of the Kuomintang after Chiang's death until about 1991, but has since liberalized its political structure and is becoming democratic.

Its population is about 20 million, and its economy has grown to that of a modern industrialized nation, with a per-capita income of about twelve thousand dollars. Japan and the United States are its major trading partners. It is emphasizing sophisticated technological development, with an aerospace program and its own aircraft industry.

Although there is indigenous public resistance to the use of nuclear power, Taiwan has an active program, with about half of its electrical power being supplied by nuclear reactors. Because of its peculiar status with relation to China, it is not a member of the IAEA or a signatory to the NPT. It has not developed a nuclear-export industry. Its nuclear plants and materials are under IAEA safeguards, and, partly because of its dependence on the United States, it is unlikely to act in violation of the NPT.

North Korea

Despite all of its resources, North Korea has been unable to develop economic strength. Under the strong dictatorship that has ruled since the Korean War, its major effort has been to develop its industrial base—transforming a previously agricultural country into an industrial nation, emphasizing heavy industry and self-sufficiency. Its only political relationships have been with other Communist countries, particularly the Soviet Union and China. North Korea has remained consistently hostile to South Korea, with which it is technically still at war. It has isolated itself further politically by terrorist acts, in particular a 1983 bombing in Rangoon that killed several members of the South Korean government, and the destruction in 1987 of a South Korean airliner over the Thai-Burmese border.

With the demise of the Soviet Union and the opening up of China, North Korea has found itself almost completely isolated. Its economy, which was closely tied to that of the Soviet Union, has suffered badly. It has insufficient capital to buy the oil it needs for its industry, which it previously got from the Soviet Union. Its present interest in obtaining nuclear reactors is, in part, a reaction to a severe energy crisis.

A brief chronology of the North Korean nuclear program follows.

1967: North Korea starts up a small research reactor provided by the Soviet Union.

1979: North Korea starts to build a nuclear reactor, but has difficulty in making it work.

1985: North Korea signs the Nuclear Non-proliferation Treaty, opening its nuclear sites to inspection.

1987: North Korea misses the first eighteen-month deadline for concluding a safeguards agreement.

1988: North Korea misses the second deadline.

1989: North Korea shuts down its reactor, ostensibly to remove some defective fuel rods, possibly a dozen. (It may have withdrawn many more. The uncertainty regarding this number is the reason we do not know whether North Korea has enough plutonium for just one or for two nuclear weapons.)

1990: North Korea threatens to withdraw from the Nuclear Non-proliferation Treaty unless the United States removes all nuclear weapons from the Korean peninsula. There are reports of North Korean tests made with high explosives that are most probably related to research on how to detonate a nuclear weapon.[14] (Later reports to the U.S. Congress indicate that the Defense Department had some information about a North Korean nuclear-weapon program.)[15]

1991: North and South Korea agree to denuclearize the Korean peninsula.

1992: In January, the United States and South Korea agree to cancel their regular "Team Spirit" joint military exercises for the year, exercises to which the North Koreans had always objected. In February, North Korea brings into force its safeguards agreement with the IAEA and promises to allow inspections. In five inspection visits from May to December, inspectors visit seven declared sites and take samples of plutonium from laboratory-scale processing equipment. (Such samples give information about the total flux of neutrons to which the fuel rods have been exposed in producing plutonium and about when the processing took place.)[16] The measurements of radioactive isotopes in the the fuel rods do not agree with North Korean statements and indicate that reprocessing has taken place in 1989, 1990, and 1991.

1993: In February, the IAEA calls for special challenge inspections (for the first time in its history). In March, "Team Spirit" exercises take place despite the protests of North Korea, which may have interpreted the 1992 cancelation as permanent. At inspections in February and March, North Korea bars inspectors from two undeclared sites that are suspected of housing nuclear waste. It also announces its withdrawal from the NPT, a process that requires ninety days' notice. In June, North Korea suspends its withdrawal from the NPT but continues to refuse full inspection. In October, inspectors say that the cameras they installed earlier are no longer reliable. In December, North Korea offers to let inspectors into five of seven declared sites, but refuses access to its reactor and a suspected processing plant.

1994: Continued agreements to inspection are followed by refusals to allow it. North Korea considers itself to be in a special case of partial withdrawal from the NPT. Finally, in May, the North Koreans shut down their reactor to remove all of the fuel rods. Requests by the IAEA that it be allowed to set aside a selected number of the fuel rods for detailed measurement are rejected. By mid-June, all 8,000 of the rods had been removed and placed in a cooling pond. By the end of the year, U.S. and North Korean negotiators reach an agreement.

As encouragement to the North Koreans, the United States will do two things. First, it will make arrangements for providing North Korea with light-water-moderated reactors with a capacity of 2,000 MWe by a target date of 2003, organize an international consortium to finance and supply the project, and conclude a bilateral agreement with North Korea for cooperation in the field of peaceful uses of nuclear energy. Second, the United States, representing the consortium, will make arrangements to replace the energy lost by the freezing of North Korea's graphite-moderated reactors until the first light-water reactor is built (a period of about nine years). North Korea will be provided with oil for use in conventional power plants, ultimately about 500,000 metric tons a year.

In return, North Korea will do four things. First, it will freeze the operation of its graphite-moderated reactors and related facilities and will eventually dismantle them. Second, it will complete the freeze within one month of the date of the document of agreement. Throughout the freeze, the IAEA will be allowed to monitor the freeze, and North Korea will cooperate fully in this. Third, it will complete the dismantling of its graphite-moderated reactors and their facilities by the time its light-water-moderated reactors are completed. Fourth, it will cooperate with the United States in finding a method of safely storing spent fuel from the 5-MWe experimental reactor during the construction of its light-water-moderated reactors, and will dispose of the fuel in a safe-guarded manner that does not involve reprocessing in North Korea.

North Korea will remain a party to the Nuclear Non-proliferation Treaty and will allow the implementation of its safeguards agreement under the treaty. In addition, both sides agree to move toward full normalization of political and economic relations. This will include opening liaison offices in the two capitals and, finally, moving their relations to an ambassadorial level.

After the contract for the light-water reactor is completed, presumably about the year 2,000, the IAEA will be allowed to resume ad hoc and routine inspections at all previously declared facilities not already being inspected.

This agreement has many strong points. With its existing graphite-moderated reactor, North Korea could have produced enough plutonium for a few weapons a year. Were a second reactor to become operational in a few years, it would have the capability of making about 50 kilograms of plutonium a year, enough for more than five nuclear weapons. Were a third, larger reactor to come on line, it would be able to make about 200 kilograms of plutonium a year.

Light-water-moderated reactors are much easier to monitor than gas-cooled, graphite-moderated ones. They use enriched uranium fuel, which North Korea must now import; in contrast, gas-graphite-moderated reactors use natural uranium, of which North Korea has its own source. The design of gas-graphite-moderated reactors makes it easy to remove individual fuel rods as soon as they have produced a small amount of weapon-grade plutonium, and before any significant amount of the plutonium 240, 241, and 242 isotopes that make the plutonium hard to use for weapons can be produced. The fuel rods for light-water reactors must be changed in the large groups in which they are assembled, and this requires a major shutdown of the facility, which can be monitored readily. In addition, light-water reactors are less efficient than gas-graphite-moderated ones in producing plutonium. The United States negotiators apparently decided to sacrifice the ability to find out how much plutonium the North Koreans might have already separated in order to be able to control their future activity.

Those opposed to the agreement decry the error of rewarding a nation for complying with a treaty it has signed but is threatening to disavow. They also point out that there is nothing to prevent the North Koreans from getting the new reactors and then, instead of turning the used fuel over to another country such as Russia for disposal under safeguards, keeping the used fuel to make a large number of nuclear weapons.

Although this is a possibility, there are several reasons why it does not appear probable. Reprocessing facilities would have to be constructed secretly, and if there was any indication that North Korea was violating its agreements, the U.S.-led coalition supplying the new reactors and the interim fuel oil would be able to withhold its needed assistance. After completion of the new reactors, compliance would be motivated by North Korea's dependence on the power supplied by what would by then be the major power source of the country, a source that could not produce power without a supply of slightly enriched uranium from abroad.

1995: During the spring, the agreement unravels somewhat because of a U.S. plan to have South Korea build the reactors for North Korea. One can see why this plan might be a sore point for North Korea, which had been competing with South Korea for over forty years. It would be a public example of South Korea's greater technical proficiency. Also at work was the perceived injustice of South Korea's being allowed to develop a complete range of nuclear technology while North Korea was prevented from even a minor development.

The cost of the planned program was so great that only those who would benefit most from it were willing to pay for it. South Korea is possibly the only source of financing, and it certainly wanted to finance the construction of reactors only by its own industry. The problem has been resolved by U.S.–North Korean negotiations, which took place in August 1995. A formal contract was signed on December 15. By the beginning of 1996, U.S. firms were repackaging the used reactor fuel, which had been sitting in a cooling pool. In some cases, the metal containing the fuel rods had been disintegrating. The rods are being put into new, more durable containers, which will be shipped abroad eventually. The Korean Peninsula Energy Development Organization, an international consortium set up by the United States, Japan, and South Korea, is in charge of building two 1,000-MWe light-water-moderated reactors, which will cost between $4 billion and $4.5 billion. This project will be financed, primarily by South Korea and Japan, by a loan with a twenty-year interest-free repayment period. The scheduled completion date of the first reactor is 2003. In the interim, the United States will provide 500,000 metric tons of fuel oil per year to some North Korean power plants.

The evidence available regarding North Korea's possible production of a nuclear weapon is this: until the much-publicized shutdown of North Korea's reactor in May 1994 for the removal of all of its fuel, the only occasion on which North Korea might have withdrawn a large number of fuel rods for reprocessing was during the 1989 shutdown. The questions of greatest concern in regard to possible weapon production are: how much fuel (with its attendant plutonium) was withdrawn in 1989; whether this fuel has been processed to separate the plutonium; whether a bomb has been made from this plutonium; and what is going to be done with the large amount of fuel that has just been withdrawn. IAEA inspectors wanted to examine selected fuel rods during the 1994 total removal of fuel, to establish whether only a small group of defective fuel rods (their number was claimed by the North Koreans to be about a dozen), or a significant part of the total fuel, had been removed in 1989. An estimate that North Korea already had enough plutonium available for one or two bombs apparently is based on the assumption that virtually all of the fuel rods were removed (and on some knowledge of the power level at which the reactor operated up to that time).

The truth of North Korea's assertion that only a few defective rods had been removed in 1989 could be established by examining the radioactivity from the fission products and plutonium produced in the fuel rods. The fuel rods are not uniformly exposed to neutrons: those at the center of the reactor are subjected to more neutron flux than those on the edges. If all of the fuel rods had been in the reactor for the same length of time, a sampling of activity in the rods would show a gradual increase from the outside to the center. If a group of fuel rods had been removed, a "canyon" of fuel rods with less activity than that expected would show up. By measuring the size of this discontinuity, an estimate could be made of how many fuel rods were withdrawn in 1989. From this a better estimate could be made of how much plutonium North Korea might have obtained.

North Korea, however, made this determination impossible by removing all of the fuel rods. In principle, with perfect information about the radioactivity of each of the fuel rods, a reconstruction of the neutron-exposure pattern might be possible. But to do so with any conceivable accuracy would be like assembling a jigsaw puzzle using pieces of poorly defined shape. There are 8,000 fuel rods.

It is also possible to determine the average time for which the individual fuel rods were exposed to neutrons. All of the rods will have been exposed for a few years, but the average time of the exposure for rods introduced later would be shorter. The radioactive fission products have many different half-lives. If, for example, the fission took place five years ago, the short-lived fission products will have decayed and all that will be left are those with half-lives of about five years or longer. A detailed measurement of the radioactivity of all of the fuel might be used to determine the average time at which fissioning took place. If there was trustworthy knowledge of the power output of the reactor over its entire lifetime, some reconstruction of what had taken place might be possible.

Because of secrecy, one can only speculate as to sources. Knowledge of the operational schedule may have come from "national technical means"—that is, spy planes or satellites, which may have been able to measure the temperature of the cooling gas or water coming from the reactor. Operational records of the reactor may have been made available to inspectors when North Korea joined the NPT. Although these records by themselves might not be reliable, when coupled with other observations they could be useful.

North Korea might be able to separate 40 kilograms of plutonium from the 8,000 fuel rods it has removed. (If North Korea had a 25-megawatt [thermal] reactor in operation from 1986 to 1994 at the power levels estimated, it could have produced about 40 kilograms of Pu-239. When it removed some unknown number of fuel rods in 1989, it might have had about 15 kilograms of plutonium.) This would provide the United States sufficient material for approximately three or four nuclear weapons. As a less-developed nation, North Korea would probably be able to make about half as many.

North Korea still had to separate the plutonium from the highly radioactive material of the fuel rods withdrawn in 1989. It has admitted to having a very small scale, laboratory-size separation system that has produced a gram or so of plutonium a year, but it claims that there is no other separation plant in North Korea except for one under construction, a thousand times larger, that it revealed in May 1992. This plant would have been able to process the fuel rods from the large reactors that were then being built, and would have had an annual capacity to separate enough plutonium for many nuclear weapons. No experienced engineer would proceed directly from a laboratory-scale demonstration to a major operating plant without an intermediate pilot-plant step. The North Koreans are considered too competent to have skipped this necessary step. This points to the existence of a small, hidden chemical-separation plant capable of separating enough plutonium for one or two bombs a year.

North Korea has repeatedly emphasized a need to reprocess its reactor fuel for safety reasons. Its reactors are similar in design to the British and Japanese graphite-moderated reactors in that the fuel is encased in an alloy that interacts with any water used to cool it. After some time the alloy will disintegrate, and the fuel will be exposed to water or air, with dangerous consequences. It is estimated that within several months the fuel must be reprocessed or cooled in some other way. Cooling is most easily done in a water cooling pond, yet because of the possibility of the fuel encasement breaking, cooling presents a serious problem. Cooling can be done in containers using recirculating gas, but this is difficult. An obvious solution, though one that may not be acceptable to the North Koreans, is to send it to a country such as Russia for reprocessing.

The primary purpose of North Korea's nuclear program has apparently been the development of nuclear weapons. They chose to build gas-cooled, graphite-moderated reactors, which easily can be used to make plutonium for weapons. Of course, these reactors also use natural, nonenriched uranium, which fits in with North Korea's desire for self-sufficiency. Another indication of their purpose is the evidence we have that North Korea may have tested methods of detonating nuclear weapons.

North Korea's fear that nuclear weapons might be used against it in case of war is an important consideration in evaluating its determination to provide itself with nuclear weapons. There is, apparently, evidence that the United States contemplated using nuclear weapons during the Korean War.[17] Many cities and installations were targeted—though this does not in itself imply that the use of the weapons was considered a reasonable option. Still, on April 5, 1951, the joint chiefs of staff did authorize the use of nuclear weapons against the Manchurian air bases of the Chinese if bombers were launched from them against U.S. forces. Fortunately, other developments, including the removal of General MacArthur as commander, intervened. Early in 1953, the U.S. high command leaked word of a new strategic plan to end the war that included the use of small atomic bombs and artillery shells.[18] This threat, apparently, was helpful in the negotiations that ended the war with the July 1953 armistice. All of this suggests that the North Koreans have built a nuclear-power program with the additional purpose of developing nuclear weapons to deter the use of such weapons by the United States, or even to deter conventional war. The United States must concern itself with whatever additional purposes the North Koreans might have in owning these weapons.

At the time of this writing, North Korea's large army is close to the South Korean border. Its position is probably motivated in part by North Korea's need, in case of war, to move troops quickly into contact with South Korea's troops and population and so prevent the United States from using nuclear weapons against its army. The same considerations probably led the North Koreans to build underground weapons factories, airplane hangars, and troop and matériel depots. As men-

tioned earlier, North Korea finds itself isolated from its previous sup-
porters, particularly Russia, and it must fear that in the case of war with
South Korea and its powerful ally, the United States, it may have to go
it alone.

The real challenge for the United States is to stop the further production of nuclear weapons by North Korea. Although there is uncertainty
about whether North Korea has a bomb, there is fairly good knowledge
that at this time it does not have sufficient plutonium for more than one
or two bombs. Two weapons are not enough to allow any aggressive
action by their owner. Once they are used, unless they cause the complete destruction of enemy forces, their user will be punished. A single
weapon's possible use in defense against an invasion, on the other hand,
could serve as an effective deterrent.

There appear to be few alternatives to the type of agreement the
United States has made with North Korea. The application of sanctions
that prevent trade with North Korea is the most forceful punitive action
that can be taken, short of war. These sanctions could be effective only
with the support of China and Russia. Russia might help in this; China
appears reluctant. North Korea has already been cut off from trade with
most of the world by sanctions. Communication with North Korea for
any normal business purpose is very difficult. It receives about $3 billion
a year in foreign exchange from trade and from the large amount of
foreign currency Korean residents of Japan send to relatives in North
Korea. The trade in military weapons accounts for more than two-thirds
of the total. Preventing the Korean Japanese from sending money is a
less serious measure than imposing trade sanctions, particularly since
the amount being sent has decreased in recent years.[19] Taking such a
step might apply pressure to the North Korean government because it
both directly affects the lives of private people in North Korea and removes a source of foreign currency. Although the Japanese are reluctant
to do this, it may be the only way to apply sanctions. To be effective, this
policy must be maintained over a long period.

Aggressive action, such as an air strike against the reactors or reprocessing plant, is not a sensible possibility, because North Korea's response would certainly be war. It should be remembered that the Korean
War of 1950–53 was one of the most bitter of this century, causing about
a million Korean and Chinese deaths. The United States and its non-
Korean allies lost over fifty thousand men. Today, the North Korean

army has equipment less modern than that of the South Koreans, but it has about twice as much of it, and it is formidable. It has over a million men, almost twice as many as the South Korean forces. A large part of North Korea's army is positioned just north of the demilitarized zone, within artillery range of the northern suburbs of Seoul. However optimistic one might be about the outcome of any protracted war in which the United States supported South Korea, it is clear that South Korea would suffer intolerable damage. There is also the chance that China would enter the war in support of North Korea.

North Korea's possession of nuclear weapons at this time presents a twofold danger: its effect on the continued observance of the Nuclear Non-proliferation Treaty by other nations, particularly South Korea and Japan; and the possibility it raises of the sale of nuclear weapons to the maverick nations of Libya, Syria, Algeria, and Iran. The latter speculation does not seem unreasonable when one considers that most of North Korea's foreign trade is in weapons.

On the other hand, North Korea has good reason to develop reactors for peaceful purposes. It needs them as a source of electrical power, having no known oil reserves or foreign currency to buy oil. In its isolation, North Korea has wanted always to be self-sufficient, and thus chose to develop nuclear reactors that could operate with natural uranium. It developed its graphite-moderated reactors without much outside assistance, using a design that is, supposedly, not very stable and is also a difficult one to make work. (North Korea could have obtained Soviet assistance in building more efficient and reliable reactors under IAEA safeguards, but these would have made the use of the reactors for the production of plutonium weapons much more difficult.) North Korea obtains its uranium from residues in its coal, which is its major fuel supply. If it felt itself in danger of being cut off from all outside assistance, it would have a good reason to reprocess its nuclear fuel and thus extend the fuel supply for its reactors. North Korea has claimed, however, that it wants to do reprocessing as a part of a breeder-reactor program. But breeder technology is so much more difficult than that of ordinary reactors that building a breeder reactor would not be a sensible project for a technically inexperienced nation like North Korea.

The problems posed by the existing fuel seem small compared with the dangers of unrestricted development. It is ironic that all of this effort must be made to arrive at a situation similar to one that we decry in the case of Iran. The situation of the two countries, in regard to reactors, however, is quite different. Iran, with its huge oil reserves, has less need of nuclear power. If Iran seized used fuel to obtain plutonium, the threat of withholding new fuel for any reactors Iran might then build would have less effect because of Iran's lack of dependence on reactors. Also, Iran, with money from the sale of oil, has more resources for developing a nuclear-weapon capability: it is able to hire nuclear engineers from the more-developed nations, and it can buy needed parts from European sources.

The alternative to the present U.S.–North Korean agreement would be to impose sanctions and let things go on as at present, relying on the complete collapse of the North Korean economy.

Neither side trusted the other in the negotiations; each step on one side was contingent upon a step on the other. The fuel oil would have to be delivered if a shutdown of the present program were to take place. As of early 1998, the program was apparently moving slowly ahead.

SOUTH ASIA: INDIA AND PAKISTAN

While Britain ruled India, interest in its northern frontiers was well expressed by the viceroy, Lord Curzon, in 1907:

> India is like a fortress, with the vast moat of the sea on two of her faces and with mountains for her walls on the remainder; but beyond these walls, which are sometimes of by no means insupera-ble height, and admit of being easily penetrated, extends a glacis of varying breadth and dimension. We do not want to occupy it, but we also cannot afford to see it occupied by our foes. We are quite content to let it remain in the hands of our allies and friends, but if rivals creep up to it and lodge themselves right under our walls, we are compelled to intervene.[20]

During the nineteenth century, the main goal of the British in the region north of Kashmir (the northernmost part of India, which sepa-rated it from Tibet and China), was to ensure that Russia did not get a foothold in that area. China and Tibet were considered suitable occu-pants (if that word can be used when speaking of a desert region that even now is virtually uninhabited). In 1899, the British Minister in Peking, Sir Claude MacDonald, proposed a boundary. The British learned, unofficially, that the local Chinese authorities in Sinkiang Province had no objection to the proposed boundary, but they never heard from Peking, which did not like boundary agreements because it felt that they usually meant a loss of territory for China, which at the time was very weak. The MacDonald boundary gave almost all of the Aksai Chin Desert to China. Subsequent surveys and proposals put most of the desert in Kashmir—a fact that, unfortunately, was not communicated to China. One of these proposals was incorporated in maps of the region. (It was through this desert region that China, in the 1950s, would build the road connecting Sinkiang Province to Tibet.)

The remainder of the Himalayan border was occupied by the friendly states of Nepal, Sikkim, and Bhutan, and a tribal region, formerly called the North-East Frontier Agency and now named Arunachal Pradesh. The British regularized the border of the North-East Frontier Agency and Burma with Tibet in 1914, again without an agreement with China; a commission, of which the British head was one Henry McMahon, established what was called the McMahon line.

When India received its independence from Great Britain in 1947, its population consisted of about 315 million Hindus and 100 million Muslims. Because of conflicts between the two groups, the British decided to allow the formation of two nations, one Muslim and the other Hindu, with people in different regions being allowed to choose their affiliation. The eastern and western parts of India had a Muslim majority and elected to become part of a single nation, Pakistan. The central, larger region, with a Hindu majority, became the present state of India. Although the newly elected governments of these areas behaved responsibly, there was terrible rioting when, as a result of the division, some 10 million Muslims, Hindus, and Sikhs changed regions; about 1 million people were killed during this transfer of populations.

A serious problem arose in the state of Kashmir during the partition. There a population that was 75% Muslim was ruled by a Hindu prince. The prince ceded Kashmir to India to gain support for himself against his Muslim population, which was being helped in rebellion by Pakistan. A cease-fire was finally agreed to in 1949, in which control of most of Kashmir was given to India. Nevertheless conflict continued, though on a smaller scale, and in 1957, despite a U.N. Security Council resolution requiring a plebiscite, India declared the portion of Kashmir that it controlled to be a part of India. Kashmir is the only part of the old British India that was not allowed the right of self-determination.

India's border problems then became much more severe than those cited by Lord Curzon fifty years earlier. It had hostile West Pakistan on its west, and in the east it surrounded East Pakistan. On the east and west parts of its northern Himalayan frontier, it had the vague borders established by the British. China, instead of being the weak nation that had earlier faced the British, had become a strong military power, and, no longer exercising a loose suzerainty, it occupied Tibet in 1950. Jawaharlal Nehru, India's prime minister, adopted a policy of friendship toward China, and when Tibet appealed to the United Nations regarding its occupation by China, India withheld its support. Furthermore, Nehru supported China's bid for membership in the United Nations over that of the Nationalists in Taiwan. India did not align itself with either the United States or the Soviet Union in the Cold War.

In 1959, China asked that a commission be set up to review, and possibly change, the frontier boundaries. India demurred, wanting no change and insisting that the most intrusive (for China) of the British boundaries were historically accurate. China negotiated boundaries with Burma and Pakistan in 1959 and 1960. To India's great anger, the new boundary in Burma used the old British-negotiated McMahon line in Burma, a line that it did not recognize where it extended between Arunachal Pradesh and Tibet. Even worse, the boundary negotiated with Pakistan was for a portion of Kashmir that was occupied by Pakistan but claimed by India. In 1962, India moved troops into the disputed area beyond the MacDonald line, claiming the relevance of maps never approved by the Chinese, and, claiming a mistake in the McMahon line, also occupied the disputed area beyond the McMahon line north of Arunachal Pradesh. Both sides kept troops in or near the disputed areas, but China had easier supply routes—from the high Tibetan plateau—than did India, which had to use trails over high Himalayan passes to supply its troops.[21]

In the fall of 1962, orders were given, apparently, for the Indian troops to attack the Chinese who "occupied Indian territory," an attack against superior forces that were better supplied. The Chinese observed the preparations of the Indians and, on October 20, preempted the attack. In a short time, the Indian troops in the eastern contested area were defeated; they had no way of regrouping and no reserves available because of troop relocations arranged by the Indian high command. The way was open for Chinese troops to course through to the plains of Assam.

The border war became for India an invasion of its territory by China. Nehru, no longer unaligned, called for American and world assistance. The United States and Britain dispatched bombers to help the Indian air force, and the United States sent an aircraft carrier. Just before midnight on November 20, the Chinese government announced that in another twenty-four hours its forces would observe a cease-fire and in another nine days would begin to withdraw. There would be a cease-fire along the entire border, and, beginning on December 1, the Chinese frontier guards would withdraw to positions twenty kilometers behind the line of actual control that had existed between China and India on November 7, 1959.

In the eastern sector, where the advance to the plains of Assam had taken place, China said that since it was going to withdraw to a line 20 kilometers back from the McMahon line, India should make a similar withdrawal. In the western sector the Indian command had been more adept, and the Chinese had cleared the Indian troops only from the region in front of the MacDonald line; the Chinese troops would withdraw 20 kilometers from that line. China suggested that the prime ministers of the two countries meet to seek a settlement, but stated that even if this did not take place it would go ahead with the withdrawal.

India's reaction was to observe the cease-fire and to refuse to negotiate except under terms that put it back into the positions it had held before October 20. The hostilities ended, but no joint agreements were made. India was left with a powerful enemy on its Himalayan frontier. In 1964, two years after the border debacle, China exploded its first atomic weapon. India then began its nuclear-weapon program.

Kashmir again became the center of conflict between India and Pakistan in 1965, when Pakistan encouraged guerrilla warfare against India, supposedly to spur U.N. enforcement of a plebiscite. India retaliated by action at the 1949 cease-fire line. When Pakistan tried to cut India's supply lines, India invaded Pakistan. China created a diversion on the frontier, bringing about a withdrawal of the invading Indian troops. With Soviet help, a peace agreement was made in January 1966. The Soviet help led to the Treaty of Peace and Friendship of 1971 between India and the Soviet Union.

That same year brought a major calamity to Pakistan. East Pakistan elected Mujibur Rahman (Sheikh Mujib) as its president, but West Pakistan, led by Agha Mohammed Yahya Khan, chose not to honor the election. In a bloody campaign, its troops arrested Sheikh Mujib in Dacca, East Pakistan's capital. Mujib called on his followers to proclaim the independence of East Pakistan as the nation of Bangladesh. Martial law was put into effect, and there was sporadic fighting until India's troops crossed the border and entered the conflict. By December they had advanced to Dacca. Zulfikar Ali Bhutto took over from Yahya and released Mujib, who in 1972 became the first president of Bangladesh.

The population of Pakistan, which previously was almost a third of India's, became less than one-sixth of India's. Two years later, after India exploded its first atomic bomb, Pakistan was faced with both the conventional and atomic power of a hostile neighbor over six times its size. A major concern of Pakistan's leaders is that it again may be cut in two in a war with India. This would produce two nations less than one-twelfth the size of India, each powerless on the international scene. It probably appears to Pakistan that the only feasible defense against the threat India poses is the possession of atomic weapons.

India's Nuclear Weapons

Before international nuclear safeguards were in effect, the Canadians sold India a 40-megawatt research reactor, which started working in 1960.[22] This reactor can produce about 9 to 10 kilograms of weapon-grade plutonium a year. When it became apparent that India was violating the agreement it had made with Canada by using the reactor to produce plutonium for weapons, Canada stopped its assistance. India had been processing the plutonium in its Trombay separation plant since 1964. It conducted its first nuclear test in 1974 and is now estimated to have five nuclear warheads. India claims that its agreement with Canada has not been violated because the purpose of the 1974 nuclear explosion was to test the design of explosives for peaceful purposes; at other times, India hints that it could produce nuclear weapons in a short time. With the nuclear-power plants India has developed since 1974, it is now assumed to have about 400 kilograms of weapon-grade plutonium, or probably enough to make over sixty weapons.

In addition to its uranium, India has very large resources of thorium, which can be used to produce uranium 233, an effective bomb material.

In spite of its denials, there is some evidence that India is building a plant to produce lithium 6, which could be useful in producing hydrogen bombs. India has aircraft suitable for delivering nuclear weapons and has developed missiles capable of carrying them as far as China.

India's Technology

India has never been active in exporting nuclear technology, although it has the ability to do so in many sectors: fuel-handling and heat-transfer equipment, pumps, valves, instrumentation, and electrical equipment. Indian companies currently lack enough experience in dealing with European firms to be able to compete in many technologies. India has joined the IAEA, but because of its nuclear ambitions opposes the NPT, despite general compliance with its injunctions. India had an agreement to provide Libya with sensitive nuclear technology, such as reprocessing, in return for oil, but withdrew when the full implications of the trade were known and made public. Only 1–2% of India's electricity is generated by atomic power.

Pakistan's Nuclear Weapons

Pakistan's ability to develop nuclear weapons was furthered by its role as an ally of the United States in the Cold War. It allowed the United States access to its northern provinces for intelligence activities against the Soviet Union; U-2 spy planes were based there, for example. The Soviet-Afghan war brought increased activity in that area when the United States supplied the Afghan rebels from bases on Pakistan's northern frontier.

The purchase of American high-tech equipment suitable for use in producing atomic weapons has been banned for a long time; with the passage of the Solarz Amendment to the Foreign Assistance Act in 1985, the restrictions regarding such equipment became even tighter. The amendment provided for the cutoff of all military and economic aid to nonnuclear nations that illegally imported or attempted to import nuclear-related materials from the United States. The Pressler Amendment, which made foreign aid to Pakistan dependent on the president's certifying that that country did not have nuclear weapons, was also passed. During the Afghan war, the Reagan administration avoided examining any information that might nullify this certification. Pakistan was thus able, during those years, to obtain American and European technology relating to the production of nuclear weapons.

Pakistan chose to concentrate on the construction of a uranium weapon rather than focus on a plutonium bomb, as India did. Arguably, the most important assistance in Pakistan's development of nuclear weapons came from a Pakistani national, A. Q. Khan, who had worked in a Urenco centrifuge plant in Holland.[23] Apparently, he brought centrifuge designs to Pakistan and helped in designing a plant. The Chinese gave some technical assistance, though how much is difficult to assess because China has always denied any participation. Probably, China's major assistance was in developing a centrifuge cascade. Pakistan has not made a nuclear test, but is assumed to have made its first nuclear weapon between 1987 and 1990; it may now have three or four weapons.

Although Pakistan has developed a nuclear infrastructure with possibly a few thousand trained technicians and engineers, its nuclear industry is not large enough to be a commercial supplier. Pakistan does have an operating centrifuge uranium-enrichment plant that uses somewhat advanced Urenco technology, and in principle it could become a supplier of enriched uranium or enrichment expertise.

The India-Pakistan Standoff

In contradiction to the argument presented earlier that nuclear weapons in the hands of less-developed nations can readily lead to nuclear war, some argue that nuclear weapons are ideally suited to maintaining the peace between India and China, and between India and Pakistan.[24] In both cases, such weapons make the cost of escalating minor border controversies extremely high. As the argument goes, if all the antagonists are content to keep their nuclear weapons unassembled, but ready for assembly, the dangers of accidental or unauthorized launching are small. Pakistan would be in the position of threatening to destroy Delhi if an attack by India threatened to again dismember it. An examination of the 1990 confrontation between Pakistan and India over Kashmir lends support to both sides of this argument.

At the beginning of 1990, Pakistan supported Muslim uprisings in Kashmir by supplying over thirty training camps in Pakistan for Kashmiris, who would then cross the border to organize demonstrations protesting Indian rule. The protests grew in number and violence between

January and April; India put Kashmir under military rule. A large Indian strike force was moved into Rajasthan, which is fifty miles from the border with Pakistan and a likely place from which to launch an invasion. In the midst of all this, Benazir Bhutto, the prime minister of Pakistan, visited a training camp inside the Pakistani-controlled portion of Kashmir, where she pledged $5 million to support the "freedom fighters."

At that time, there were reports that the Pakistanis had designed a nuclear warhead that could be carried by one of the advanced F-16 fighters that the United States had sold to them. In a speech to the Indian parliament, India's prime minister warned Pakistan that it could not take Kashmir without a war, and commented that India would not allow Pakistan to achieve nuclear superiority. One parliamentary leader threatened that, if there was war, Pakistan would cease to exist.

It is not clear what happened next. The most striking version of the sequence of events comes from an article by Seymour Hersh.[25] Hersh states that early in 1990, information reached Washington from a reliable source that the technicians at Pakistan's Kahuta nuclear-weapon plant had been authorized to put together nuclear weapons, and that Pakistan was prepared to use them if India invaded Pakistan. U.S. intelligence efforts were stepped up. Evidence was found of the movement of trucks from what was a suspected nuclear-weapon storage site to a nearby Pakistani air-force base. There were reports of F-16s armed for delivery, on full alert. At this point President George Bush sent Robert Gates as his personal emissary to confer with Pakistani and Indian leaders. Gates told the Pakistanis that they would get no support from the United States in a war with India. He insisted that they agree to stop supporting terrorism in Kashmir. He told the Indian leaders to stop infiltrating the border region of Pakistan and to withdraw their troops. So that a mutual withdrawal could be confirmed, he told both sides that the United States would give each side access to the best U.S. intelligence on the other side's activities. Both sides withdrew.

This version of what occurred has been contested in an article by Devin T. Hagerty.[26] Hagerty writes that Robert Oakley and William Clark, U.S. ambassadors to Pakistan and India, respectively, during the 1990 crisis, "directly contradict Hersh's central claims." Both ambassadors were very much involved in trying to calm the dangerous situation. Hersh claims that General Mirza Aslam Beg of Pakistan authorized the assembly of nuclear weapons, but according to Hagerty, General Beg "has staunchly denied" Hersh's version of the events. Hagerty suggests that Pakistan possibly "undertook certain actions that were suggestive of nuclear-delivery preparations, so that Washington would intervene to resolve the crisis." His view is that Hersh exaggerated the nuclear dimensions of what was in other regards a real crisis. The conflicting evidence makes it unclear whether the presence of nuclear weapons contributed to the dimensions of the crisis or prevented it from escalating.

That crisis clearly demonstrates the danger of having a weak national leadership. A similar crisis in 1987 had brought about large-scale troop buildups in the same region. At that time both India and Pakistan were controlled by strong leaders, Pakistani President Mohammad Zia-ul-Haq and Indian Prime Minister Rajiv Gandhi, and the crisis was resolved without much outside intervention. In 1990, the leadership of both nations was weaker: in Pakistan, Prime Minister Benazir Bhutto was not kept informed of nuclear and military development by President Ghulam Ishaq Khan and the military leaders; in India, Prime Minister V. P. Singh had recently been elected with help from the support of a militant Hindu party. Intelligence sources on both sides heated up the conflict with unreliable reports.

SOUTHEAST ASIA

None of the nations of Southeast Asia, an area that extends from Myanmar (formerly Burma) through Thailand, Laos, Cambodia, Vietnam, Malaysia, and Singapore to Indonesia, Brunei, and the Philippines, has shown any interest in having nuclear weapons. In most cases, the state of these nations' economic and technological development would make the production of such weapons impossible. Indonesia, with its 200 million people and almost $100-billion gross domestic product (enhanced by large oil revenues), has considerable economic potential but relies primarily on an agricultural economy. The city-state of Singapore has become a technologically advanced society and markets materials useful for nuclear-weapon development. It has shown no interest, however, in developing its own weapons.

On December 15, 1995, ministers of these nations signed a treaty forming a nuclear-weapon-free zone encompassing most of this region.[27] The treaty encompasses not only the national territories of the signatories, but ocean areas much larger than those that would result from the application of the twelve-mile limit, including regions over two hundred miles from land. Both China and the United States objected to the terms of the treaty, claiming that it would prevent the movement of their nuclear-armed warships and submarines through the region. This objection was made in spite of the treaty's statement that

> nothing in this Treaty shall prejudice the rights or the exercise of these rights by any State under the provisions of the United Nations Convention on the Law of the Sea of 1982, in particular with regard to freedom of the high seas, rights of innocent passage, archipelagic sea lanes passage or transit passage of ships and aircraft, and consistent with the Charter of the United Nations.

China also objected because the treaty suggested that China did not have sovereignty over some parts of the South China Sea. An additional reason for the United States' objection is that the treaty includes a region that surrounds nations that are not signatories to it: the protocols that nuclear-weapon states are asked to sign include an assurance by the signer "not to use or threaten to use nuclear weapons against any State Party . . . within the Southeast Asia Nuclear Weapon-Free Zone." The treaty will go into effect when ratified by seven of the ten signatories.

THE MIDDLE EAST AND THE NORTH AFRICAN COAST

The Middle East is an acknowledged danger spot for the start of a war, conventional or nuclear. The nations there, except for Turkey, Iran, and Israel, are all Arab-speaking, and all except Turkey have been hostile toward Israel. Upon its founding in 1948, Israel was attacked unsuccessfully by five of the Arab states: Lebanon, Syria, Jordan, Egypt, and Iraq. It preempted an attack in 1956, and it was attacked unsuccessfully again in 1967. The OPEC-induced rise in oil prices in the 1970s brought money into several Arab states and Iran, money that these states used to increase and modernize their armed forces; these funds were augmented in some cases by Soviet military aid. Meanwhile, the United States gave assistance of many kinds to Israel.

Early on, this situation drove Israel to try to obtain nuclear weapons. Algeria, Iran, Iraq, Libya, and Syria have all at some time had nuclear ambitions, in most cases stimulated by Israel's nuclear-weapon program.

TABLE 8

Selected Statistics for the Nations
of the Middle East and North African Coast

Nation	Population (millions)	GNP (billions of dollars)	Literacy (%)
Algeria	28	53	52
Bahrain	0.5	3	74
Egypt	55	37	44
Iran	60	80	54
Iraq	20	35	60
Israel	5	47	92 (Jewish)
			70 (Arab)
Jordan	3	4	71
Kuwait	2	20	71
Lebanon	3	3	75
Libya	4	24	60
Morocco	26	25	89
Oman	1.5	68	20
Qatar	0.5	7	76
Saudi Arabia	18	79	62
Syria	13	20	64
Tunisia	8	10	62
Turkey	59	178	81
United Arab Emirates	2.4	28	68
Yemen	10	5	38

Table 8 gives some statistical information regarding the nations of the region. All of the nations except Israel, which is a modern, technically educated society, could be classified as developing countries. Of the other countries in the region, Iraq before the Gulf War was, arguably, the most developed. It had a secular regime, a strong central government capable of controlling its diverse ethnic groups, and adequate education and health facilities for most of its citizens.

Israel

The French helped Israel substantially, both in building a nuclear reactor and in the design and construction of a chemical-separation plant for plutonium.[28] South Africa may have helped in the testing of Israel's weapons. Some American Jewish businessmen may have helped raise money for the Israeli nuclear program. The greatest help from the United States may have been in its looking the other way during the development of the program. Israel is believed to have made its first nuclear weapon in about 1968, and it is estimated now to have over 150 warheads. Israel has never admitted to having weapons, and it would seem unlikely that any weapons could be operational without technical training of personnel in Israel's citizens' army. In a citizens' army such training would be difficult to keep secret.

Israel has the technical capacity to be a major nuclear supplier. It markets gas separation, solution purification, tritium manufacture, radioactive-materials handling, radiation protection, and waste-disposal systems. It also sells technology in high-vacuum engineering, precision machining, pulsed power, and robotics. The volume of this trade is small, and the trade is almost completely in dual-use items—that is, items that can be used for purposes other than nuclear construction. Israel had a close relationship with South Africa in the development of military technology, but there are only rumors of a close nuclear collaboration as well. Although it has not signed the NPT, Israel would be unlikely to export technology in opposition to U.S. policy.

Iraq

Iraq has been interested in nuclear energy since 1959, when the Soviet Union agreed to provide it with a research reactor. The reactor was eventually delivered, but it did not begin operating until 1968. By this time, Iraq had signed the Nuclear Non-proliferation Treaty, making its reactor subject to safeguards under the IAEA. The small 2-megawatt (thermal) reactor was located at the Tuwaitha Atomic Center near Baghdad. It was upgraded to 5 megawatts in 1978 and then operated with 80%-enriched fuel. A small radio-isotope laboratory was also provided, and the reactor was used primarily for the production of radio-isotopes for medical purposes.

In an attempt to get a more powerful reactor, the Iraqis sought French help in 1976. They asked for a 500-megawatt, gas-cooled, graphite-moderated natural-uranium power reactor. The French were aware, of course, that this type of reactor is excellent for producing plutonium, but not so useful for providing electricity because it is very hard to control. They refused to provide the kind of reactor Iraq wanted and suggested instead a light-water-cooled-and-moderated reactor. In 1976 the Iraqis accepted the French proposal and in addition requested a smaller reactor of the same type; they called the reactors Tammuz I and II, respectively. (The French had named the first reactor Osirak because it was modeled on a French materials-testing reactor called Osiris.) Tammuz I used highly enriched uranium as fuel and therefore was not well suited to producing plutonium for weapons. (The fuel would be primarily U-235, not the U-238 from which plutonium is made.) But by using a uranium blanket placed over the reactor, rather than the fuel itself, for plutonium production, the reactor, with its 70 megawatts of power, would be capable of making enough plutonium for at least one bomb a year. The reactor operated with about 15 kilograms of 93%-enriched uranium, in itself enough for a single uranium weapon. The fuel would be under safeguards, but it would be difficult to control the material in a blanket that might cover the reactor and be exposed to its neutrons. Showing concern about proliferation, the French agreed to ship only enough fuel at one time to keep the reactor operating; and, more important, they planned to operate the reactor jointly with the Iraqis for the first ten years.[29]

Iraq's nuclear effort had been furthered in 1976 when the Italian nuclear agency signed a ten-year assistance agreement by which it agreed to help Iraq in the construction of a fuel-fabrication laboratory (not needed for the reactor operation) and a radiochemistry laboratory, including three lead-shielded "hot cells." This equipment made it possible for the Iraqis to make fuel pellets and, after exposing them to neutrons, to separate the plutonium thus created. Estimates of the plutonium output of the reprocessing facilities ranged from less than a kilogram a year to several kilograms. (When the Italian government was criticized for the sale, it claimed to have consulted with the U.S. government before going ahead with it.)

These Iraqi projects experienced many difficulties. Explosions destroyed the cores of the Tammuz I and Tammuz II reactors on April 6, 1979, when they were being assembled in La-Seyne-sur-Mer on the French Mediterranean coast. Delivery to Iraq was delayed for about six months. In June 1980, Yahya el-Meshad, an Egyptian nuclear expert working for Iraq, was murdered in Paris. On September 30, 1980, just after the start of the Iran-Iraq war, Iranian aircraft bombed the Tuwaitha Atomic Center, causing minor damage. It is assumed that the Israelis were involved in all three actions. Their involvement was clear in the fourth and most effective action, that of June 7, 1981. On that day Israeli aircraft dropped sixteen 1-ton bombs on the Tammuz reactors. This, coupled with the Iran-Iraq War, probably halted the reactor program in Iraq. There has been speculation that Iraq built a hidden reactor and accompanying reprocessing facility after the destruction of its Tammuz (Osirak) reactor, but these have not been found in the aftermath of the Gulf War.

What Iraq is known to have done is start a multifaceted uranium-enrichment program.[30] Some information about this program had leaked out before the war, in particular about a centrifuge-development program. Remnants of the program were found after the war, but it was apparent that the Iraqis had been a long way from making successful centrifuges. They had obtained the high-strength maraging steel needed for one type of centrifuge and carbon fibers for another. They also had obtained designs of the successful Urenco centrifuges; they had had considerable assistance from German companies in this development. (Until the Gulf War, the member nations of the Nuclear Suppliers Group sometimes violated the spirit of the group's guidelines by not requiring safeguards on exports of components of devices that themselves required safeguards. Germany was particularly adept at this.) At the time of the Gulf War, Iraq's centrifuge program was still a long way from being able to enrich a useful quantity of uranium.

That the Iraqis had also been developing another technique—the use of calutrons—was not discovered until after the war. At the time of the war, students of proliferation did not believe that calutrons offered a useful method of enriching uranium. Although this was probably true for a developed nation, for a country such as Iraq, the calutron was a possible enrichment method. The calutron had the advantage of its technology not being secret. Most of the components could be made indigenously or had benign uses and thus could be imported without triggering safeguards. By the time the war had begun, Iraq had installed about a third of the calutrons it estimated it would need to be able to separate enough uranium for a bomb every two years. This estimate was probably very optimistic.

Although Iraq's nuclear program was brought to a halt by the Gulf

War, the situation there cannot be viewed complacently. Iraq now has, possibly, five thousand trained engineers—the most important element in any program for developing nuclear weapons. Before the war, it had developed a whole technological infrastructure for nuclear-weapon work: machine shops, laboratories, supplies, and trained technicians. Although much of this was destroyed during the war, it can be rebuilt for far less than its original cost. Iraq had been spending at least $1 billion a year for several years on its nuclear program, much of it on gaining experience in technologies, and this experience remains, despite present sanctions and the destruction of facilities.

Iran

The possibility of Iran's becoming a nuclear power is circumscribed by its not having been able to institute any coherent economic or development policies since the end of the Iran-Iraq war in 1988.[31] This disastrous war saw the end of control by fundamentalist radicals and the death of Iran's powerful religious leader, the Ayatollah Khomeini. Because of serious internal divisions, Iran lacked direction under the more moderate president, Hashemi Rafsanjani, who took office in 1989. The effect of the 1997 election of an even more moderate and possibly more forceful president, Mohammad Khatami, has yet to be seen.

The constitutional changes of 1988 reduced the power of the parliament relative to that of the president, but the country is seriously divided, with the lower classes and a fundamentalist radical clergy on the left, a central group of technocrats allied to the well-off middle class, and a conservative and powerful Islamic component on the right. Stirring this mix is a merchant class that profits from a disorganized financial structure. The political division is compounded by the peculiar leadership system: political and economic affairs are controlled by the president, and religious affairs by a supreme religious leader. This latter role, which Khomeini fulfilled in such a dominant way, is now occupied by the Ayatollah Khamenei, a political cleric rather than a religious authority. His religious pronouncements have little weight, and he is forced to rely on political maneuvering to exert power. The policies of President Rafsanjani could, however, be successfully thwarted by the country's religious leaders when they characterized those policies as untrue to Islamic principles. Rafsanjani once somewhat plaintively remarked:

There are two ways of criticism. One is that you accuse someone of overlooking the values of the Revolution, or of turning his back on the policies of the late Imam, or of going against Islam. This is a bad method. The [second] reasonable way is to prove that a particular action might have certain consequences. If someone uses this method, it is not displeasing.[32]

There has been no coherent development of industry in Iran since the war. Even the oil industry has not been well maintained, and Iran is increasingly unable to market its allotment of OPEC oil. Iran's economy is completely dependent on its oil sales, which account for 85% of its foreign exchange. Oil produces an annual revenue that fluctuates unpredictably between $12 billion and $18 billion. Iran's problems are compounded by the increase in its population from 35 million to 60 million in the sixteen years since the revolution. This represents an average annual increase of 3.4%.

The resulting poverty, paradoxically, increases the pressure on Iran to obtain nuclear weapons. It sees its most threatening enemy as the United States, whose great superiority in conventional weapons enables it to control the Persian Gulf, Iran's lifeline. Iran does not have the money to compete successfully in conventional weapons, whereas nuclear weapons, which are more affordable, do offer Iran a way of defending itself against U.S. domination. According to estimates by the CIA and other agencies, it will take Iran eight to ten years (by the year 2005 or so) to make a nuclear weapon, unless it can get fissile material from the former Soviet Union. Because of the disorganization there, this is a possibility. The United States has instituted a dual containment policy against Iran and Iraq. Other Western powers have not joined in and point out the inconsistency of this policy, in that the United States is one of Iran's largest trading partners.

The history of Iran's nuclear development begins under Shah Reza Pahlavi. During the 1960s, the United States provided Iran with a 5-megawatt reactor and "hot cells" that could be used for separating plutonium from irradiated fuel rods. Iran signed the NPT and negotiated a safeguards agreement with the IAEA. The shah planned the construction of large reactors as a source of electrical power and, possibly, of plutonium for bombs as well. West Germany agreed to construct two 1,300-MWe power plants. In 1974, Iran bought a share in the gaseous-diffusion uranium-enrichment company EURODIF. Work was stopped on the power plants after the Ayatollah Khomeini rose to power in 1979, and from 1980 to 1990 Iran refused to accept and pay for the partially enriched uranium it had contracted for with EURODIF. This 3%-enriched uranium, though suitable for reactors, would not have been usable in weapons. If an enrichment program had been planned, however, the 3%-enriched uranium for power reactors would have reduced the effort needed to produce weapon-grade uranium by a factor of two to four, depending on the enrichment method used. The partially finished reactors were damaged by Iraqi bombing raids during the Iraq-Iran war. After the war, West Germany refused to continue work on the reactors, in part because of its suspicions of Iran's intentions to produce nuclear weapons. In 1991, Iran tried to get EURODIF to supply it with partially enriched uranium, but EURODIF refused.

Evidence now points to a nuclear-weapon development program in Iran. Work may be in progress at the Tehran Research Center and a new center that was started at Isfahan in 1984, during the Iran-Iraq War. Political leaders have urged the development of atomic weapons, and although many technicians and engineers left Iran when the religious extremists took power, some are returning under the persuasion of more moderate regimes. China has been assisting the "peaceful" program by training technicians, and in 1991 it delivered a small calutron for use in isotope separation. This calutron is not useful for producing enriched uranium, though it is suited to separating radioactive isotopes for medical and other probably peaceful purposes. The small calutron might be of some use in giving experience and understanding of the problems that would occur in a larger and more effective one.

Iran has good relations with Pakistan and gets some technological assistance from that country, but Pakistan is unlikely to give it much help in getting nuclear weapons. Pakistan would probably not want another neighbor, even a Muslim one, as a nuclear power. Iran has solicited the help of Muslim countries of the former Soviet Union for its nuclear-weapon program.

An effort by Iran to develop a capability to build its own nuclear weapons is of real concern. It has employed many engineers and technicians from the former Soviet Union, and it continues to receive some help from China. In late 1994, Iran negotiated with Russia for the completion of the light-water reactors started many years ago under the shah. These reactors will produce about 1,000 MWe each, and enough plutonium for over forty nuclear weapons a year. Even though the plan is for Iran to ship the used reactor fuel to Russia for reprocessing, thus putting the recovered plutonium under external control, there is no guarantee that the Iranians will do this. If electrical power was desperately needed, the external supply of fuel for the reactors would allow some control. But Iran has large supplies of oil to fuel conventional electrical generators. Even if it was cut off from further supplies of low-enriched uranium as a result of its retaining the used reactor fuel for plutonium production, its economy might not be hurt.

In addition, Iran was at the same time asking for Russian assistance in the contruction of a centrifuge plant for enriching uranium. Although this plant was, nominally, to be used only to make low-enriched uranium as fuel for the reactors, it would enable Iran to be independent of outside supplies of fuel, and thus of any international control. Moreover, the enrichment plant could readily be changed to accommodate the making of weapon-grade uranium. The United States protested to Russia about its possible assistance in this program, and in a meeting between Presidents Bill Clinton and Boris Yeltsin in May 1995, an agreement was reached that Russia would not help with the centrifuge plant. Although there is some controversy regarding Iranian intentions, the U.S. government claims evidence of Iran's nuclear ambitions. There is little doubt that Iran has a nuclear-weapon program. Although it is unlikely to have any weapons for several years unless it can get the fissile material from an outside source, a future Iran with a large supply of nuclear weapons could endanger the entire Middle East.

Libya

In spite of being a signatory to the NPT, Libya has made repeated attempts to get atomic weapons. But its technology is at so low a level that it must buy turnkey facilities; it has virtually no technological infrastructure. Libya can consider the acquisition of nuclear weapons entirely on the basis of its large oil exports. It manufactures little other than agricultural products and small consumer goods. Its technical development is limited to an ability to perform maintenance on vehicles and to modify them on a small scale. It produces cement and building materials as well as some aluminum pipe and fittings, electrical cable, bricks, and glass.

Libya's dictator, Muammar Qaddafi, has attempted to hire engineers to work on nuclear weapons. In a 1975 interview, he said that he planned to entice Arab scientists away from the United States and Western countries to make Libya a nuclear power. In 1979, he reportedly ordered Yassir Arafat to assemble a group of Arab scientists to make an atomic bomb. In 1985, Qadaffi advertised in a U.S. engineering journal for academicians to teach and work in Libya.

Libya has no appreciable uranium resources; its desire for uranium may be one of the reasons for its invasion of Chad, which has extensive resources in its northern region, which borders Libya. At the present time, the only possibility of Libya's obtaining nuclear weapons is by the outright purchase of weapons stolen from the former Soviet Union or produced by some friendly nation such as North Korea. Libya is, apparently, prepared to use its income from oil sales for this purpose.

Algeria

Algeria has a small, 1-megawatt research reactor supplied by Argentina in 1989, and a larger one supplied by China. It recently acceded to the NPT, and both reactors are under IAEA safeguards.[33]

Syria

Syria started training nuclear specialists in the 1970s, and in 1981 it signed a nuclear-cooperation agreement with India. It is not now known to have any significant nuclear facilities. It is a signatory to the NPT.

SUB-SAHARAN AFRICA

Of the forty-two nations in sub-Saharan Africa, only three—Cameroon, Nigeria, and South Africa—have a gross national product of over $10 billion, certainly the minimum needed to be able to develop nuclear weapons. Nigeria, with its oil-rich economy of $66 billion, might have had the potential, but has never had any interest. Instead, it has spent its resources on bad investments and civil war.

Four other sub-Saharan nations provide sources of uranium—Congo, Gabon, Namibia, and Niger. Congo has large uranium reserves. Gabon, however, has one of the world's richest uranium deposits. About a billion years ago, the ore in this deposit was so pure that, with the greater natural enrichment in U-235 that it had at that time, it apparently became critical, producing a natural-uranium chain reaction. The companies that mine and sell uranium in Gabon are primarily French. Namibia is a major exporter of uranium; foreign companies from Canada, France, the United Kingdom, and especially South Africa are involved in the mining, processing, and marketing of uranium there. In Niger, one of the world's major exporters of uranium, French companies have carried out most of the exploration for the ore, as well as its mining and marketing.

South Africa

In 1993, President F. W. de Klerk of South Africa acknowledged that his country had built six nuclear weapons. (The first probably was assembled in 1982.) De Klerk claimed that these weapons had been dismantled and that the nuclear material had been "recast and stored according to internationally accepted measures." All of this had been done, he said, because of the change in the international situation and because of South Africa's desire to sign the NPT.[34] (He claimed that the weapons had been dismantled before South Africa signed on September 16, 1991.) Although German engineers had helped in the development of South Africa's vortex-tube uranium-enrichment process, de Klerk denied collaborating with any nation on nuclear-weapon development and has consistently denied that any tests were made. The only obvious foreign involvement in producing the weapons seems primarily to have been the purchase of dual-use equipment from Europe.

However, it has been suggested, but not documented, that Israel collaborated to some extent with South Africa in the construction and testing of an atomic weapon.[35] According to one version of the story, the Israelis tested their first weapon off the coast of South Africa with the participation of South African scientists and the South African navy. What we know is that on the morning of September 22, 1979, a U.S. VELA nuclear-detection satellite observed a double flash, characteristic of a nuclear explosion, over the Indian Ocean about fifteen hundred miles off the east coast of South Africa.[36] A panel of U.S. scientists was set up to assess whether there had indeed been a nuclear explosion. The panel found no confirming evidence, such as the seismic signals, electromagnetic disturbances, or fallout that usually accompanies a nuclear explosion; it finally decided that the flash was probably not caused by such an explosion. Others have claimed that an air explosion of a small weapon in such a remote region could not be expected to cause much observable peripheral effect.

Waldo Stumpf, chief executive officer of the Atomic Energy Corporation of South Africa, Ltd., has given a very convincing description of South Africa's nuclear program in an article in *Arms Control Today*.[37] In the article he describes the international isolation and fear of Soviet-sponsored aggression, through Cuban troops in Angola, that contributed to South Africa's decision to build atomic weapons. Stumpf states that the weapons were made with uranium, at first enriched only to 80% U-235 by the vortex-tube technique. The weapons did not have a neutron trigger; supposedly, they would deliver only about 10 kilotons of explosive equivalent. He claims that no tests were made, and points out that if a test of what he calls a crude weapon had caused the detected double flash over the Indian Ocean, fallout should certainly have been observed. Stumpf points out that the cost of the entire program was about $500 million. The South Africa case illustrates the ability of a technologically developed nation to build a few bombs for a fraction of the cost of a less-developed nation's program—for example, Iraq's.

In joining the NPT, the de Klerk government granted the International Atomic Energy Agency broad access to its facilities and, although not required to do so, revealed its past programs. In a 1993 report, the IAEA wrote that the amount of highly enriched uranium that could have been produced was consistent with that reported by South Africa, and it accepted the completeness of South Africa's inventory of materials and facilities.[38]

South Africa has very large uranium deposits, although they are of low grade. They are commercially viable only because the uranium is mined along with gold ore. In 1951, South Africa became one of the major uranium suppliers for the U.S. nuclear-weapon program. It also produces zirconium and hafnium, both important for nuclear technology. In the process of producing nuclear weapons, South Africa has developed a complete nuclear industry. It has built its own nuclear reactors, and, with large enrichment facilities that make use of both the vortex-tube and centrifuge processes, it has more than enough capacity to take care of its own reactor-fuel needs. It has signed the NPT and a comprehensive safeguards agreement and will soon be in a good position to export enriched uranium and other materials and components useful for the production of nuclear power. Its power reactors have been operating long enough to have generated about 3 tons of plutonium, which are still, however, contained in the fuel rods.

Nuclear-Weapon-Free Zone

In June 1995, the Organization of Africa Unity, which includes nations from all of Africa, approved a treaty establishing a nuclear-weapon-free zone for the entire continent of Africa and the islands near its coasts, such as Madagascar, Mauritius, and the Cape Verde and Canary islands. The treaty is usually called the Pelindaba Treaty, after the location of the South African Atomic Energy Corporation headquarters, where negotiations on the final draft were carried out. The treaty enters into force when twenty-eight of the African nations have signed it. It was opened for signature in 1996.

The treaty prohibits the development of nuclear weapons and their being stationed on the territory of any signatory. At this time, these provisions are meaningful only for the nations of the North African coast and for South Africa. The other significant provisions are a prohibition on bringing nuclear wastes into Africa for dumping, and control of the movement of wastes across national boundaries in Africa. The extreme poverty of some of the African states makes them susceptible to agreeing, for a fee, to permit wealthier countries to dump nuclear waste on their lands.

LATIN AMERICA AND THE CARIBBEAN

In the Americas south of the U.S.-Mexico border, only six countries might have the economic potential and technological development for producing nuclear weapons: Argentina (GNP, $70 billion), Brazil ($390 billion), Chile ($28 billion), Colombia ($43 billion), Cuba ($27 billion), and Mexico ($236 billion). In the fall of 1962, the United States learned that the Soviet Union had placed nuclear missiles in Cuba with the approval of the Cuban government. The missiles were withdrawn in late October, after the so-called Cuban missile crisis. During the past few years only Argentina and Brazil have been of concern in regard to proliferation.

The Treaty of Tlatelolco

Under the initiative of the government of Mexico, the presidents of Bolivia, Brazil, Chile, Ecuador, and Mexico issued a joint declaration on April 29, 1963, agreeing "to announce forthwith that [their] governments are prepared to sign a multilateral Latin American agreement whereby [their] countries [would] undertake not to manufacture, receive, store or test nuclear weapons or nuclear launching devices. . . ."

In November 1964, the Mexican government convened in Mexico City a "preliminary meeting" on "the denuclearization of Latin America." Four meetings of a preparatory commission were held in the Tlatelolco section of Mexico City between March 1965 and February 1967, when the Treaty of Tlatelolco was opened for signature. Since that time the treaty has been signed by all the nations of Latin America and ratified by all except Cuba.

The Treaty of Tlatelolco attempts to establish Latin America and the Caribbean as a nuclear-weapon-free zone. It prohibits contracting parties in this region from producing, testing, or possessing nuclear weapons in their territories. It forbids the receipt, deployment, or installation of any nuclear weapons. The contracting parties agree to use any nuclear material and facilities under their jurisdiction exclusively for peaceful purposes.

The treaty relates only to the construction of nuclear weapons; it does not prevent the production of highly enriched uranium or plutonium. The requirement is that these materials be destined for peaceful uses. It does require each contracting party to "negotiate multilateral or bilateral agreements with the International Atomic Energy Agency for the application of its safeguards to its nuclear activities." Most of the nations of Latin America have joined the NPT.

After World War II, the most technologically developed nations in South America, Argentina and Brazil, both vying for leadership, started nuclear-weapon programs. In both countries, the military played an important role in this contest. Argentina was under a military dictatorship from 1976 to 1983. A transition to civilian control took place in 1983, in part because of the disastrous outcome of the Falklands War. But the military still exerted considerable power, and the desire to have nuclear submarines was a motivating force for the production of highly enriched uranium. In Brazil, a part of the stimulus for nuclear development was competition with Argentina. Brazil was under a military dictatorship between 1965 and 1985, and the military's influence has been considerable at other times.

The election of Carlos Saúl Menem as president of Argentina in 1989 reestablished civilian control there, and in 1990 Fernando Collor de Mello was elected president of Brazil. In both cases, the election resulted from the failed economic policies of the preceding regimes. Both Menem and Collor de Mello placed greater emphasis on economic improvement than military posturing. Argentina signed the Treaty of Tlatelolco in January 1994 and the NPT in February 1995. Brazil, its policy unchanged after Collor de Mello resigned and was replaced as president by Itamar Franco in 1992 (who was then replaced by Fernando Enrique Cardoso in January 1995), signed the Treaty of Tlatelolco in May 1994. Although Brazil has not yet signed the NPT, the Tlatelolco Treaty provides many of the same restrictions.

Argentina

By 1983 Argentina had two operating nuclear-power plants and a gaseous-diffusion uranium-enrichment plant. The first nuclear-power plant to go into operation was a natural-uranium-fueled, heavy-water-moderated 320-MWe plant bought from West Germany. This facility started up in 1974. Argentina's second reactor, which began operation in 1983, is also natural-uranium fueled and heavy-water moderated. It has a power of 600 MWe and was bought from Canada. The reactors provide somewhat less than 15% of Argentina's electrical power. The plants are now under safeguards. A third power reactor is under construction.

Construction of a gaseous-diffusion plant was started secretly in 1978 under the military government then in control of Argentina. The existence of this plant was not revealed until 1983, when the civilian government of President Raul Alfonsin took over. This plant's construction indicates that the military government had a goal of making nuclear weapons, because Argentina's power reactors do not require enriched uranium. The plant was intended to produce 20%-enriched uranium (which is not in itself sufficiently enriched for use in a nuclear weapon), at a rate of about 500 kilograms per year. Although it now produces uranium at the expected enrichment level, it puts out less material than it was designed to produce. Argentina had some foreign assistance in building this plant, but primarily used its own technology. At one point with design help from West Germany and Italy it also started to build a plant for reprocessing reactor fuel to produce plutonium. Construction was suspended in 1990.

The civilian government in 1983 had also suspended, to some extent, Argentina's nuclear-weapon program. To reduce the danger of a nuclear-arms competition with Brazil, reciprocal confidence-building visits were arranged, but Argentina would not sign the Treaty of Tlatelolco at that time. One of its reasons for refusing, apparently, was its desire to have nuclear-powered submarines, which would operate with highly enriched uranium fuel.

Even though Argentina later became a party to the Treaty of Tlatelolco and signed the NPT, it had gone a long way toward producing nuclear weapons before this occurred. As a result of its now-discontinued nuclear-weapon program, it has mastered a broad range of technologies relevant to the production of nuclear power. It mines uranium and markets enriched-uranium fuel using gaseous-diffusion enrichment. It also sells research reactors, special welding machines, furnaces to sinter UO_2 pellets, radiological-protection equipment, and engineering services. The latter make up a very important part of its exports. Its expertise includes uranium-ore processing and chemical reprocessing. In 1967, Argentina created what it called a multinational program in metallurgy, and it now offers courses in metallurgy, thermodynamics, instrumentation, crystallography, x-ray diffraction, metal defects, diffusion, and so forth. This program appears to be part of a long-range plan to achieve an international reputation for competent engineering in a broad range of technologies.

Argentina has no supply of separated reactor plutonium, but its nuclear development is sufficient to allow it to produce nuclear weapons within a year or two should it decide to do so. Its two reactors have accumulated about 5 metric tons of plutonium in their used fuel.

Brazil

Brazil started to build a jet-nozzle uranium-enrichment plant with German help in 1975. This safeguarded method has now been discontinued. At the same time that it started work on this method of enrichment, Brazil began, ostensibly on its own, an unsafeguarded program to build a centrifuge enrichment plant for military purposes. By the mid-1980s, it had also started to build a laboratory-scale plutonium-enrichment facility. Obviously, Brazil was attempting to achieve a completely indigenous ability to produce nuclear weapons. Although Brazil has not yet signed the NPT, all of these facilities are now under safeguards.

Brazil has a well-developed nuclear industry, just as Argentina does, and with a change of regime would be well on its way to producing nuclear weapons. It has the world's fifth-largest uranium reserves, with 8% of the world's total. It exports uranium yellowcake to Europe and Asia, and is developing the process of converting yellowcake into UF_6. With the world's largest thorium reserves, Brazil now may be able to export thorium for use in fast breeder reactors. It exports lithium, beryllium, and zirconium. A fuel-element plant has been in operation since 1982. Brazil makes a range of auxiliary equipment, such as piping, pressure vessels, and heat exchangers, and provides engineering services in mining, milling, and processing. Its nuclear industry is not as large as Argentina's.

Only about 2% of Brazil's electrical power is generated by nuclear reactors, although two new large reactors will come on line by the end of the century. It has about 300 kilograms of plutonium in its used fuel elements.

AUSTRALIA, NEW ZEALAND, AND THE PACIFIC ISLANDS

Since 1952, Australia and New Zealand have been joined with the United States in a Pacific defense pact, the ANZUS (Australia, New Zealand, U.S.) Treaty.[39] Australia has relied on the United States as a partner in its defense ever since World War II. It supported the United States in the Korean, Vietnam, and Gulf wars, and it allowed the United States to set up bases for surveillance of U.S. missile tests and for other Cold War purposes. None of the nations in the region produce any materials that are useful in building nuclear weapons except Australia, which markets uranium from its extensive mines.

Antinuclear sentiment in the South Pacific region grew in the 1980s, in part in protest at the U.S.-Soviet standoff, but also as a result of the French nuclear tests in the Pacific and the possibility of Japan's dumping nuclear wastes in the South Pacific. An expression of this sentiment was publicized in February 1995, when New Zealand refused to allow the

U.S. destroyer *Buchanan* to make a port visit because it felt the ship was probably carrying nuclear weapons. Australia had earlier opposed U.S. deployment of the MX missile as destabilizing and refused to make staging facilities available to U.S. forces monitoring MX-missile tests.

In August 1984, the thirteen member states of the South Pacific Forum (Australia, New Zealand, Fiji, Papua New Guinea, the Solomon Islands, Vanuatu, Tonga, Western Samoa, Kiribati, Tuvalu, Nauru, the Cook Islands, and Niue) endorsed an Australian proposal to establish a nuclear-free zone in the South Pacific. The treaty, signed at Rarotonga in the Cook Islands on August 6, 1985, produced the second nuclear-free zone in a populated area.[40] (The first had been created by the Treaty of Tlatelolco; the other nuclear-free zones at the time covered the unpopulated areas of the Antarctic, and outer space.) The area covered by the Treaty of Rarotonga encompasses Australia, with a line north from Western Australia to the equator through the boundary of Indonesia and Papua New Guinea, then eastward slightly north of the equator until it intercepts the Latin American zone, then south to the Antarctic treaty zone, then west and, finally, north along Western Australia.

Several of the treaty's provisions are different from those of the Treaty of Tlatelolco. It prohibits the dumping of nuclear wastes at sea. A signer agrees not to manufacture any nuclear explosive device, not to provide special fissionable material to any state unless it is subject to safeguards, not to allow the stationing or testing of any nuclear explosive device on its territory, and not to assist in the testing of any nuclear explosive device. The treaty allows each signatory nation to decide for itself "whether to allow visits by foreign ships and aircraft to its ports and airfields, transit of its airspace by foreign aircraft, and navigation by foreign ships in its territorial sea."

There was no opposition from either the Soviet Union or the United States when the treaty was signed. The United States accepted the treaty as a reasonable compromise between the extremely divergent views of those nations that wanted no treaty and those that wanted a more complete ban on activities related to nuclear weapons.

Table 9 summarizes the level of nuclear development in various countries around the world. Since the end of World War II, the world's nuclear-development situation has changed from one in which the United States was the only owner of nuclear weapons and the only

TABLE 9
Nuclear Development around the World, 1995

Country	Nuclear Non-Proliferation Treaty[a]	Safeguards agreement[b]	Nuclear Suppliers Group[c]	Uranium mines	Uranium enrichment type and output[d] (SWU/year)	Reprocessing output[d] (tons of heavy metal/year)	Level of nuclear technology	Separated plutonium, civilian plus military[e] (kg)	Nuclear warheads[f]
Argentina	NPT	SA	NSG	yes	diffusion 20k	—	medium	?	0
Armenia	NPT	SA	—	no	—	—	—	0	0
Australia	NPT	SA	NSG	yes	—	—	low	0	0
Austria	NPT	SA	NSG	no	—	—	low	0	0
Belarus	NPT	—	—	no	—	—	low	0	0
Belgium	NPT	SA	NSG	no	—	100 (shut down)	high	2,000–3,500	0
Brazil	—	—	NSG	yes	centrifuge (planned)	—	medium	0	0
Bulgaria	NPT	SA	NSG	no	—	—	low	0	0
Canada	NPT	SA	NSG	yes	—	—	high	0	0
China	NPT	—	—	yes	diffusion, 0.2M	yes	medium	0	300
Czech Rep.	NPT	SA	NSG	yes	—	—	low	0	0
Denmark	NPT	SA	NSG	no	—	—	low	0	0
Estonia	NPT	—	—	yes	—	—	—	0	0
Finland	NPT	SA	NSG	no	—	—	low	0	0
France	NPT	SA	NSG	yes	diffusion, 11M	1.6	high	42,000⁺ 6,000	570
Gabon	NPT	—	—	yes	—	—	—	0	0
Germany	NPT	SA	NSG	no	centrifuge 0.5M	40 (shut down)	high	1,800	0
Greece	NPT	SA	NSG	no	—	—	low	0	0
Hungary	NPT	SA	NSG	no	—	—	low	0	0

				thorium						
India	—	—	—		—	275	—	low	300	6?
Ireland	NPT	SA	NSG	no	—	—	—	low	0	0
Israel	—	—	—	no	—	yes	—	medium	300	50–100
Italy	NPT	SA	NSG	no	—	10	—	medium	0–1,000	0
Japan	NPT	SA	NSG	no	centrifuge, 0.8M; chemical, 2k	planned	—	high	5,000	0
Kazakhstan	NPT	SA	—	yes	—	—	—	—	0	0
North Korea	NPT	SA	—	yes		?	—	—	0	1?
South Korea	NPT	SA	NSG	no	—		—	medium	0	0
Kyrgyzstan	NPT	—	—	yes	—	—	—	—	0	0
Lithuania	NPT	SA	—	no	—	—	—	low	0	0
Luxembourg	NPT	SA	NSG	no	—	—	—	low	0	0
Namibia	NPT	—	—	yes	—	—	—	—	0	0
Netherlands	NPT	SA	NSG	no	centrifuge, 1.2M	—	—	medium	0–700	0
New Zealand	NPT	SA	NSG	no	—	—	—	low	0	0
Niger	NPT	—	—	yes	—	—	—	—	0	0
Norway	NPT	SA	NSG	no	—	—	—	low	0	0
Pakistan	—	—	—	no	centrifuge, 5k	—	—	low	0	0
Poland	NPT	SA	NSG	no	—	—	—	low	0	0
Portugal	NPT	SA	NSG	yes	—	—	—	low	0	0
Romania	NPT	SA	NSG	no	—	—	—	low	0	0
Russia	NPT	SA	NSG	yes	centrifuge, 14M	large	—	high	22,000+ 125,000	6,669
Slovakia	NPT	SA	NSG	no	—	—	—	low	0	0
Slovenia	NPT	—	—	no	—	—	—	low	0	0
South Africa	NPT	SA	NSG	yes	vortex, 0.3M	—	—	medium	0	0
Spain	NPT	SA	NSG	yes	—	—	—	low	0	0
Sweden	NPT	SA	NSG	no	—	—	—	medium	0	0

TABLE 9 (cont.)

Country	Nuclear Non-Proliferation Treaty[a]	Safeguards agreement[b]	Nuclear Suppliers Group[c]	Uranium mines	Uranium enrichment type and output[d] (SWU/year)	Reprocessing output[d] (tons of heavy metal/year)	Level of nuclear technology	Separated plutonium, civilian plus military[e](kg)	Nuclear warheads[f]
Switzerland	NPT	SA	NSG	no	—	—	medium	0–1,000	0
Tadjikistan	—	—	—	yes	—	—	—	0	0
Ukraine	NPT	—	NSG	yes	—	—	low	0	0
U.K.	NPT	SA	NSG	no	centrifuge, 0.9M	1,500	high	44,000+ 2,800	300
U.S.A.	NPT	SA	NSG	yes	diffusion, 19M	>5,000	high	1,500+ 100,000	8,402
Uzbekistan	NPT	—	—	yes	—	—	—	0	0

[a]This column indicates whether a country has ratified the Nuclear Non-proliferation Treaty; the abbreviation *NPT* signifies ratification. Data primarily from *SIPRI 1997 Yearbook* (Oxford: Oxford University Press, 1997).

[b]This column indicates whether a country has a safeguards agreement with the International Atomic Energy Commission; the abbreviation *SA* signifies the presence of a safeguards agreement. Data primarily from *SIPRI 1997 Yearbook*.

[c]This column indicates whether a country is a member of the Nuclear Suppliers Group; the abbreviation *NSG* signifies membership. Data primarily from *SIPRI 1997 Yearbook*.

[d]Data primarily from *World Nuclear Industry Handbook*, ed. James Varley (Sutton, Surrey, England: Nuclear Engineering International, 1995).

[e]Data primarily from Albright, Berkhout, and Walker, *World Inventory of Plutonium*. The authors give estimates of the ownership of reprocessed plutonium in 1990 (reprocessing is generally done in the United Kingdom or France), but the actual location of the plutonium is not always clear. The authors point out (p. 201): "Each year, the IAEA and Euratom publish aggregate figures for the plutonium and HEU [highly enriched uranium] they safeguard. They are barred by rules of confidentiality from disclosing the amounts safeguarded in individual countries."

[f]Both the United States and Russia have many more weapons than those listed here. The numbers given here are for strategic weapons that are in place. Both countries have removed many of their strategic weapons, and all of their tactical ones, from their active arsenals. Weapons not in place or in active arsenals are being or have been disassembled, but their pits (the nuclear centers of the warheads) are being stored intact.

supplier of technology to one where thirty-four nations are members of the Nuclear Suppliers Group (there are over forty-two nuclear suppliers), twelve nations now enrich uranium, six nations process plutonium, sixteen nations own supplies of plutonium, and eight nations own nuclear weapons. Although the latter category has not seen an increase in recent years, knowledge of nuclear technology is growing steadily, and nations generally are edging closer to being able to build nuclear weapons readily in case the world's security systems change radically.

The developments that have taken place in the past thirty years give some information about what we may expect in the future. Since 1965, only three new states have obtained nuclear weapons. Both Argentina and Brazil have given up their nuclear-weapon programs, South Africa has given up its nuclear weapons, and the nations of the former Soviet Union have completed the return of the nuclear weapons on their territories to Russia. This is of great importance. It must be understood, however, that neither stopping development programs nor giving up weapons is the same as never having them in the first place; the knowledge and expertise remain.

Control of proliferation by control of access to technology is now directed primarily toward maverick nations such as Iran, Iraq, Libya, and North Korea, but this method will become increasingly difficult. We now have forty-two nations marketing nuclear technology; in 1969 there were only about seven. About five thousand Iraqi technicians are estimated to have been employed on weapons construction in that country, and Pakistan certainly has an equal number of capable employees. The design of the Urenco centrifuges, possibly the world's best, is now available in Pakistan and is partially so in Iraq. Some of the trained Urenco people, and even the centrifuge design itself, may be available to other Muslim nations. There is also the possibility of the theft of nuclear materials from the former Soviet Union and of design help from its unemployed nuclear engineers.

8

The Theft of Nuclear Materials and the Effects of Uncontrolled Proliferation

The end of the cold war has removed the danger of a nuclear exchange of thousands of weapons that might put an end to civilized life, but it has increased the likelihood that a nuclear weapon will be used. This is a terrifying irony. The collapse of many controls in Russia after the breakup of the Soviet Union has left its stockpiles of nuclear weapons and weapon material exposed to theft and subsequent sale to terrorists and maverick nations.[1]

THE THEFT OF NUCLEAR MATERIALS IN RUSSIA

By U.S. standards, methods of guarding nuclear materials in the Soviet Union were very lax. In the Soviet police state there was little danger of theft. Movement was restricted, so it would have been hard for anyone stealing nuclear material to take it anywhere. Borders were closely watched, and permission to leave the country was difficult to obtain. Furthermore, living conditions for nuclear workers were better than those of the ordinary citizen. The military was adequately housed, and its officer corps had great prestige. Both the possibility and the temptation for theft were slight.

The breakup of the Soviet Union changed all of this. Movement became unrestricted; borders were no longer sealed. Scientists and other nuclear workers received salaries lower than the country's average. Payments were often months in arrears, even in the military service.

As conditions in Russia deteriorated, Western observers began to hear hair-raising stories of the casual way in which the dangerous materials were being handled. News items detailed the arrests in Western Europe of persons trying to sell stolen "nuclear" materials. Most of these arrests involved people trying to sell as weapons material any radioactive substance they could get their hands on.

It was clear that control was breaking down in Russia, but the Russian agencies in charge of nuclear material became defensive and were unwilling to assume any responsibility. Between 1991 and 1994, the German government reported 700 instances of attempted sales of stolen Russian material.[2] Although many of these cases were fraudulent, about half involved actual nuclear smuggling. The following two cases suggest the nature of the problem:

1. During a three-and-one-half month period in 1992, Leonid Smirnov stole approximately 3.7 pounds of 90%-enriched uranium from the Luch Scientific Production Association at Podolsk, Russia. He removed this uranium from the plant in small quantities on over twenty separate occasions. When he tried to take the accumulated material to Moscow, he was apprehended at the Podolsk railway station. This is the only case of fissile-material theft that Minatom (the Russian Ministry of Atomic Energy, the agency in charge of safeguarding much of Russia's nuclear material) has acknowledged.

2. A supply of unused, 20%-enriched reactor fuel for nuclear submarines was stored at a Murmansk shipyard. The shipyard was enclosed by a fence with several gates, some of which were unguarded. The storage building itself was surrounded by another fence, unguarded and with several holes in it. Entry to the building was controlled by a door with a padlock. In 1993 Captain Alexei Tikhomirov of the Russian Navy broke into this building. His brother, a civilian working at the shipyard, had told him of the negligible security arrangements and had described the location of the reactor fuel. Tikhomirov managed to steal some of the fuel and got away successfully, but, panicking, he neglected to relock the entry door. The theft, which otherwise might have gone unnoticed for some time, was detected the next day. He was arrested some months later when he and two accomplices sought to sell the fuel for $50,000.

These two cases are typical of the smuggling that has been intercepted. The situation is not surprising, given a poorly guarded supply of nuclear material, marginal security arrangements, insider knowledge, and people without money and with no knowledge of methods of disposing of the stolen material. For a while, many of the thieves were caught by sting arrangements of the German police. This became so prevalent a way of catching the criminals that Russia finally objected, pointing out that the market provided by the stings encouraged the thefts.

No thefts of nuclear weapons have yet been reported. The Russian Ministry of Defense apparently protects its weapons more effectively than do the civilian agencies or the naval stores, although a story coming out of Russia calls this into question. It has been reported that inspectors from the Russian Ministry of Defense found a battery of nuclear-armed SS-25 mobile missiles completely deserted because all the operators and guards had left to find food.[3]

A problem associated with Russian compliance with the Start I Treaty is that, after weapons are dismantled, the nuclear cores pass into the hands of Minatom. The security Minatom provides is described in testimony given to the House Committee on Appropriations in 1992: "Set up under Soviet rule for a strictly regimented, closed society worried only about external threats, the security often amounts to little more than barbed wire fences and armed guards, providing scant protection against insiders and their accomplices who hope to get rich by smuggling out nuclear materials for sale on the black market . ."[4] Victor Mikhailov, head of Minatom, has more recently reported a great decrease in the number of incidents of theft. Unfortunately, this data can also be read as an indication that professional criminals with established export routes have gotten into the act, replacing the bumbling, amateurish efforts of earlier days.

It is a serious matter if a large amount of even low-enriched, reactor-grade uranium is actually available. Almost a ton of this uranium would be needed to get enough U-235 through enrichment to build a nuclear weapon. However, with its 3% to 4% enrichment of U-235, low-enriched uranium more than cuts in half the size of a centrifuge plant needed to produce weapon-grade uranium. If techniques such as enrichment by EMIS (calutron) or laser separation are used, the size of plant needed would be more than four times smaller.

The supply of nuclear material in Russia (and in the United States) is immense: Russia has about 200 metric tons of separated weapons-grade plutonium and the United States has about 100 tons. For highly enriched uranium, Russia has about 1,000 metric tons compared with 500 tons in the U.S.[5] There is the Russian stockpile of nuclear weapons controlled by the Ministry of Defense, containing between 15,000 and 25,000 weapons (compared with about 7,000 strategic weapons mounted on delivery vehicles). Minatom controls a growing stockpile of weapons-grade fissile material which it extracts from dismantled nuclear weapons. About 15 tons of plutonium and 45 tons of highly enriched uranium are shifted to this stockpile from the Ministry of Defense each year. Minatom also has custody of the plutonium from Russian nuclear power reactors, about 30 tons of which are produced each year. In addition to the material under Minatom's control, fissile material is scattered across Russia in laboratories and scientific institutes. These locations provide only the most rudimentary security for this fissile material.[6] The problems are compounded by the rampant corruption of officials and the presence of organized crime in Russia today.

It is very difficult for the United States to improve the security of Russian weapons material. To do so would require interfering in the internal affairs of a country that is suspicious of the motives of its former enemy (a suspicion made more intense by our plans for expanding NATO). The Nunn-Lugar Program, set up in 1991, seems an excellent plan. The legislation initiating the program describes it as follows: "That it is in the national security interests of the United States (a) to facilitate on a priority basis the transportation, storage, safeguarding, and destruction of nuclear and other weapons in the Soviet Union, its republics, and any successor entities, and (b) to assist in the prevention of weapons proliferation."[7] The best example of implementation of a program of this sort was the purchase and removal to the United States in 1994 of 600 kilograms of Russian bomb-grade uranium from Kazakhstan.[8] This had been found almost unprotected in Ust-Kamenogorsk. The price paid was in the low tens of millions (funded by money from the Departments of State, Defense, and Energy); this was a bargain, considering the amount of material it took out of circulation. An interesting sidelight to this transaction revealed the status of Soviet inventory control: when an accounting was made of all of the material purchased, 104% of what had been paid for was received.

Another similar but much larger transaction shows what has been wrong with the United States's operation of the Nunn-Lugar Program. In 1992 the United States arranged to buy 500 tons of bomb-grade uranium from Russia for $12 billion. The plan was to use the uranium, blended down, as reactor fuel. Delivery would be spread out until the year 2014. The United States entrusted management of this deal to the U.S. Enrichment Corporation (USEC), a corporation set up in 1993 to take over the U.S. enrichment plants from the Department of Energy. In overseeing the uranium purchase, the USEC was in effect competing with itself. The cost to the USEC of the Russian low-enriched uranium under the deal is about $82/SWU, while the cost of uranium from its own facilities, which are subsidized by the U.S. government, is about $60/SWU. This purchase got caught up in American bureaucratic blunders, with the Department of Commerce opposing the transfer as "dumping" that would affect American companies (on the basis of bizarre accounting rules that converted a higher cost into a lower one). This, of course, infuriated Minatom's director, Victor Mikhailov, thereby increasing the difficulty of any subsequent negotiations with him. Even had this transfer gone smoothly, it would have done little to alleviate the present security problem, because the scheduled removal of the material from Russia will not be completed until 2014.

The Nunn-Lugar Program's effectiveness also has been dampened by restrictions. It is conditioned on Russian arms-control compliance, for example, and is subject to onerous auditing and to "buy-American" rules. In the atmosphere of present-day Russia, the best way to overcome resistance to a proposal is to have some financial rewards attached to it. Unfortunately, this can also be said of the United States.

One of the more successful ventures in improving security has been a series of U.S.-funded collaborative research projects between Los Alamos and the Lawrence Livermore Laboratory, on the one hand, and their Russian counterparts, Arzamas-16 and Chelyabinsk-70, on the other. Although these projects were focused more on fundamental physics problems than on nuclear-material security, they generated a degree of rapport that allowed the start of a joint project to develop a Russian materials-security system at Arzamas-16 and at the Kurchatov Institute. This has also led to a center for training in materials-security problems in Russia that is funded under the Nunn-Lugar Program.

The possible migration of Russian nuclear workers to maverick countries increases the danger of proliferation. There is little work for the 50,000 nuclear engineers and technicians in the former Soviet Union. About 1,000 to 2,000 of these engineers are capable of taking charge of a major part of a weapons-production program. It is possible that unemployed Russian nuclear engineers have accepted jobs in the unstable nations that are of major concern in efforts to prevent proliferation. The *Boston Globe*, in late 1992, cited the arrest, shortly before takeoff, of a planeload of Russian nuclear experts bound for North Korea.[9] The combined experience of these scientists and engineers could have reduced the time and effort needed to establish either a standard nuclear weapons program or a program making use of stolen material.

Economic support could influence Russian behavior with regard to materials-security, but the United States has provided very little money for this. Although the Clinton administration favors such activities, they are not high on its list of priorities. Money must come from Congress, which is often reluctant to give any assistance to our former enemy. The administration seems unwilling to expend what credits it may have in Congress for this, rather than for its numerous other important programs. The total U.S. money spent from 1992 through 1996 was $633 million, with $184.50 million in 1996, mostly Nunn-Lugar money.[10] The Defense Department's total budget for 1996 was $285,733 million. The cost of prosecuting a war against a rogue country that is believed to be about to assemble a nuclear bomb would run into tens of billions of dollars and would probably lead to great loss of life on both sides. In the hands of a terrorist group making an attack on a New York City skyscraper, a nuclear weapon might cause the loss of hundreds of thousands of lives and billions of dollars worth of property, and it might bring to an end New York's eminence as a place of business.

The theft and subsequent sale of nuclear material expands the dangers associated with nuclear proliferation. It allows shortcutting the elaborate and expensive procedures necessary to produce fissile material. Present procedures have made it very difficult for an underdeveloped nation to build nuclear weapons, and have made it impossible for terrorist groups, even those as highly organized as the Japanese *Aum Shinrikyo,* to build one. The availability of weapon-grade uranium, however, would make it possible for a medium-sized group to build a Hiroshima type of weapon. All that would be needed is about 100 lbs. of highly enriched uranium, some neutron-reflecting material, a gun barrel measuring a few inches in diameter, and some high explosive. Some understanding of metals, of nuclear physics, and of the action of explosives would complete the list. The calculations for designing the Hiroshima bomb were so straightforward that it was not thought necessary to test a prototype in 1945.

Past efforts, which have concentrated on preventing nations from developing or purchasing the technology to build nuclear weapons, have been remarkably effective. But the availability of stolen nuclear material from the former Soviet Union may now be allowing terrorist groups and maverick nations to circumvent all of the controls and to buy nuclear materials for a small fraction of what they would otherwise cost.

The great success of the previous effort was that nations generally have been made to feel they will be more secure without nuclear weapons than with. Almost all of the developed nations are able to build their own weapons, some needing only a few month's time. Most have relied on the shield provided by the deterrent nuclear strength of one of the nuclear powers. But the deterrent shield (i.e., the threat of retaliation) is lost when the enemy is a terrorist group. If terrorist groups, or countries such as Libya, Iraq, or North Korea, are known to have nuclear weapons, an obvious reaction might be a rush by all nations to arm themselves.

THE EFFECTS OF UNCONTROLLED PROLIFERATION

If almost total proliferation does occur, the status of a nuclear-weapon nation in regard to other nations will fall into one of four categories: (1) the nation is the sole possessor within a group of competitors; (2) the nation has a great many more weapons than its competitors; (3) it and one or more of its competitors have equal numbers of nuclear weapons; or (4) the nation is primarily concerned with terrorist groups.

One can consider as an example of the first case the relationship of the United States to all of the nonnuclear powers. We have not used nuclear weapons since we dropped two bombs on Japan during World War II. We have not made a no-first-use statement, however, and during the Korean War, apparently, we threatened China indirectly with the use of nuclear artillery to force an end to the war. The possible use of such weapons was also probably implied during the confrontation between China and Taiwan over the islands Quemoy and Matsu. In similar circumstances, would any of the world's less stable nations show the restraint the United States did in these situations?

The second case, that of a nuclear power with many weapons in a confrontation with a weak nuclear power, is of particular concern to the United States. It would appear that the weaker power, fearing complete obliteration, would not dare to attack the larger one. The larger power would not be so constrained from attacking unless the smaller nation could make its weapons so secure as to threaten unacceptable damage against its larger enemy. The smaller power might also use a nuclear weapon as a defensive method of last resort—if, for example, it was being invaded.

In the third case, that of two countries having equal numbers of weapons, the reasons not to use the weapons are somewhat more compelling. However, one of these nations might use nuclear weapons if it anticipated complete national defeat by conventional warfare.

The final case, possession by a terrorist group, is in many ways similar to possession by a rogue nation that might anonymously act as a terrorist. The rogue nation, however, might hesitate to launch a terrorist type of attack because of the devastating consequence of its being discovered. Terrorist groups with sufficient resources could operate independent of the wishes of any of the maverick nations, but the fear of being connected to the terrorist groups might inhibit funding sufficient for an independent nuclear venture. It certainly would make a maverick country reluctant to allow a terrorist group to base nuclear operations on its soil.

The Danger of Anonymous Attack

The first three cases just described assume a straightforward confrontation, and nuclear attacks that allow the victim to identify the attacker. But nations and certainly terrorist groups can make an attack that conceals the identity of the attacker; in any situation where a powerful nation has several enemies, an anonymous attack may be possible. The threat of retaliation does not prevent such an attack unless the hostile nation can be convinced that it will ultimately be identified. The possible victim might in turn use a barbarous method to deter attack. It might, for example, indiscriminately threaten all terrorist-sponsoring nations with retaliation if an attack was made and the perpetrator not identified. At best this might cut off much of the funding of terrorist groups. It would have no effect, however, on the private U.S. militias that might have the resources and the will for nuclear attack.

The multiple-retaliation threat would be most needed and possibly most effective in a situation where two or more maverick nations were allied only in hatred of a nuclear power; they might even be mutual enemies. An example would be Israel, probably a major nuclear power, confronted with nuclear-armed Iraq and Iran. In such a situation, retaliation against both nuclear-armed maverick nations for an attack by one would not seem more immoral or irrational than the "mutually assured destruction" (MAD) strategy practiced by the United States and the Soviet Union during the Cold War. MAD was not really a defense, but an assurance to an enemy that even if he destroyed most of your country you would be able to retaliate and destroy most of his. This strategy was justified by the assumption that it would prevent a nuclear war from ever taking place. A threat to destroy several antagonists might be justified by the same perilous logic.

Maverick nations that now sponsor terrorism would be unlikely to exercise the restraint and care in the use of nuclear weapons shown by the United States and the Soviet Union in their Cold War confrontations. An accidentally launched weapon or a preemptive strike would be much more likely in the Middle East. To be effective, the policy of retaliation against two or more enemy nations for a nuclear strike by one must be announced. This announcement, however, puts the announcer at risk of a preemptive strike by either of the two target nations. A maverick nation, in addition to being the possible target of a preemptive nuclear strike by the enemy target nation, is at risk of a blind retaliatory strike by that nation as the result of the action of the other maverick nation or terrorist group which it does not trust and over which it has no control. Such a situation could result in the settling of differences between the maverick nations and the formation of an alliance. It could, on the other hand, lead to nuclear war.

Defenses against Nuclear Attack

The best defense against nuclear weapons is the threat of retaliation. (In most of this discussion, I assume that no retaliation would be made unless the attacker could be positively identified.) When only two nations or power blocs are involved, the identity of the attacker is always known, and defense by the threat of retaliation is effective. Under these special circumstances, the possession of nuclear weapons by two powers, although dangerous, can be stabilizing, as we saw during the Cold War competition of the United States and Soviet Union. But now, even when only a two-way confrontation occurs, the situation is much more dangerous than it was for the United States and the Soviet Union. The nations involved may be very close to each other geographically, so that little time would be available for an evaluation of an indicated attack. Inexperience in handling nuclear weapons and a less-developed and less-controlled military structure make the possibility of an accidental or unauthorized launching of a nuclear-armed missile or plane much more likely.

Most of the nations now trying to get nuclear weapons are different in character from those currently owning them; they are maverick nations that support terrorism. They may have ambitions that are thwarted by the nuclear powers. Their primary reason for wanting the weapons is probably defensive: to prevent other nations from coercing them. They may consider nuclear weapons as weapons of last resort, to be used even against a great nuclear power if their nation is about to be overrun and destroyed, but they may also have plans for using nuclear weapons aggressively.

In discussing proliferation, I shall deal principally with the situation that the United States, its allies, and the rest of the developed world face with regard to the hostile states that support terrorism. I shall assume that the present major nuclear powers would not use their nuclear weapons except when attacked with a nuclear weapon.

In the next few decades, any new nuclear powers will probably have a much smaller number of weapons than the United States and its allies or Russia. The retaliatory threat, therefore, even by Israel, France, or Great Britain, would be one of the complete destruction of any new nuclear state. Being the target of one hundred nuclear weapons would concentrate the mind of even a Qaddafi. It is doubtful that the new owners would use their weapons in a way that invited retaliation, except in defense against a devastating attack with conventional weapons.

Although a missile attack against the United States now seems unlikely, there currently is discussion in the United States about the construction of not only ground-based but also space-based missile defenses. Circumstances are significantly different from those the United States confronted vis-à-vis the Soviet Union during the Cold War. Then the threat was of a possible missile attack with thousands of sophisticated weapons. No defense could have been impenetrable. Defense against an attack of only a few missiles, however, is possible, and can probably be made with a ground-based defense system. (Such a system would violate the anti-ballistic-missile treaty.) Unfortunately, a terrorist type of attack is more difficult to defend against than one by a few ICBMs.

If a nation with a small number of weapons chose to use them aggressively against a major nuclear power, it would conceal its identity as the attacker. When the identity of the culprit must be concealed, the possible methods of attack are limited. It can be assumed either that the maverick nations would not have submarines capable of launching missiles or that, if they did, it would be possible to keep the submarines under observation. Under these circumstances, no attack would be made by a ballistic missile, because reverse plotting of a measured final trajectory could locate the source. It would not be made by a massive flight of aircraft, because the route and source of the flight might easily be determined. A possible method of attack would be by a Scud-type missile launched from a ship; a flotilla of ships could not be used, however, because it would be detected. If a cruise missile had sufficient range to fly by a devious route and thus conceal its origin, it might be a threat. Accurate guidance systems for missiles will probably soon be available. The Global Positioning System, for example, which now can tell you where you are anywhere in the world within about 15 meters, would be useful in this regard.

It is unlikely that an attack would be made by a terrorist group sponsored by a maverick nation, because the terrorist-supporting nations would probably not trust such an organization, realizing that it would act according to its own agenda. Most likely, any attack would be made by a pseudo–terrorist group, a part of the military of a maverick nation. In either case, the risk to the developed world would be the same. The devious politics of the Middle East could lead to a nation's attempting to make an attack appear to be from one of its neighbors.

The attack could be by a nuclear weapon carried in a truck driven or shipped to the victim country. The weapon could be in a ship, itself to be exploded in a harbor of the victim nation. Although it would be too large to be loaded in ordinary passenger baggage, the weapon could be carried in a cargo plane. The weapon would not necessarily be loaded on the ship or plane in the maverick nation, but might be sent first to another nation to be shipped from there. There are many possible scenarios. If a missile is launched from a ship, the ship itself must be scuttled to prevent detection of its origin. It could be sent in a small boat launched from a ship offshore or traveling along the coast from another nation, probably not directly from the attacker country. It is unlikely, in the next two or three decades, that any of the maverick nations would be able to develop a light, "suitcase" weapon that could be carried in personal luggage on an airliner, but it might be possible to design a weapon that could be assembled from small parts light enough to be easily carried into the country to be attacked.[11]

A defense against such attacks has to be one that convinces the attacker that the source of the weapon will be found and the attacking nation punished. If controls are set up, and it they are sufficient to stop, say, one in four possible attempts, and if the maverick nations can be made to understand this, the 25% chance of detection and the threat of subsequent retribution would in itself be deterring. A decision to retaliate would be a very difficult one to make because even what might seem to be compelling evidence could prove to be otherwise, and a devastating retaliatory attack might be made on an innocent nation.

An even more effective defense might be to remove any possibility of anonymity by improving espionage to such an extent that there is a complete understanding of what is going on in the maverick nations. Information as to which nations are funding terrorist groups would be most useful, because such a nation could be told that it would be held responsible for any actions of the terrorist group. This is a tall order, but the task can probably be reduced to having sufficiently good espionage that the maverick countries think we are likely to know what is going on. If technical and other means of spying could be much improved, the international community would be able to get information about nuclear-weapon development early enough to apply effective pressure to stop it or at least to take preemptive military action against it.

Defending the United States

To further the reader's understanding of the possible defenses against nuclear anarchy, I shall now examine how various nations might cope with it, using the United States as my first example. The oceans that separate this country from what are now the trouble spots of the world give the United States a great advantage in relation to other nations. Its major defense is the threat of massive retaliation. For many years to come, any new nuclear states that might threaten the United States will have only a few weapons. There is no possibility of their being able to disarm the United States with them. A deliberate intercontinental missile attack is most unlikely, but as the number of countries with nuclear weapons increases, the chances of an accidental or uncontrolled launch become greater. To give a sense of security, some type of ground-based ballistic-missile defense will probably be set up in the United States. The most difficult threat to counter will be that of anonymous attack. The extreme means that might be considered appropriate for preventing such an attack can best be understood when one realizes that the explosion of a single nuclear weapon in the United States might cause the same number of American deaths as were caused by the Korean and Vietnam wars combined.

The most important means of reducing the chance of a terrorist type of attack are increased spying, as suggested earlier, and border controls both at home and abroad. Effective border controls to prevent nuclear weapons from being brought into this country or near its shores would be very costly. The United States would probably not institute such controls until a terrorist type of attack with a nuclear weapon was made somewhere in the world. The problems of installing an effective system are enormous. To be effective, however, the system would need to be capable of detecting only a fraction of the total attempts to import weapons, because the maverick nations would not dare to risk being caught. An idea of the scale required for such a system can be had from the fact that once the control system was in place, it would almost completely eliminate drug imports and illegal immigration.

With a highly developed information system and a great deal of international cooperation, we may be able to know the identity, the country of origin, and the contents of ships and planes approaching the United States. This knowledge would have to be obtained before entry, because once a ship carrying a weapon reached our shores, it would be too late. A system of examinations of ships before they leave port to come to the United States would be useful. If a weapon was being shipped in parts, to be assembled in the United States, only a very detailed inspection would reveal this. The Untied States has annual imports that are worth about $500 billion and weigh about 300 million tons. The attempt would be to detect a single nuclear weapon or its components in all of this cargo.

It would probably be possible to set up reliable security arrangements with all of the major trading partners of the United States, and thus reduce the amount of inspection and allow open trade. Our partners would be facing some of the same dangers, and would gain from reciprocal security measures. It would be possible to prevent the approach to the United States of ships from hostile countries. Transshipment of weapons through countries friendly to the United States could be prevented by cooperative measures, such as controls at the borders of those countries. The shipment of a weapon might be prevented by allowing U.S. inspectors to examine a ship's cargo while it was being loaded. Once certified as "clean," the ship would be allowed to travel directly to a U.S. port without offshore inspection.

A sealed box capable of remote access by U.S. Coast Guard aircraft, in some ways similar to the responders used during World War II to distinguish friendly and enemy aircraft, could be installed on each ship. The responder would indicate criteria necessary for the ship's being allowed to land: whether the ship had passed inspection, whether any attempt had been made to move the box or to tamper with it, whether the ship's route had included any intermediate stops.

Before being allowed into port or even near the United States, ships without such code boxes would have to be searched, and the deck cargo inspected on the high seas—an almost impossible procedure even in good weather. Cargo to Caribbean and Mexican ports would be subject to search. These searches would probably not cause much international uproar, because any nation in close proximity to the United States would be anxious to avoid any chance that a nuclear weapon could be launched against the United States from its territory.

Aircraft would present a different problem. If passenger planes were modified so that large pieces of baggage or cargo could not be carried, it might be possible to exempt such planes from preflight inspection, although inspection upon arrival would be necessary to prevent a weapon's being shipped in many pieces. It would, of course, be possible to perform an inspection for general baggage similar to the one now used for carry-on baggage. Cargo planes would have to be inspected as they are loaded—a particularly touchy problem for flights that stop in other foreign countries before arriving in the United States.

Our concerns cannot be limited to imports from Europe and the Orient. About a quarter of our imports come from Mexico and Canada, with both of which we have almost open frontiers. It might be possible to arrange cooperative agreements with Canada whereby Canada and its imports are subject to the same controls we set up for ourselves. This would allow our border with Canada to remain open and unguarded. To do the same with Mexico would require a much greater effort.

The use of border controls would need to be coupled with greatly expanded espionage both at home and abroad. The technical spy methods that were useful during the Cold War could be expanded and improved. The infiltration of political and religious groups similar to what was done before the World Trade Center bombing could be very much increased.

All of these means of defense would have major effects on American society. Foreign trade would decrease, and travel would be restricted. The most serious effect, however, would be the changes in American society brought about by the threat of nuclear attack by terrorist-supporting nations. The threat of a terrorist attack is more intimate in nature than the threat of attack from outside. The latter makes people band together in defense, but the threat of a terrorist attack would make people suspicious of each other. Minority ethnic groups would be suspect. Because of a perceived threat of sabotage, the United States interned all people of Japanese origin during World War II. In this new world, an even more paranoid reaction might occur. If the suspected maverick nations were Arab or Muslim, all people who merely resembled Arabs or Muslims would come under suspicion. During World War II, the anti-Japanese hysteria abated after a few years, but fears of nuclear attack would last for as long as we suspected that nuclear weapons might be in the control of a hostile maverick nation.

The consequent atmosphere of suspicion might well make us tolerant of government surveillance: the tapping of telephones, the infiltration of innocent organizations, and the collection of data files on all residents would be accepted as routine. Witch-hunts might again occur, depending on the ethnic or national groups suspected. If in spite of these precautions a terrorist nuclear explosion did occur in the United States, the government would probably curtail civil liberties even further.

Problems Facing Europe

Europe's security problems in the face of uncontrolled proliferation would be even greater than those of the United States. In the best case, the threat of nuclear danger might unify Europe. With the removal of customs barriers between members of the European Economic Community, there would be a single external barrier, with free flow of goods and weapons inside. All European nations would be constrained to a single foreign policy, because any nation that antagonized one of the maverick states could be attacked by weapons brought in through the ports of its neighbors. The whole community would need to have a single policy regarding the inspection of cargoes and the receiving of goods from maverick nations. On the other hand, if nations became critical of their neighbors' security arrangements, the danger might tend to strain the union. European nations are dependent in differing degrees on the maverick nations for their oil, and for that reason will differ on security measures directed against specific oil suppliers. Not having the fortunate isolation of the United States, Europe will find it much more difficult to keep uninspected ships a safe few hundred miles from its shores.

European nations will find it very dangerous to risk antagonizing nuclear-armed maverick nations. Europeans will have to be careful that public statements or laws do not offend the religious or political sensitivities of the Muslim world. Certainly there will be no European participation in embargos or police actions against a nuclear-armed maverick state such as Libya.

If a single nuclear weapon exploded in Europe, the European Community might disintegrate as each member nation tried to increase its own safety from attack. Disagreements over security might cause each nation to go its own way and put in place its own trade barriers and its own policy toward terrorists. The number of deaths resulting from such an attack, however, would not be anywhere near as large as the number of deaths experienced by Europe during either of the last two world wars.

Problems Facing Israel

Israel is in the most exposed position of all of the democratic nations. Its presence may not be the real cause of much of the terrorist activity in the Mideast, but it symbolizes all that the maverick nations hate about the West. If the current standoff between Israel and the Muslim states continues, the presence of even one nuclear power among the maverick nations will be a severe threat to Israel.

If Israel were faced with only one hostile nuclear power, it could assume that nation to be the source of any attack, and hence retaliate effectively. Israel's great problem is its many enemies. A ballistic-missile attack probably would not be made against it as long as Israel has a much larger number of weapons than its antagonists. Israel, however, would be particularly vulnerable to an attack by a single plane or by a long-range cruise missile from one of its hostile neighbors. Any of them could conceal the source of the attack by sending a plane or missile on a devious route over another country.

For the same reason, it would be difficult to trace the origin even of a Scud attack from a freighter—which could have come from Lebanon, Syria, or Egypt, all of whose coasts are close to Israel. Defense against attack by a single plane or a cruise missile would require highly developed radar and a continuous air alert, or a superior defensive missile system. Such defense is viable only because an attack with more than one nuclear weapon would be unlikely if the attacker was trying to conceal its source. A more probable defense would be a continuous surveillance of the hostile countries to find out if development or purchase of cruise missiles was taking place. It could then be made clear to any country found to be engaged in such activities that a cruise-missile attack would be attributed to that country. Of course, if more than one country was developing or buying cruise missiles, this defense would not be effective.

An attack by a ship containing a bomb would be difficult to prevent. Such an attack might involve sending a nuclear weapon to one of Israel's trading partners, from which nation it would then be transshipped (possibly innocently) and delivered to the target. To prevent this, Israel would need the cooperation of all countries with which it traded. Europe and the United States would, in all likelihood, already have increased their surveillance, so obtaining cooperation there would be relatively easy. Israel would want information similar to that sought by the United States—complete data on all air and ship traffic coming into its ports.

A terrorist type of attack would be possible only if Israel had several nuclear enemies. It is therefore to be expected that Israel would go to extreme measures to avoid facing more than one nuclear adversary. Because one new nuclear power in the region would encourage others, Israel would probably use force to stop any proliferation in the region.

The possible proliferation of nuclear weapons to the Muslim nations of the Middle East brings to mind many other risks for Israel. The fear of losing Arab oil has already weakened European support for Israel, and the possibility of becoming a target of nuclear terror as a result of supporting Israel could reduce the support of the United States. The effect of a nuclear attack on Israel would be much more severe than on a larger nation. Most of Israel's population lives in a region no larger than the San Francisco peninsula. Although an attack by a 20-kiloton nuclear weapon would kill only a small fraction of the population, it could contaminate a large region with radioactivity. The threat of another attack might be sufficient to produce a mass exodus, however successful Israel's retaliation. The Israelis are certainly aware of the risks, and one should not be surprised at extreme reactions from Israel if any of its antagonists move toward possessing nuclear weapons.

The Problem of North Korea

Besides the Middle East, the other present danger spot is North Korea. That country's probable possession of one or two nuclear weapons does not cause much threat to its neighbors; a single weapon is significant only as a defense, to be used to repel an invasion. If North Korea were to initiate a nuclear attack, it would cause great damage, but the country would then be exposed to determined retaliation. As discussed earlier, there is apparently some evidence that North Korea was at one time planning to operate a more powerful reactor and to increase its facilities for separating plutonium from used reactor fuel. With several weapons, North Korea could become a real threat to its neighbors. If this should happen, a domino effect would be set in motion, and South Korea and Japan would be under immense pressure to build their own nuclear weapons. With their present state of industrial development, this would not take them long. However, in any conflict, even with this degree of proliferation, the threat of retaliation would make nuclear attacks unlikely. Alternatively, North Korea might consider anonymous attacks. Also, arms now account for most of North Korea's foreign sales, so it is possible that it might start selling finished weapons to the highest bidder.

Much of this discussion has focused on dangers to the United States and its allies, but the arguments presented here also apply to the other nuclear powers, Russia and China. On the other hand, newly armed countries with few nuclear weapons do not have the means for an obliterating massive retaliation; their problems will be different. If their weapons are assembled and ready to mount in planes or missiles for delivery, they present an attractive target for a preemptive strike by an enemy. Only by greatly dispersing aircraft and protecting missiles in silos can their retaliatory capacity by maintained. The only safe posture short of this is to store the nuclear weapons in secure deep repositories, separate from their delivery systems. Otherwise, the possession of nuclear weapons can make for an unstable situation, one in which there is an advantage in being the first to strike. In addition, such countries face the same threat as do the better-armed nations—the danger of anonymous attack.

9
Improved Control
of Atomic Energy

T he effort to prevent nuclear proliferation must thus far be considered a success. In the last twenty-five years, only three additional nations have acquired nuclear weapons. The international community has been successful in persuading the nations of the former Soviet Union to turn their weapons over to Russia, convincing them that they will not gain in security by keeping them. South Africa has given up its weapons. Argentina and Brazil have dismantled their programs. The major concern remaining is the possibility of terrorist groups getting stolen nuclear material and the possession of nuclear weapons by nations that operate outside regular international norms, such as the maverick states of Iran, Iraq, North Korea, and Libya. These states want nuclear weapons in order to strengthen themselves against regional enemies, or, sometimes, to combat the hegemony of the United States, whose conventional weapons they feel are too powerful to be opposed. The principal effort in preventing proliferation should be directed toward the terrorist groups and these nations. The result of possible unrestricted proliferation to such nations, many of which have committed terrorist acts, has been discussed in the previous chapter.

What is not often discussed is how close many nations are to having nuclear weapons. There are at least fifteen nations that could quickly, possibly in less than a year, get them. The reason they have not done so is that they feel more secure without such weapons than with them. This is the optimal situation, and one that should be maintained. It is fortunate that, at this time, the developed nations that can get nuclear weapons readily are, almost without exception, democratic. Even South Korea and Taiwan, which did not fit this description just a few years ago, now have governments that, by most standards, are democratic. Argentina and Brazil have governments much more representative now than they were a decade or more ago.

Most of these nations have security arrangements with the nuclear powers that give them protection from attack. The European states, for the most part, have the protection of the NATO alliance, with its three nuclear powers. Japan and South Korea also have security arrangements with the United States. Taiwan probably feels it will get more protection from the United States if it has no nuclear weapons than if it were to have a few.

The two greatest challenges for the future with respect to proliferation are to prevent the maverick nations from getting nuclear weapons, which will become increasingly difficult as sources of technological help multiply; and to assure security for the developed world so that it will continue to feel no need for nuclear weapons. Methods that achieve these ends will also prevent any major conventional war from breaking out. Although proliferation is now contained, the world is close to a situation in which all developed nations have nuclear weapons. If this should occur, and a general war take place, the world could witness the explosion of hundreds of nuclear weapons.

In the first section of this chapter, I discuss improved methods of preventing proliferation to the maverick nations. In the following section, I talk about general methods of enhancing security. The implications for U.S. policy are covered at the chapter's conclusion.

OTHER METHODS OF PREVENTING PROLIFERATION

Both the strength and the weakness of our present methods of surveillance are apparent in the current standoff with North Korea. This difficult situation also illustrates the hard choices we will have to make to prevent proliferation.

The United States apparently had some information about the North Korean nuclear-weapon program as early as 1985.[1] It is somewhat surprising, then, that the United States did not make more effort earlier on to prevent the North Koreans from going ahead with their nuclear development, although it would have been more difficult at the time to get the cooperation of the United Nations and the IAEA. (The sensitivity of these bodies to the problems of clandestine proliferation has increased markedly since the Gulf War and the discovery of Iraq's nuclear program.) In addition, the legal basis for any U.S. insistence on inspection, or actions such as sanctions, would have been very tenuous because, although North Korea signed the NPT in 1985, it did not make a safeguards agreement with the IAEA until 1992. Moreover, there would almost certainly have been a veto by the Soviets or Chinese.

Questions about the accuracy of U.S. information on the North Korean program also complicated the matter. A secret report to a congressional committee would have been less compromising to U.S. intelligence sources than evidence presented to the IAEA or the U.N. Security Council. For the United States to have proceeded effectively, it would have needed convincing evidence—if intelligence sources were not to be compromised, several kinds of evidence.

Information not derived from inspections such as those that have been done recently by the IAEA in North Korea comes from many sources, the best of which are probably people working at the North Korean reactor who are spies for the United States or South Korea. Useful information could also be gained by a knowledge of North Korea's imports. The physical size of North Korea's reactor, however, cannot be estimated from imports of uranium, because the country is reported to have its own uranium ore. The reactor is a gas-cooled, graphite-moderated type. Possibly, special graphite had to be imported; knowledge of the amount imported would reveal the size of the reactor. The power level that a reactor can maintain is, in any case, more closely related to the cooling system than to the reactor size, so a knowledge of the fan size, if it is gas-cooled, would be important. Some of the information that contributed to an estimate of the reactor's capability undoubtedly came from the satellite surveillance developed by the United States during the Cold War. This is the method most often used in studying weapons development in closed societies.

The present situation in North Korea teaches a tough lesson: action against North Korea's nuclear-weapon program should have been started much earlier. Had China supported the United States in this, North Korea might have been dissuaded from initiating an atomic program, or its program might at least have been impeded enough to make it ineffective. An earlier start, however, would have required definite information about the program, much more than our current methods of surveillance allow.

Satellite, Aerial, and Intrusive Inspection

The best technical method of evaluation now available is the use of satellite detectors, especially optical detectors. The most effective of these, cameras in satellites orbiting two hundred miles above the earth, are able to resolve details of a fraction of a meter and, in good weather, can gather a great deal of information. Unfortunately, in order to remain in a fixed location, a satellite carrying such a camera would need to be in geosynchronous orbit over the equator, which would put it more than 20,000 miles from the earth.[2]

In order to provide accurate pictures of the earth, satellites need to be no farther than two hundred miles from the earth; at this distance they circle the earth in about ninety minutes, and therefore are above a single point on the earth's surface for only a short time. By the time they arrive at the same point in their orbit again, the earth will have revolved beneath them, and they will see a different part of its surface. Because an individual satellite can view a single spot on the earth's surface only infrequently, many satellites are required to view a spot more consistently. Another problem is that any ordinary optical system will not be able to penetrate clouds. Special infrared sensors can be used to scan the earth's surface at night, but the resolution available is worse than that of a camera operating in the visible region of the spectrum.

Although with a radar system it is possible to determine what is beyond clouds, ordinary radar is not useful in aerial surveillance because it cannot resolve small objects. If, for example, a radar antenna with a diameter of 1 meter were used with a radar wave having a wavelength of 3 centimeters, the smallest detail it could resolve from a height of 200 miles would be 2 miles in diameter. With an antenna 10 meters in diameter, the smallest details would be 0.2 miles in diameter. An antenna about 1,000 meters in diameter would be needed to resolve an object 3 meters in diameter. A very clever invention called Synthetic Aperture Radar almost reaches this resolution. It produces the effect of an antenna with a very large diameter by combining signals received as the satellite moves through space. If the radar used can combine signals during the time the satellite moves 1,000 meters, the effect will be the same as having an antenna 1,000 meters in diameter. The radar must have a stable platform, because the position of the transmitter and receiver must be accurately known over this interval. Used with a satellite, which provides an ideal platform, this special radar has achieved a resolution of a few meters. Satellites are also used for intercepting radio communications. Even when the messages intercepted are coded and unintelligible, the volume and time of the radio traffic will reveal information about some special activity below.

Although these remarkable devices are helpful, by using them one cannot do more than spot-check what is going on around any buildings that appear to be part of a nuclear-weapon enterprise. Checks made when buildings are being constructed reveal more. If the building is to house a reactor, there might be some indication of what part of the enclosed space is to be used for the reactor and what part for the support activities, and thus allow an estimate of the reactor's size. If the reactor is to be used to produce electricity, the electrical transformers and power installation would reveal the amount of power to be transmitted. If it is a research reactor, one that is not to be used for power production, it might be air-cooled. In this case, power would be needed to operate the cooling fans. Observing and tracing the power lines by satellite-borne sensors might give information about whether power was being produced by the reactor or being used by it, and could also reveal the amount of power involved.

Once a reactor is in operation, it produces a lot of heat. This must be gotten rid of by water or air cooling; if water is used, the heated water must be dumped somewhere, probably back into the river or lake from which it came. The temperature of a body of water or of the air can be measured from space by instruments carried in a satellite.

Information gathered in these ways allows only an educated guess as to what is going on. Still, this information would probably be useful in initiating a demand for inspection and, if this were not granted, a promise of punitive action. Much closer surveillance of sites of suspected nuclear-weapon production is what is really needed. In a situation in which the suspect nation wants IAEA approval, on-site inspection can probably be arranged. However, even a nation that wanted IAEA approval might balk at many inspections, and if more detailed inspection is called for, low- flying airplanes could be effective. This type of inspection, which allows the collection of much more continuous and detailed information than that available by satellite, is planned for use on Eastern European borders under the Open Skies Treaty. This agreement, which applies to the area of NATO and the former Warsaw Pact countries, allows adherents to make a restricted number of low-altitude flights over other states to make sure that no unannounced military developments are taking place. Although the altitude of the flights is not restricted, the resolution of the instruments is. Preliminary flights have already occurred, but, although the treaty has been ratified by most of its signers, it cannot go into effect until three crucial states, Russia, Ukraine, and Belarus, have done so. Both Russia and Ukraine have been reluctant to ratify the treaty until it is part of a larger agreement on European security. Belarus is expected to go along with Russia.

Low-altitude inspection by airplane allows the measurement of other characteristics of a nuclear-weapon program. If reactor fuel rods are being reprocessed to separate their plutonium, gases that accumulate in the irradiated material as a result of the fissioning of uranium will be released. Many of them recombine with other elements, but the gas krypton 85, a so-called noble gas, will not combine with anything. It would be released into the air in most installations. Samples of air taken by a low-flying plane could be used to determine whether chemical reprocessing is going on. Low-flying planes could also measure the power being carried in transmission lines. They might be able to detect electrical signals from the motors driving centrifuges, or even the sound of the centrifuges themselves. The magnets for calutron-enrichment spectrometers would emit some fields when operating, which should be readily detectable.

A nation that has not made an agreement with the IAEA would not allow inspections or low-altitude flights of foreign aircraft over its facilities, so surveillance would have to be carried out against the nation's wishes. Pilotless aircraft, able to fly independently to their destination at a very low altitude to avoid radar detection, might be used. They could be designed to take detailed pictures, or to take air samples. They would be expensive to use, but so are surveillance satellites.[3]

Other types of devices would be useful for inspecting possible nuclear-weapon programs in non-IAEA-cooperating nations. It is probably possible to design remotely operated equipment that can be dropped off near a road and can even, in some circumstances, burrow into the soil for concealment. This equipment could monitor traffic and possibly measure the radioactivity of loads being carried on the road. Devices might be designed to take soil samples from areas where groundwater might be contaminated by radioactive waste from reprocessing, or to listen in on telephone calls to the site.

It is probably more feasible to use *lidar* (laser radar) for remotely analyzing emissions from suspect installations, chemical as well as nuclear. This technology is under development. In an application for detecting gaseous emissions, a laser beam in a carefully selected part of the optical spectrum is projected from a distance through the air above a suspected installation. The suspect gases in the air will absorb certain parts of the spectrum from the laser, and the laser beam, proceeding farther, will be back-scattered from the air or possibly a conveniently located object to be detected by the sender. Ranges of over 10 km seem possible. The utility of such a device will be very dependent on the range. Whether it will be possible to get the 150-km range needed for surveillance by satellite is not clear. Unfortunately this system does not appear suitable for detecting noble gases such as krypton.

A variant on this system can possibly be used to detect the very small particles of aerosols, with the laser beam exciting fluorescence from the aerosols either in the air or after they have been deposited in a layer on the ground. The fluorescence would be detected remotely from the laser location.

Efforts are also being made to develop small, portable detectors of various sorts to enable inspectors to analyze samples while doing their inspection rather than collecting samples to be analyzed after the inspection has been completed.

If samples of clothing, hair, and so forth can be obtained surreptitiously from workers in a suspect plant, detailed analyses similar to those done forensically in criminal investigations might yield clues to the activity at the installation.

At some point it may become necessary for a nation or group of nations attempting to stop nuclear-weapon development to use further actions such as embargoes or even invasion. These extreme actions cannot be taken without verifiable information, so every method of gathering accurate information must be explored.

Getting technical information about a nation's nuclear program during that program's initial development would also allow early efforts to recruit people willing to act as spies. Without exact information supplied by entirely credible sources, putting into force the military action that might be required to shut down a nuclear-weapon program would be unthinkable. In most cases, our information-gathering methods, be they technical or human, are not accurate enough for us to act upon.

Table 10 summarizes the relative detectability of various parts of a nuclear-weapon program.

TABLE 10

Detectable Traces of Various Components of Nuclear Technology

Component	Physical Traces Visible from Air	Imports	
		Hard to Conceal	Easier to Conceal
Large reactor	Large building	Entire facility*	—
Small reactor (30 MW thermal)	Thermal signal in cooling water; large building; vent stack	Special graphite; remote handling equipment	Uranium
Chemical separation	Radioactive krypton	Remote handling equipment	—
Electromagnetic enrichment (calutron)	Power poles and transformers; cooling water; large, high-bay building	Heavy steel; magnet wire; power supplies; magnetic-field measuring devices; high-vacuum pumps	Machine tools; pumps and valves
Gaseous-diffusion enrichment	Large, low-bay building	Diffusion barriers; pumps	Valves; flow meters; cooling units; piping in large quantity
Centrifuge enrichment	Medium-sized, low-bay building	Rotors of special material; bearings; damping systems	Pumps; valves; flow meters; special machine tools
Chemical (uranium enrichment)	Small building	Special resins and chemicals (some proprietary)	Chemicals and chemical equipment
Laser isotope separation	Small building	High-power lasers; special optical parts; crucible	Pumps
Bomb construction	Explosive-test facility	Fast capacitors and switches	Special machine tools

*Any large reactor will of necessity be purchased outright, its purchase a matter of public record.

Sanctions, Embargoes, and Preemptive Strikes

If convincing information about a maverick nation's clandestine nuclear program could be acquired by the methods suggested here, the support of a group of other nations in enacting sanctions or a trade embargo against that country might be forthcoming. As explained earlier, the Nuclear Suppliers Group already requires safeguards on material used for nuclear development and refuses to sell equipment that is clearly to be used for bomb production. By restricting the maverick nation's trade in other important commodities, additional pressure could be applied. In considering possible action that might have been taken by the international community against North Korea, one can see that this policy has its difficulties. It would have been difficult to get China to go along with sanctions or an embargo against North Korea. In addition, the fact that North Korea had very little international trade except with other maverick countries would have made such actions rather ineffective. The key to interdicting a nuclear program's lines of supply is to get an early start.

In some situations, an extreme version of an embargo could be produced by a blockade. But this would usually be considered an act of war, and there are, as well, many situations where it would not be effective. In the war in the Balkans, the United Nations effectively set up a blockade on oil going up the Danube to Serbia, but Serbia's neighbors allowed a flow of oil through their territory that mitigated the effect of the embargo.

Finally, there is the possibility of a preemptive strike or a military invasion to destroy the nuclear facilities of the renegade state. The United States was fortunate in being able to get international cooperation in the Gulf War. This was possible mainly because of Iraq's clearly aggressive action of invading Kuwait, but also because of threats to European oil supplies. After the war, we saw how difficult it can be to find the appropriate facilities to destroy, even with almost complete access to a country. It appears that a military invasion would work only against a small, weak country.

INTERNATIONAL CONTROL

A world in which all nations that want nuclear weapons are able to have them would be hazardous to the United States as well as to most countries of the world. But restricting the supply of technology has been successful only in slowing down nuclear proliferation. We have reached a delicate situation, one in which many nations can readily get nuclear weapons if they feel threatened. If a threatening situation should arise, the result could be nuclear war. Thus it is in the interest of the United States and of all nations to prevent nuclear proliferation.

More serious attempts must be made to restrict the demand for nuclear weapons. If it were possible for the United States, acting alone, to enforce a ban on nuclear proliferation, it most likely would do so; but this is not possible. Embargoes and sanctions—actions short of preemptive strikes or invasion—can be effective only if they are supported by most of the world's nations. It is essential, therefore, that the United States proceed in its enforcement efforts with as much help from other countries as it can muster. These efforts should be coupled with measures to assure international security.

The First Attempt

The several recent proposals for international control of nuclear weapons recall the first attempt at international control, made just after World War II. The new proposals are realistic in suggesting that only very minor control, certainly nothing that violates the sovereignty of the major nuclear powers, be attempted as a first step. Before examining these recent proposals in detail, I shall review that first attempt and discuss why it foundered.

The Acheson-Lilienthal Plan

When World War II ended, the American government recognized that the atomic bomb had radically changed diplomacy and international relations. On September 11, 1945, Secretary of War Henry L. Stimson wrote to President Truman proposing control of the use of atomic weapons. His proposal read as follows:

> My idea of an approach to the Soviets would be a direct proposal after discussion with the British that we would be prepared in effect to enter an arrangement with the Russians, the general purpose of which would be to control and limit the use of the atomic

bomb as an instrument of war and so far as possible to direct and encourage the development of atomic power for peaceful and humanitarian purposes. Such an approach might more specifically lead to the proposal that we would stop work on the further improvement in, or manufacture of, the bomb as a military weapon, provided the Russians and the British would agree to do likewise. It might also provide that we would be willing to impound what bombs we now have in the United States provided the Russians and the British would agree with us that in no event will they or we use a bomb as an instrument of war unless all three Governments agree to that use. We might also consider a covenant with the U.K. and the Soviets providing for the exchange of benefits of future developments whereby atomic energy may be applied on a mutually satisfactory basis for commercial or humanitarian purposes.

I would make such an approach just as soon as our immediate political considerations make it appropriate.[4]

In December 1945, Dean Acheson, then undersecretary of state, was asked to study which policies the United States should follow. The following month, David Lilienthal, who had gained a wide reputation as head of the Tennessee Valley Authority, was made a special consultant to assist Acheson. Robert Oppenheimer, who had been thinking about the political implications of atomic weapons for a longer time than almost any other American, was an important assistant in and coauthor of this effort.

The result was the Acheson-Lilienthal Report, produced in March 1946. The report concluded that the only way to make sure that nuclear energy would not be used for weapons purposes was to create an international body that would have a monopoly over nuclear research and development relating to atomic energy. Most of the dangerous activities, such as the enrichment of uranium, would be undertaken by the international agency. The report suggested that if such activities were performed by national or other bodies, the level of inspection required to assure that no material was being diverted would anger the country being inspected. (It was estimated, for example, that three hundred inspectors would be required to police a diffusion plant.) In an attempt to avoid the necessity of such inspection, the report suggested that work relating to atomic energy be divided into "safe" and "dangerous" activities. Dangerous activities would include:

the provision of raw materials;
the production of plutonium and U-235 in suitable quantity and
    quality for use in explosives;
the use of plutonium and U-235 in making nuclear explosives.

The report pointed out that the transition from U.S. to international control of the governing body would take some time, possibly about three years, and that the transfer of control should be gradual. The report continued:

Should the worst happen and, during the transition period, the entire effort collapse, the United States will at all times be in a favorable position with regard to atomic weapons.[5]

The Baruch Plan

Bernard Baruch was appointed U.S. representative to the United States Atomic Energy Commission, to deal with the question of international control of atomic energy. On June 13, 1946, he made a proposal, based on that of Acheson and Lilienthal, for setting up an International Atomic Development Authority. Among the requirements he outlined for such an undertaking, he described a key one:

When an adequate system for control of atomic energy, including the renunciation of the bomb as a weapon, has been agreed upon and put into effective operation and condign punishments set up for violations of the rules of control which are to be stigmatized as international crimes, we propose that:
1. Manufacture of atomic bombs shall stop;
2. Existing bombs shall be disposed of pursuant to the terms of the treaty; and
3. the authority shall be in possession of full information as to the know-how for the production of atomic knowledge.[6]

What would prove the major stumbling block was the following statement:

> It would be a deception, to which I am unwilling to lend myself, were I not to say to you and to our peoples, that the matter of punishment lies at the very heart of our present security system. It might as well be admitted, here and now, that the subject goes straight to the veto power contained in the Charter of the United Nations so far as it relates to the field of atomic energy. The Charter permits penalization only by concurrence of each of the five great powers—the Soviet Union, the United Kingdom, China, France and the United States.
>
> I want to make very plain that I am concerned here with the veto power only as it affects this particular problem.[7]

He then submitted the following measures (which I have abbreviated somewhat here) as representing the fundamental features of the plan.[8]

General. The Authority should set up a thorough plan for control of the field of atomic energy.

Raw materials. The Authority should have as one of its earliest purposes to obtain and maintain complete and accurate information on world supplies of uranium and thorium and to bring them under its dominion.

Primary production plants. The Authority should exercise complete managerial control of the production of fissionable materials.

Atomic explosives. The Authority should be given sole and exclusive right to conduct research in the field of atomic explosives.

Strategic distribution of activities and materials. The activities entrusted exclusively to the Authority because they are intrinsically dangerous to security should be distributed throughout the world. Similarly, stockpiles of raw materials and fissionable materials should not be centralized.

Non-dangerous activities. A function of the Authority should be the promotion of the peacetime benefits of atomic energy.

Definition of dangerous and non-dangerous activities. Provision should be made to assure constant reexamination of the questions, and to permit revision of the dividing line as required.

Operations of dangerous activities. Not only must any plant dealing with uranium or thorium after it once reaches the potential of danger-ous use be subject to the most rigorous and competent inspection by the Authority, but its actual operation shall be under the management, su-pervision, and control of the Authority.

Inspection. By assigning intrinsically dangerous activities exclusively to the Authority, the difficulties of inspection are reduced. If the Author-ity is the only agency that may lawfully conduct dangerous activities, then visible operation by other than the Authority will constitute an unambiguous danger signal. Inspection will also occur in connection with the licensing functions of the Authority.

Freedom of access. Adequate ingress and egress for all qualified repre-sentatives of the Authority must be assured.

Personnel. The personnel of the Authority should be recruited on a basis of proven competence but also so far as possible on an interna-tional basis.

Progress by stages. Once a charter for the Authority has been adopted, the Authority and the system of control for which it will be responsible will require time to become fully organized and effective. The plan of con-trol will, therefore, have to come into effect in successive stages. These should be specifically fixed in the charter or means should be otherwise set forth in the charter for transitions from one stage to another.

Disclosures. In the deliberations of the United Nations Commission on Atomic Energy, the United States is prepared to make available the information essential to a reasonable understanding of the proposals which it advocates. Further disclosures must be dependent, in the inter-est of all, upon the effective ratification of the treaty. As the successive stages of international control are reached, the United States will be prepared to yield, to the extent required by each stage, national control of activities in this field to the Authority.

International control. Purely national authorities for control and devel-opment of atomic energy should to the extent necessary for the effective operation of the Authority be subordinate to it.

The Soviet Plan

Andrej Gromyko, on June 19, 1946, made the Soviet response to the Baruch Plan. Its essence is conveyed in three of the eight articles he proposed.

Article 1: The high contracting parties solemnly declare that they will forbid the production and use of a weapon based upon the use of atomic energy, and with this in view, take upon themselves the following obligations:

a. Not to use, in any circumstances, an atomic weapon;

b. To forbid the production and keeping of a weapon based upon the use of atomic energy;

c. To destroy within a period of three months from the entry into force of this agreement all stock of atomic energy weapons whether in a finished or semi-finished condition.

Article 2: The high contracting parties declare that any violation of Article 1 of this agreement shall constitute a serious crime against humanity.

Article 3: The high contracting parties, within six months of the entry into force of the present agreement, shall pass legislation providing severe punishment for the violation of the terms of this agreement.[9]

The Outcome

It soon became clear that a control treaty between the United States and the Soviet Union would be impossible because of a fundamental disagreement between them. This disagreement was based on two questions: when the United States would destroy its atomic weapons or turn them over to international control; and whether a veto would be allowed in the Security Council regarding the enforcement of the treaty. Undoubtedly, there would also have been disagreement about the terms of inspection, for neither the Soviet Union nor U.S. industry was eager to subject itself to inspection.

The United States controlled the Security Council on this issue. The members were the United States, Great Britain, France, China, and the Soviet Union. In 1946, a civil war was under way in China between the Nationalists under Chiang Kai-shek and the Communists led by Mao Tse-tung. The Nationalists, supported by the United States, had been winning until 1947; they lost power in 1950. Until that time, four of the five members of the Security Council could have been considered anti-Communist and willing to vote with the United States on issues involving the Soviet Union. In addition, Stalin feared that the inspection of installations in the Soviet Union by an international body controlled by the Security Council would breach the mantle of secrecy that he felt enhanced Soviet power.

The Acheson-Lilienthal Report had proposed a transition period before international control came into effect, but it made no specific reference to removing the Security Council's unanimity rule when atomic energy was concerned (Baruch's plan would have removed the requirement of unanimity). In an article about the Acheson-Lilienthal Report, Robert Oppenheimer wrote:

> If this plan works, the first step which would have to be taken by a nation bent on aggression is either the seizure of the facilities belonging to the Authority or the violation of the convention by which the nations agreed not to build certain kinds of plants, not to mine certain ores. Now this may happen—but I don't think it will, because the nation doing it will be coming out and saying, "We're going to make atomic war," and gives you a clear warning.[10]

In retrospect, a Soviet rejection of almost any proposal made at this time would have been inevitable. The Soviets preferred to negotiate international control from the position of an equal. A treaty that would have prevented their achieving this equality would have left them dominated by the United States. As a matter of fact, in 1946 the Soviets had already started their own development of a nuclear weapon, and three years later they carried out a successful test.

New Proposals

Although there have been many proposals for international control since 1946, often under various forms of world government, almost all people seriously involved in the policies of the U.S. and Soviet governments have concentrated their efforts on trying to control the arms race. Only since Mikhail Gorbachaev's coming to power and the subsequent collapse of the Soviet Union has the possibility of some kind of international control seemed real. A great many proposals relating to this kind of control have been made in the past few years. One approach has been to examine the possibility of getting rid of all nuclear weapons. This utopian goal has been considered in some detail in *A Nuclear-Weapon-*

Free World.[11] This most optimistic proposal requires the assistance of individual whistle-blower citizens in each nation, motivated in part by rewards and by assurances of subsequent protection by the international community. The conditions under which this protection might be relied upon appear to require societal changes more remote in prospect than any of those required for the international control of nuclear weapons by other means. This goal of preventing nuclear proliferation by eliminating all nuclear weapons does not appear to be a practical one at this time.

In this section I shall review some of the other recent proposals—proposals that depend on successful experience to produce a climate in which more complete control can be put into effect. All of these proposals would probably be useful in preventing nuclear-weapon proliferation, especially because the United States and Russia share an interest in achieving this goal. However, the proposals do have a common weakness: for any of them to be successful, China must be involved.

The Roland Timerbaev Proposal

The most modest suggestions have come from a long-time Soviet arms-control negotiator, Roland Timerbaev.[12] Appropriately, because Timerbaev has been involved in the evolution of the IAEA almost since its inception, he urges that further international control be achieved through an extension of the IAEA's activities and authority.

He points out that the Nuclear Non-proliferation Treaty's safeguards system contains very far-ranging provisions: special inspections are authorized when the IAEA needs to verify material described in a report submitted by a state, or when the agency considers the information provided not sufficient for it to fulfill its responsibilities. He feels that the provisions covering the second of these situations may lead to far-reaching verification measures, and points out that under full-scope safeguards the IAEA has the responsibility to make sure that safeguards are applied to all nuclear materials involved in all peaceful nuclear activities of a state, whether those activities are carried out within its territory, under its jurisdiction, or under its control anywhere. He argues that safeguards agreements do not make a distinction between declared and undeclared material; that since the IAEA has the right to ensure that all material subject to safeguards is in fact under safeguards, it has the right of access to any place where such material may exist, and may use its special inspection authority to gain access to such locations.

He also emphasizes the need for the IAEA to have access to national intelligence information that has a bearing on any request for a special inspection. He gives a short but, in his words, "by no means exhaustive" list of other problems that the IAEA might address:

1. The safe and secure dismantling and destruction of nuclear weapons.

2. Safeguarded storage of weapon-grade nuclear materials released from dismantled warheads, and their subsequent use for peaceful purposes.

3. The safe, secure, and safeguarded management, control, storage, and eventual disposal of civilian plutonium.

4. The secure cleanup of nuclear debris caused by nuclear activities, both military and civilian, on land and seabed.

5. The foolproof safety of nuclear reactors.

6. Waste management and final waste disposal.

Timerbaev explores the limits of what might be possible with something resembling the present IAEA. He does not directly address the problem of reducing the demand for proliferation. He does not confront the problem of enforcement that has so sharply been brought into focus by the current standoff with North Korea. Timerbaev relies on safeguards, and it is in enforcing safeguards that all attempts to prevent proliferation run into trouble.

The Gerard C. Smith Proposal

Gerard C. Smith, who directed the Arms Control and Disarmament Agency during the first Nixon administration, faces the problem of nuclear proliferation indirectly, proposing that a multilateral regime obtain control of nuclear weapons. His ideas can be summarized as follows.[13]

A gradual process would be started that would lead, eventually, to the abolition of nuclear weapons. Weapons would continue to exist, under multilateral custody, for an indefinite interim period. Following the precedents of the World Bank and the International Monetary Fund, a specialized agency of the United Nations might be an appropriate home for the multilateral regime. Nonmilitary uses of atomic energy would continue to be under the aegis of the International Atomic Energy Agency. The abolition of weapons would be achieved in three steps.

First, weapons now part of existing forces, including those of nations other than the superpowers, would be reduced in yield and numbers. Before reductions had been completed, all nuclear testing, production, and deployment of new systems would be halted.

Second, the remaining small national forces would be assigned to a multilateral force. Only airborne delivery systems, no missiles, would be allowed. In spite of the assignment to a multilateral force, individual nuclear-weapon nations would control their own forces, but the nations supplying the forces would jointly make any decisions to fire the weapons. The weapons would be used only in retaliation for aggression. A nation could withdraw its forces if its supreme national interest required it to do so. A nation could elect not to involve its forces in the event of a decision to use the weapons.

Third, the international organization would act as the safe deposit for nuclear weapons during the relatively long period until abolition seemed practical.

Smith implies, but does not spell out, the antiproliferation measures that would have to be a part of this multilateral control. More seriously, he does not address the problems inherent in the fact that nations could keep nuclear weapons on their own territory under their own real control, even though they were nominally controlled by an international agency. Some form of permissive-action links (PALs) would have to be a part of the multilateral agreement. The PALs could provide a method of majority control for launching an air strike—a necessity for making this plan one of real international control.

The Jonathan Dean Proposal

Jonathan Dean, a long-time State Department negotiator and advisor for international security issues to the Union of Concerned Scientists, has suggested a gradual approach to the virtual elimination of nuclear weapons.[14] In most situations, his approach emphasizes methods of control that have been tested. He suggests that nuclear disarmament might proceed in three stages. The first would ensure that the START reductions with Russia were irreversible. The second would institute a post-START arms-control program that would bring in the other nuclear powers. The third would aim not at getting rid of nuclear weapons completely, but at making them very much less threatening by separating the warheads from their delivery systems and keeping the warheads in internationally monitored storage. In greater detail, the stages he describes are as follows.

Stage 1. A U.S.-Russian system of monitoring the stocks of warheads and fissile materials of both countries would be set up. This system would use a portal-perimeter monitoring system similar to that used under the Intermediate Range Nuclear Force Treaty. Monitoring would be designed to assure that warheads and fissile materials were not withdrawn from storage contrary to the joint agreement. Because storage would be on each nation's own territory, neither nation could be prevented from violating the agreement, but the monitoring system would warn the other nation.

A comprehensive data exchange would be set up between the United States and Russia on their holdings of warheads (both deployed and stored) and fissile materials. The information would be subject to mutual verification.

The United States and Russia would have to agree to dismantle all strategic warheads reduced under the START and other treaties and put this material under controlled storage. These actions would have to be coupled with a cutoff of fissile material. Additionally, the United States and Russia would have to agree to destroy all missiles withdrawn from deployment and end production of missiles.

These procedures would lead to a much less reversible reduction of nuclear weapons than the United States and Russia would otherwise have.

Stage 2. The other three nuclear powers—the United Kingdom, France, and China—would get involved. They would need to freeze nuclear development or reduce the level of deployment by possibly 10%. To encourage this, the United States and Russia would need to further reduce their nuclear weapons to about one thousand each. All warheads and fissile material of all five countries would be put under some form of international monitoring.

Stockpiles of plutonium for civilian nuclear reactors would have to be transferred to IAEA control, to ensure that nations would not have unmonitored material for nuclear-weapon production.

At this point, all nuclear weapons and fissile material of the five nuclear powers would be monitored, their numbers would be known, and they would thus become, to some extent, nonthreatening. The weapons of the undeclared powers would not be so controlled.

Stage 3. Drastic further reductions would now be required, particularly by the United States and Russia. Each of the five nations would reduce its nuclear weapons to a total of two hundred, separate the warheads from the delivery systems, and place all warheads and the fissile material from the dismantled weapons under international monitoring while the reductions were being made. (The number two hundred was chosen because it would require all five to make some reductions.) The staff of the IAEA would have to be increased significantly in order to carry out the monitoring and verification tasks. In the final stages of these reductions, the undeclared nuclear states—Israel, India, and Pakistan—would be given the choice of putting their weapons in similarly monitored storage or of eliminating them.

The proposal does not then proceed to the complete elimination of nuclear weapons. All nations that now have nuclear weapons would still have them on their national territory. The warheads would be separated from the delivery systems, and, although the proposal does suggest that arrangements could be made for replacement of old weapons under some international control, the production of new weapons would be prevented.

The proposal also suggests that the storage sites be dispersed and located deep underground so that no nation that possessed concealed weapons or had managed to avoid controls and manufacture new ones would be able to make a preemptive strike and destroy a stockpile.

The Ashton Carter, William Perry, and John Steinbruner Proposal

A proposal for international cooperation in reducing the risk of conventional war and preventing nuclear proliferation has been made by Ashton B. Carter, William J. Perry and John D. Steinbruner.[15] Their main point is that the control of nuclear weapons and the prevention of proliferation can best be accomplished by a general security regime that can satisfy the security needs of all nations by controlling conventional as well as nuclear weapons. They set this thesis forth as follows:

The central purpose of cooperative security arrangements is to prevent war and to do so primarily by preventing the means for successful aggression from being assembled, thus also obviating the needs for states so threatened to make their own counterpreparations. Cooperative security thus displaces the centerpiece of security planning from preparing to counter threats to preventing such threats from arising—from deterring aggression to making preparation for it more difficult. In the process, the potential destructiveness of military conflict—especially the use of weapons of mass destruction—is also reduced. Cooperative security differs from the traditional idea of collective security as preventive medicine differs from acute care. Cooperative security is designed to ensure that organized aggression cannot start on any large scale. Collective security, however, is an arrangement for deterring aggression through counterthreat and defeating it if it occurs.

Clearly the one idea does not preclude the other and both are, in fact, mutually reinforcing.[16]

In this proposal for cooperative security, the only legitimate use for armed forces is the defense of national territory. The goal would be to have all forces so configured that they could defend their territory but could not attack that of anyone else. Nuclear weapons would be used only in response to an attack by nuclear weapons. Such a posture, the authors of this proposal acknowledge, is difficult to achieve. It is hard to distinguish between defensive and offensive weapons, and many nations would find such a posture unacceptable. Under these criteria, it would be hard for the United States to justify more than a small defensive force. It could not justify its present offensive-force structure, which is designed for deep strikes into enemy territory to destroy organizational structure rather than the enemy's front-line firepower. Israel's whole military posture is designed for preemptive offense to prevent fighting on its very small territory. Even Russia and China, whose enormous territories are suitable to a purely defensive posture, would probably find it difficult to accept such an arrangement.

The authors suggest a way of replacing some of the security that might be lost by the elimination of advanced-strike weapons: the internationalization of all air-traffic control, military and civilian, and the creation of an international surveillance system. It is impossible for any modern army to launch an offensive without reconnaisance and advance preparations; such activities would be detected by the air-traffic control and surveillance. In addition, an air force cannot control its strike or other aircraft without air-traffic control. If controls were also imposed on location, movement, and density of forces, there would be advance knowledge of any impending strike and, therefore, time to impose international sanctions on the perpetrator. In some cases, such as a threatened attack on Israel, the distances involved are so short that it might be necessary to guarantee a rapidly launched international air strike in support of the victim.

The cooperative-security proposal does not envision the sudden setting up of a worldwide security regime. Ideally, there would be an agreement between the five major nuclear powers, possibly begun as an extension of the type of agreements that already exist and gradually growing to include more regions and more controls. If treaties between a small group of nations are seen to offer major security benefits, others will find it desirable to join the effort. At the stage where an international retaliatory strike force is envisioned, almost all nations would probably want to be included.

These considerations lead to an essential part of the plan: an international response to aggression. The plan envisions contributions from many nations to such a response, in part according to their expertise. The response force would be organized around the reconnaisance strike complex (i.e., the ability to strike deep within enemy territory, as employed by the United States in Desert Storm). The United States would provide most of the airlift equipment, the tactical-intelligence data, and the Stealth aircraft. Coalition partners would participate in achieving air and naval superiority and would provide most of the ground forces. Russia, for example, has highly capable aircraft; Russia, Germany, France, China, and India might provide the bulk of the ground forces. The United Kingdom, Italy, and Japan might make major contributions to naval forces. The United States, Russia, and the United Kingdom might provide the global strategic-intelligence capability.

Nuclear weapons would play no part in the normal defense forces, being used only for retaliation against nuclear attack. In preventing nuclear proliferation, it would be of major importance to assure that nuclear weapons could not be used in aggression, and the cooperative regime would make this a primary concern. The proliferation of other weapons would also have to be controlled. The cooperative-security proposal suggests that the control of chemical, biological, and nuclear weapons, of missiles, of conventional weapons, and of dual-use technology be integrated in such a way that information could more easily be shared, common procedures for monitoring and inspections used, and common lists of controlled items prepared. Of great importance in achieving integrated controls would be a combined effort to "marshall political pressure behind cooperative control efforts."[17]

The authors acknowledge that the regime they describe can be approached only gradually. They point out that we already have many agreements that fit the description of a cooperative-security regime. Among those are most of our nuclear accords, including Start I and Start II. There are also the Conventional Forces in Europe (CFE) agreement, which imposes national ceilings on ground forces; the Conference on Security and Cooperation in Europe (CSCE) talks; the Confidence and Security-Building Measures (CSBMs); and other agreements with similar intentions. The authors urge that cooperative security be the organizing principle for international security in the post–Cold War era. They suggest some first steps:

Superpower denuclearization. Of immediate importance is helping the former Soviet Union live up to its commitments to denuclearize under Start I, and to complete a further Start II agreement. A goal should be to reduce the number of nuclear weapons in Russia and the United States to about two thousand each, with some reductions for the United Kingdom, France, and China. Without a serious commitment from the United States and Russia to reduce the number of their nuclear weapons, there will be little chance of stemming nuclear proliferation.

Ground-force relocation. The former Soviet Union needs help in relocating its ground forces, particularly in providing housing for relocated officers.

Greater military-to-military contacts and planning dialogue. The major military establishments should together engage in explicit discussions of force size, defense-budget levels, and military doctrine.

Common warning and intelligence functions. There should be collaboration in tactical warning of missile test launches. An improved capacity is needed for determining, when there is heightened suspicion and some evidence of attack preparation, whether a strategic attack is or is not under way. The common management of all civil and military air traffic in Europe west of the Urals is possible. This would make it much more difficult for nations in that area to secretly prepare to mount an attack.

Arms registration. In December 1991, the U.N. General Assembly passed a resolution calling for the voluntary registration of all arms imports and exports. One hundred fifty countries voted to approve. Only China, Cuba, and Iraq abstained. More diplomatic effort should be directed toward making registration meaningful.

A single proliferation-control regime. Six independent proliferation-control regimes now exist. A single control regime could be more effective.

Regional cooperative-security arrangements. Both Russia and the United States are powers in Asia as well as Europe. We should be considering the possibility of extending something like the CFE agreement to Asia as well. There may also be other regions where such agreements would be useful.

The Roger Speed Proposal

A slightly different approach has been advocated by Roger D. Speed, a physicist and senior defense analyst at Lawrence Livermore Laboratory.[18] Although Speed agrees with the concept of cooperative security expressed by Carter, Perry, and Steinbruner, he emphasizes the setting up of a new international-security regime, to be accomplished in three phases.

Phase 1: The making of a new agreement between the nuclear and nonnuclear powers, with the objective of establishing a new international security regime that would eliminate nuclear weapons as instruments of policy, provide security guarantees against nuclear threats, and preclude the development of new national nuclear arsenals. This international bargain would be formalized in a comprehensive document called the International Security Treaty (IST). The basic provisions of the Nuclear Non-proliferation Treaty would be included within the IST, but the new treaty would be broader in scope and provide for increased enforcement powers. The treaty would establish an independent agency called the International Nuclear Authority (INA), which would report directly to the U.N. Security Council and have the responsibility of overseeing the implementation of the treaty.

One purpose of the treaty would be to "create an environment that minimizes the insecurity of nations and lessens their motivation for acquiring or maintaining nuclear weapons."[19] The treaty would establish that "nuclear weapons are no longer to be considered legitimate instruments of state policy."[20] The nuclear powers would have to agree to: (1) sign a "no first use" statement; (2) reduce nuclear arsenals to a low level; (3) dismantle all retired nuclear warheads and place nuclear material under international control; and (4) stop all nuclear-weapon tests by a specific date.

In addition, all parties to the IST would have to agree to: (1) take joint action against any state or group that was the first to use nuclear weapons; and (2) use military force in actions designed to support U.N. Security Council resolutions.

The main focus of the treaty, however, would be on the detection of clandestine nuclear activities. There would be a global regime to control fissile material by establishing that all such material, of all states, would be accounted for and any surplus material placed under international control by the INA and the IAEA. The global regime would also prohibit the further production of plutonium and highly enriched uranium for use in weapons.

Once the IST was ratified by two-thirds of the member states and all five permanent members of the Security Council, it would become binding international law and would apply to all states, whether they had signed the treaty or not. Attempts to obtain or illegally retain nuclear weapons would be subject to U.N. economic, political, and military sanctions.

Phase 2. The creation of a retaliatory force. Called the International Nuclear Deterrent Force (INDF), it would have absolutely no coercive, functions. Providing credible assurances that the INDF would be restricted to its retaliatory role would be central to its acceptance. The force would be under the command of the U.N. Security Council and under the physical control of the INA. Sophisticated permissive-action links would be installed on all weapons to prevent their unauthorized use. Only in the event of first use of nuclear weapons by an outlaw state could the Security Council authorize the retaliatory use of the INDF.

After confidence had been built that the INDF would not be misused, work on the final phase could begin.

Phase 3. National nuclear disarmament. Because of the possibility of some renegade nation's retaining a few nuclear weapons, movement toward complete disarmament could take place only by reliance on the INDF and its weapons for retaliation. Under the proposed International Security Treaty, once retaliatory action had been considered by the Security Council, it could go forward despite a veto by one of the permanent members. If Permissive Action Links had been installed on the weapons, however, all members would have to agree to their use; therefore action could proceed only through the permanent members' use of their own nuclear weapons. When the only nuclear weapons are in the hands of the INA, it might be desirable that weapons be launched if a majority of the five permanent members approved.

Speed offers two further suggestions. First, in conjunction with the IST the international community should begin to move toward a more cooperative security regime that would emphasize defensive, as opposed to offensive, forces. Second, the Security Council should pledge to resist international aggression when it occurs. (This pledge would not necessarily apply to nonparticipants in the treaty.)

Speed points out that his proposal does not require the international ownership of nuclear facilities. International ownership would probably be needed, however, in a situation where all nuclear weapons were supposed to be destroyed, because the possessor of even a very small number would be extremely powerful. When the International Nuclear Agency retains control of some nuclear weapons, the diversion of a small amount of nuclear material would be less serious, because the INA could retaliate for any possible use of this material.

The Kosta Tsipis–Philip Morrison Proposal

Kosta Tsipis and Philip Morrison have made a proposal that they characterize as attacking the demand for, rather than the supply of, nuclear weapons. Its main points can be seen in their "11-Step Program" for the United States.[21]

1. Stop the developing, testing, and production of new nuclear weapons.

2. Obtain an agreement among all nuclear powers for a no-first-use policy.

3. Start negotiations for the eventual verified elimination of nuclear weapons.

4. Support the admission of Germany, Japan, and some nations from

unrepresented regions as permanent members of the U.N. Security Council.

5. Strengthen nonproliferation measures by ending most arms sales, policing secondhand transfers, and controlling dual-use technologies when possible.

6. Direct conventional-weapon development to improvements in reliability and immunity to countermeasures.

7. Establish a worldwide credit and banking embargo against excessive weapons purchasers.

8. Increase large-scale civilian aid to developing countries and stop military financial aid.

9. Help the United Nations to develop measures for conflict resolution.

10. Start negotiations through the United Nations to establish a permanent international security force, possibly with regional commands, and assign U.S. military units—marine corps, air force, navy, and space assets—to this force.

11. Start consultation with Britain, Russia, France, and China on assembling an international nuclear deterrent force of ballistic missile–armed submarines to be controlled by the expanded U.N. Security Council.

It is an interesting list, mixing noncontroversial measures with ones that many arms-control enthusiasts might consider impossible to achieve or even counterproductive. For example:

1. The cessation of tests of nuclear weapons has been proposed many times and has general support.

2. The proposal of a no-first-use policy is complicated by the presence of chemical and, especially, biological weapons. Under some circumstances, the new biological weapons are more destructive of human life, weight for weight, than are nuclear weapons. Should we develop biological weapons to counter biological-weapons threats so that we can have a no-first-use policy? The answer might be to have *no-first-use* refer more generally to any weapons of mass destruction, including both nuclear and biological weapons. The generalization of the no-first-use policy to allow retaliation for a chemical or biological weapons attack, however, contradicts the many statements by the United States that it will never use nuclear weapons against any signatory to the NPT except in retaliation for a nuclear attack.

3. The total elimination of nuclear weapons is a desirable goal, but how can it ever be known that all have been destroyed?

4. The admission of Germany and Japan as veto-holding members of the Security Council is probably inevitable, but the addition of other veto-empowered members will increase the likelihood of paralysis on the Security Council when difficult decisions must be made.

5. Strengthening supply-side nonproliferation measures is probably noncontroversial, although, with regard to some dual-use materials, arguments can be made against enforcement that is too stringent.

6. The purpose of the proposal to focus conventional-weapons research on problems of reliability is not clear. The proposal by Carter, Perry, and Steinbruner to emphasize defensive weapons appears a more direct move to prevent intensive development of new attack weapons.

7. Organizing a banking and credit embargo against extravagant weapons purchasers would have the effect both of reducing the possibility of armed conflict and of directing spending toward economic development.

8. Phasing out military aid and loans seems to be a good idea, but there could be circumstances in which such action would have undesirable results.

9. Strengthening the United Nations' abilities in conflict resolution is clearly noncontroversial.

10 and 11. The final two suggestions (of raising a common, conventionally armed international security force and setting up an international nuclear deterrent force) are similar to those in the proposals offered by Carter, Perry, and Steinbruner, and by Roger Speed.

The least comprehensive of the six plans, Timerbaev's, is the one most likely to be put into effect. Many of his suggestions have already been adopted. Smith's suggestion of a multilateral force, although it deemphasizes the IAEA, also may have a chance of success because it does not give a timetable for real international control. (To achieve such control, a method of majority control of launching an air strike seems to me to be essential.) Dean's proposal has a more limited objective than any except Timerbaev's, and is more complete in many ways than all the others. It suggests the use of techniques that have been successfully used before, and it interferes minimally with national sovereignty. Tsipis and Morrison make a number of recommendations for moving to a more internationally controlled regime, but do not outline the steps that must be taken for nations to develop enough confidence in the system to be willing to give up the amount of sovereignty required for the system to be effective.

Both Speed and Carter, Perry, and Steinbruner suggest some confidence-building measures. There is little difference in the final outcome of these two plans, but the methods for reaching that outcome are quite different. In Carter, Perry, and Steinbruner's plan, the control of proliferation is an important result of a successful cooperative-security agreement that emphasizes conventional weapons. Speed's plan, however, is aimed directly at the problem of nuclear weapons. It will be very hard to motivate the international community to effect that plan's first phase. Probably, barring a change in Russian politics that would lead to an antagonistic regime, some progress can be made toward the cooperative-security regimes suggested by Timerbaev, Dean, and Carter, Perry, and Steinbruner. At this time, however, any rapid movement toward complete international control seems unlikely except as a reaction to some cataclysmic use of nuclear weapons.

It is ironic that some international control of nuclear weapons may come into being only because the major nuclear powers want to keep their monopoly and thus prevent proliferation. International control for the purpose of preventing proliferation is an issue on which the permanent members of the United Nations Security Council might be expected to be unanimous. But for each of them the thought of turning their own nuclear weapons over to international control is very difficult. The irony is not lost on the nonnuclear nations. Their concerns must also be taken into account if we are to achieve the cooperation needed to prevent proliferation.

IMPLICATIONS FOR U.S. POLICY

Present U.S. policy for preventing nuclear proliferation relies almost completely on controlling the technology. Had this policy been seriously applied thirty years ago, it might have prevented some of the proliferation that has taken place since then. Although the various U.S. administrations over the past thirty years have tried, generally, to prevent proliferation, considerations of political and international policy have sometimes blocked consistent efforts. The Johnson administration's policy of ignoring CIA evidence of Israel's construction of a reactor and chemical- separation plant for the production of plutonium and the Reagan administration's decision to forgive Pakistan's construction of a centrifuge uranium-enrichment plant in return for support during the Afghan war are examples of considerations that have overridden a consistent non-proliferation policy.

With the collapse of the Soviet Union, it may be possible for the United States to be more rigorous in its resistance to nuclear proliferation, but it will do so under much more difficult circumstances than it faced twenty to thirty years ago. The underdeveloped world is not so underdeveloped anymore. Sources of technological assistance have multiplied even more than the relatively large number of countries currently represented by the Nuclear Suppliers Group would indicate. It is evident that, even with effective enforcement of restrictions on technology, within twenty to thirty years almost any nation with enough money will, if it wants to, have nuclear weapons.

This does not mean that we should stop restricting the supply of nuclear technology. Indeed, we must restrict it even more vigorously in order to give ourselves time to do those things that will reduce and, finally, remove demand. It will be a very difficult and slow process. We must construct a world in which every nation clearly sees that it will not gain in security, power, or prestige by owning nuclear weapons. We can do this only by making the possession of nuclear weapons useless as an instrument of international policy.

Immediately after World War II, it might have been possible for the United States to enforce a ban on the development of nuclear weapons by other nations. But this enforcement would, quite possibly, have led to a war with the Soviet Union, and such a course would probably not have been wise or even politically possible. Any action taken now to enforce a ban must be taken in alliance with the other nuclear powers. There must be some sort of international control, and the United States must choose a group with which to ally itself. This could be the United Nations, or it could be a smaller group. In either case, the controlling nations would, to some extent, have to be the same: the permanent members of the U.N. Security Council. If either Russia or China was left out, enforcement would be merely regional.

All nations must be made to understand that international control provides them with security, and that the possession of nuclear weapons ultimately causes insecurity. To achieve this understanding throughout the world, the nuclear powers must show that they also know that their own security is, in the long run, reduced by their possession of these weapons. They can best do this by reducing the number of their own nuclear weapons, and by instituting an accompanying ban on their development of new and improved ones. Each of the international-control proposals discussed earlier implies these actions. All of them have as an eventual goal the international control of all weapons. The proposals differ only in the ways they suggest for reaching that goal.

Carter, Perry, and Steinbruner suggest that the best way to reduce the chance of international conflict would be to rearrange all national forces to make them defensive. Such rearrangement would be very difficult, particularly for the United States, which has a long tradition of maintaining an offensive force. How will William Perry, after being secretary of defense, deal with this earlier suggestion by him and his colleagues? Carter, Perry, and Steinbruner were wise in not setting forth a timetable for their suggested changes. They emphasize instead keeping in mind a long-term goal while making short-term policy.

I believe that the proposal by Carter, Perry, and Steinbruner, with both its long- and short-term goals, would serve as a good basis for U.S. policy. The entire Jonathan Dean proposal could then be implemented in conjunction with this more general program.

Timerbaev's proposal to expand the activity of the IAEA is gradually being put into effect in conjunction with efforts to prevent a North Korean nuclear buildup. This expansion will continue as long as the U.N. Security Council is able to work without the interference of a veto. The use of the IAEA is essential. It is an existing agency, one that the Soviet Union has worked with for a long time. Moreover, its charter gives it broad powers, much more far-reaching than those it has used up to this time.

Gerard Smith's proposal for multilateral control appears to provide a method for deemphasizing the importance of nuclear weapons to national policy. It could be adopted in conjunction with other methods of reducing international tension.

The other three proposals are more ambitious in nature. Each of them suggests useful approaches toward creating a regime with more international control. Most of their suggestions do not conflict. It might be useful, therefore, to combine proposals, adding portions of the Speed and Tsipsis-Morrison proposals to the Dean and Carter-Perry-Steinbruner proposals when appropriate. The resulting program, with its long-term goals, would not be a mere smorgasbord. The most utopian of its goals would be to have all weapons—conventional, biological, chemical, and nuclear—under international control. Gaining firm control of just the nuclear ones would be a worthy intermediate step.

Following are two suggested channels for proceeding with the proposals discussed earlier. They could be followed simultaneously. Progress in either channel is independent in most ways, but in both channels it is tied to the dynamics of major power relationships. The first channel chiefly follows the suggestions of Jonathan Dean; the second is based primarily on the Carter-Perry-Steinbruner proposal, supplemented by suggestions from other proposals.

Channel A

The IAEA will have to be gradually strengthened as more operations come under its supervision.

1. Institute a worldwide no-first-use policy for weapons of mass destruction, a worldwide nuclear test ban, and a worldwide halt to the development of new nuclear weapons.

2. Proceed with stage 1 of Dean's proposal: make the START treaty irreversible. Set up a U.S.-Russian system of monitoring stocks of warheads and fissile materials. Set up a data exchange on holdings. Dismantle all strategic warheads reduced under START and put the fissile material under controlled storage. Destroy all missiles withdrawn from deployment. End production of strategic missiles.

3. Begin stage 2 of Dean's proposal: get the three other nuclear powers involved. Reduce the number of U.S. and Russian nuclear warheads to about one thousand each. Get all warheads and fissile material of all five nuclear powers under some form of international monitoring. Transfer stockpiles of plutonium for civilian reactors to IAEA control.

4. Begin stage 3 of Dean's proposal: institute further reductions. Reduce the number of warheads of each of the five nations to two hundred. Separate all warheads from delivery systems. Put pressure on the undeclared nuclear states to either eliminate their weapons or put them under storage and control conditions identical to those of the major powers.

Channel B

1. Initiate greater contact among the military establishments of the superpowers.

2. Institute common warning and intelligence functions among the superpowers—for example, warnings of missile tests and space launches.

3. Internationalize air-traffic control and include both civilian and military traffic.

4. Institute international surveillance of border areas where there is a potential for conflict.

5. Set up a system for complete international registration of all arms transfers.

6. Organize a combined proliferation-control regime for nuclear weapons, chemical weapons, biological weapons, ballistic-missile technology, and standard conventional munitions.

7. Extend the restrictions on conventional forces to the rest of the world.

8. Reach agreements to focus conventional-weapon development toward more defensive values.

9. Initiate a global banking and credit embargo against extravagant weapons purchasers.

10. Phase out military aid to developing nations and increase aid for nonmilitary development.

11. Initiate the development of an international security force. This force can have a limited role at first, but, as experience with its command is gained, its role can be increased. Among its responsibilities could be military support of the enforcement of non-proliferation agreements.

If progress in both channels is successful, further steps toward nuclear disarmament may be taken. At some point these would include the creation of a very small international nuclear-deterrent force to ensure the security of those nations that do not have their own deterrent forces or treaty arrangements.

It will be extremely difficult to reach the goals outlined here. The further goals of eliminating nuclear weapons and controlling conventional ones, if they are reached at all, will probably be reached under circumstances that are impossible to predict now. If proliferation can be held in check, there will be time to approach the goal of international control of nuclear weapons step by step, building the confidence of present nuclear powers as well as of aspiring ones. All steps must contribute to an understanding that the controlling international agency will not favor a single group and that the nuclear force it controls will be used only in response to a nation's use of nuclear weapons. In time, one hopes, experience with a very small international nuclear force, a proposed first step, will lead to worldwide reliance on a larger force that will replace national nuclear forces.

Appendix A
Separative Work Unit

The *separative work unit* (SWU) was devised by P. A. M. Dirac during World War II as a way of comparing enrichment techniques.[1] It is applied to separation devices producing a small amount of enhancement as a part of a "cascade" of units that, in combination, produce a large enhancement. As might be expected, it is based on the concept of entropy, a measure of the amount of disorder in a system. For two different elements or isotopes, the entropy increases as the elements are mixed (i.e., as their disorder increases).

The theoretical minimum energy required to separate two different gases can be calculated on the basis of the decrease in entropy needed. This amount of energy is generally much less than what is needed in the ideal operation of any practical system. In addition, a comparison based on this does not address the fact that the real apparatus doing the separation will be performing separative work even when one of the isotopes is a very small fraction of the total. Identical pieces of apparatus, operating at the same efficiency in a large group, will be enhancing the amount of an isotope in the face of differing incident amounts. A unit that attributes the same amount of work to the separation device regardless of the composition of the incident material is essential.

With these considerations in mind, Dirac suggested such a unit, the separative work unit (SWU), that takes into account the concentration of the isotopes being separated and assigns the same separative ability to a piece of apparatus regardless of the concentration of the isotopes it is processing.

The SWU for a two-component gas being enriched is obtained by dividing the change in entropy by the combined probability of finding each component—for example, the probability of finding a molecule containing U-235, combined with that of finding one with U-238—at the enrichment barrier. This can be represented by $N(1 - N)$, where N is the fractional component of the first molecule and $1 - N$ that of the second. If S is the entropy and F is the total amount of gas entering the separation stage, the separative work done (U) is: $\delta U = (F \, \Delta S) / [R_g N (1 - N)]$ where δU is used to represent the small amount of separative work, U, for which this equation is appropriate. **(A.1).** The gas constant, R_g, is present in the entropy, and the entropy is divided here by R_g to make the expression dimensionless, except for F. This can be defined as one wishes, possibly as the number of moles or the number of kilograms of gas being enriched. By definition, $S = R_g[N \ln N + (1 - N) \ln(1 - N)]$. (A.2).

This unit is most logically applied to an enrichment device that is itself a stage in a cascade of such devices with the feed, F, entering, and the product, $P = \theta F$, where θ expresses what fraction P is of F, and the waste, $W = (1 - \theta)F$, leaving. From equation (A.2), the change ΔS in entropy of the gas is

$$F \Delta S = \theta F S (N + \Delta N_1) + (1 - \theta) F S (N - \Delta N_2) - F S (N),$$

where ΔN_1 and ΔN_2 are the changes in the fractional components of the two gases. (A.3). If ΔN_1 and ΔN_2 are small, $S(N + \Delta N_1)$ and $S(N - \Delta N_2)$ can be obtained by expansion in a Taylor series:

$$F \Delta S = \theta F S (N) + \theta F \Delta N_1 S' (N) + 1/2 \, \theta F (\Delta N_1)^2 S''(N)$$

$$+ (1 - \theta) F S (N) - (1 - \theta) F \Delta N_2 S' (N) + 1/2(1 - \theta) F(\Delta N_2)^2 S''(N) - FS(N).$$
$$\textbf{(A.4).}$$

where, in differential notation, $S' = dS/dN$ and $S'' = d^2S/dN^2$. The first, fourth, and last terms cancel out, and $\theta F \Delta N_1 - (1 - \theta) F \Delta N_2 = 0$, because of conservation of the light isotope. This leaves:

$$F \Delta S = 1/2 \, [\theta F (\Delta N_1)^2 + (1 - \theta) F (\Delta N_2^2] S'' (N). \textbf{ (A.5).}$$

By differentiation of equation (A.2) with respect to N,

$$S''(N) = R_g/[N(1 - N)]. \textbf{ (A.6)}$$

From equation (A.1) and the above relationship, one obtains

$$\delta U = 1/2 \, F[\theta (\Delta N_1)^2 + (1 - \theta) (\Delta N_2)^2]/[N(1 - N)]^2. \textbf{ (A.7).}$$

From the conservation of mass, $\theta \Delta N_1 = (1 - \theta) \Delta N_2$, yielding

$$\delta U = 1/2 \, F\theta (\Delta N_1)^2/[N^2(1 - N)^2(1 - \theta)]. \textbf{ (A.8).}$$

An enrichment factor α is defined by the relationship

$$\alpha = [N_1/(1 - N_1)]/[N/(1 - N)]. \textbf{ (A.9).}$$

Using equation (A.9), ΔN_1 can be expressed in the following way:

$$\Delta N_1 = (\alpha - 1)N(1 - N_1) = \epsilon N(1 - N_1). \text{ (A.10).}$$

To the extent that $(1 - N) \approx (1 - N_1)$, equation (A.8) can be expressed as

$$\delta U = (SWU) = \epsilon^2 F \theta / [2(1 - \theta)]. \text{ (A.11).}$$

Equation (A.11) relates to the separative work for a single stage in a cascade where the change in enrichment is small. To obtain an expression for the effect of many stages or the entire cascade, one must, in effect, integrate this differential relationship. To do this, a value function (V) is introduced, such that the separative work $U = PV(N_p) + WV(N_w) - FV(N_F)$. **(A.12)**. Equation (A.12) can be applied to the separative work done by a single stage or a cascade. For a single stage, the separative work is given by the following expression:

$$\delta U = \theta F V (N + \Delta N_1) + (1 - \theta) F V (N - \Delta N_2) - F V (N). \text{ (A.13).}$$

This equation is of the exact form of (A.3), and, with the same approximations, can be solved in the same way to give

$$\delta U = \{\varepsilon^2 F \Theta / [2(1 - \Theta)]\} N^2 (1 - N_1)^2 V''(N). \text{ (A.14).}$$

V must be of a form that will satisfy this equation. To obtain the same value of δU given the equation (A.11), one equates

$$N^2 (1 - N_1)^2 V''(N) = 1. \text{ (A.15).}$$

When this is integrated, one gets equation **(A.16)**, as follows:

$$V(N) = (2N - 1)\ln[N/(1 - N)] + bN + a,$$

where a and b are arbitrary constants of integration. These terms drop out in calculations of separative work using equation (A.12) because of the following relationships:

$$P + W = F \text{ (conservation of total material, A.17), and}$$
$$PN_P + WN_W = FN_F \text{ (conservation of the isotope being enriched (A.18).}$$

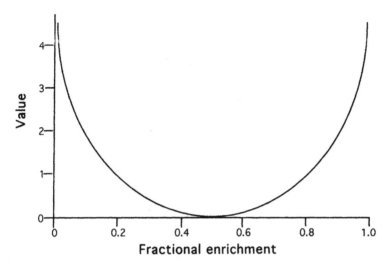

FIG. 39. Simplified value function of equation (A.19), expressing the value as a function of the fractional enrichment.

The value function used for calculations, therefore, can be simplified to $V(N) = (2N - 1)\ln[N/(1 - N)]$. **(A.19)**.

This relationship would be obtained if one assumed the value to be zero at $N = 0.5$; the relationship is shown in figure 39. It is easier to think of "value" in terms in which "value" is zero at the value of the feed. This results in the constants a and b expressed in the following equations (A.20) and (A.21), and in the relationship expressed in figure 40. N_O is the fractional enrichment assigned a zero value. For natural uranium fuel this would be 0.0072. Equation **(A.20)** is

$$a = -\ln((1 - N_O))/N_O) - (1 - 2N_O)/(1 - N_O),$$ and equation **(A.21)** is
$$b = 2\ln((1 - N_O)/N_O) + (1 - 2N_O)/(N_O(1 - N_O)).$$

When N_O has the value 0.0072 of natural uranium, these equations give $a = 5.933$, $b = 149.72$ and the value function shown in figure 40.

The relationships expressed in figures 39 and 40 produce the same result when used to calculate the SWU required in a cascade.

All of these relationships were derived for cascades that enriched by many stages, each producing a very small enrichment. Equation (A.12), using the value function, however, can be applied to any enrichment process, because it merely states what the separative work would have

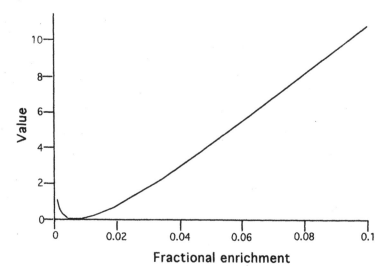

FIG. 40. Alternative value function with constants $a = -5.933$
and $b = 149.72$; constants chosen to give a value
of zero at $N_F = 0.72\%$.

been had it been done in small stages. There is also a useful approximate
relationship that allows the calculation of the number of stages required.

First, let me define a few of the symbols to be used. The "relative
isotopic abundance" R equals $N/(1 - N)$. R is not to be confused with R_g
used earlier to express the value of the gas constant. N is the symbol used
earlier for the fractional abundance of an isotope of a gas. In the case of
U-235 in natural uranium, $N = 0.0072$. α, which we have also used
earlier, is R_{n+1}/R_n, where the subscript n refers in this case to a stage in a
cascade of many stages. We also can refer to a "single-stage separation
factor" q, which equals R_P/R_W. Here the subscripts refer to the product, P,
and waste, W, from a single stage in a cascade. The product is up one
stage and the waste is down one, so $q = \alpha^2$. These definitions are for an
"ideal" cascade for which the separation factor is the same at each stage.
Real cascades are close enough to being ideal that these relationships are
useful although not completely accurate.

For many stages, m, the relative isotopic abundance, can be expressed as

$$R_{n\pm m} = \alpha^{\pm m} R_n. \text{ (A.22)}.$$

If, for example, the feed enters the cascade just below stage $n = 0$, and the product emerges at stage G,

$$R_P = \alpha^{G+1} R_F. \textbf{(A.23)}.$$

If the last stage of the stripping section is number T,

$$R_W = \alpha^{-T}. \textbf{(A.24)}.$$

The total number of stages needed in the cascade is then

$$G + T + 1 = \ln(R_P/R_W)/\ln \alpha. \textbf{(A.25)}.$$

It must be emphasized that these relationships are valid only for ideal cascades and are useful approximations for actual ones.

The discussion and figures that follow relate to the SWU needed for enrichment as a function of the enrichment of the feed, the product, and the waste.

Using the relationships expressed by these figures, one can obtain the separative work (208 kilograms) required, for example, to separate natural uranium, F kg, with its 0.72% U-235 ($N_F = 0.0072$) into a product, $P = 1$ kg, with 90% U-235 ($N_P = 0.90$) and waste, W kg, with 0.25% U-235 ($N_W = 0.0025$). From our point of view, the 208 kilogram is just a number; 208 metric tons of separative work would, for example, produce slightly less than 1 metric ton of 90%-enriched U-235.

As we saw in figure 19, few SWU are required to produce 1 kilogram of enriched fuel for a nuclear reactor at an enrichment level of 3–4%. If one considers instead the SWU needed to produce enough 3–4%-enriched uranium to be used itself as a feed to produce 1 kg of 90%-enriched uranium, a much larger amount is required, as shown in figure 20.

The SWU required to obtain 1 kilogram of 3% enrichment (reactor grade) is 3.9 kilograms. To obtain 1 kilogram of 90%-enriched with 0.25% enriched waste, 32.6 kilogram of 3%-enriched uranium will be required. Multiplying 3.9 and 32.6 gives the 127 kilograms SWU shown in figure 20.

The availability of partially enriched uranium, such as that used for a reactor, can reduce the remaining effort needed to go to weapon-grade. This is expressed in figure 41, which shows the SWU needed to go from a level of feed N_F to 90%-enriched weapon-grade. With reactor-grade fuel, 3–4% enriched, as a feed, almost two-thirds of the separative work

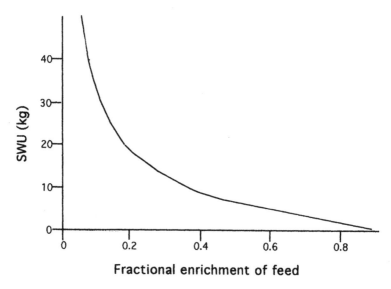

FIG. 41. SWU required to produce 1 kilogram of 90%-enriched
uranium as a function of enrichment of the feed.
Waste is 0.24% U-235.

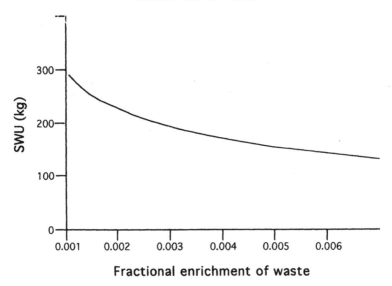

FIG. 42. SWU required to produce 1 kilogram of 90%- enriched
uranium as a function of waste enrichment. Feed is 0.72% U-235.

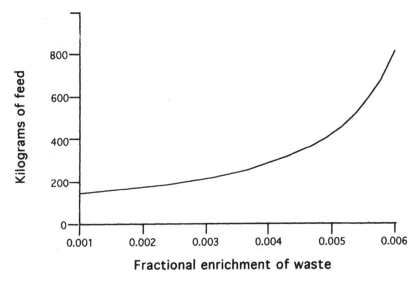

FIG. 43. Kilograms of feed required to produce 1 kilogram
of 90%-enriched uranium as a function of waste enrichment.
Feed is 0.72% U-235.

has been done. This enriched feed can be very useful to a developing
country attempting to make weapon-grade uranium.

The relation of the separative work to the enrichment of the waste is
shown in equation (A.26) and in figure 42:

$$U = -3.11 + 0.8929(4.87 - (2N_W - 1)\ln(N_W/(1 - N_W)))/(N_W - 0.0072).$$

$$(A.26).$$

Producing waste with more U-235 in it means that less U-235 is ex-
tracted and results in the need for increased feed, as shown in figure 43.

Appendix B

Supplemental Information on Calutrons

Figures 44 through 47 show the operating record of the beta calutron units at the Oak Ridge facility over a two-year period.[1] (The beta units were in groups of thirty-six vacuum chambers, each with two beams.) Over two years, as shown in figure 44, their average current increased from 0.03 to 0.075 amperes. Individual units would have operated at higher currents.

The numbers in figure 44 do not represent the average production rate. For that, one must look at the fraction of time the units operated after being turned on, the "innage" percentage of run time, figures for which are given in figure 45. Here the value rose in two years from 65% to 95%. Similar curves for the alpha units (which performed the initial separation) show currents rising from 0.045 to 0.09 amperes, and innage percentages from 60% to 85%.[2]

These results describe the effectiveness of the units only from the time they are started to the time they are terminated. Also to be considered is the time for servicing the units between runs. For the beta units, this ranged from about sixty hours in 1944 to about fifteen hours in 1946, and the alpha units had similar performance. Average runs were of about fifty-five hours, so the total time lost went from about 50% to 20% during this period. Combining the effects of down time, then, after two years the effective average current would have been about half of the nominal 0.1 amperes.

The crucial criterion is enhancement, defined as the ratio of the relative abundance of U-235 after and before enrichment.[3] Beta-unit enhancement is shown in figure 46 to have improved from zero to about 65 over two years. The alpha units were of two types, one with two ion beams, and the other with four. Enhancement improved from about 20 to 35 for the first type, and decreased in the other from 20 to about 13. The decline in enhancement was the result of a big push to increase the output of the four-beam units. (Apparently the plan was to increase the enhancement of the beta units to compensate for the alpha-unit decline.)

A large part of the U-235, in passing between the ion source and the collector, ends up being deposited, together with the U-238, all over the

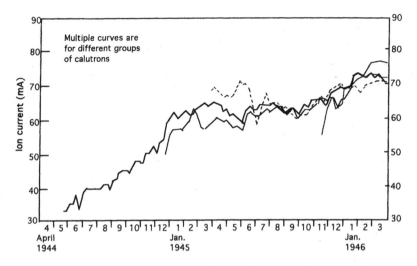

FIG. 44. Average ion current for beta calutrons at Oak Ridge from 1944 to 1946. Multiple curves are for different groups of calutrons.

From R. S. Livingston, J. E. Rodgers, and E. G. Struxness, "Performance of the Beta Ion Source," in *Separation of Isotopes in Calutron Units,* ed. H. Wesley Savage, National Nuclear Energy Series, div. 1, vol. 7 (Oak Ridge, Tenn.: USAEC Technical Information Service, 1951), p. 123, fig. 5.4.

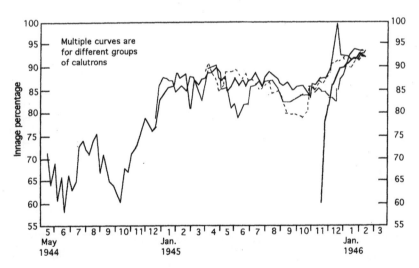

FIG. 45. Average "innage" percentage of run time for beta calutrons at Oak Ridge from 1944 to 1946. Multiple curves are for different groups of calutrons.

From R. S. Livingston, J. E. Rodgers, and E. G. Struxness, "Performance of the Beta Ion Source," in *Separation of Isotopes in Calutron Units,* ed. H. Wesley Savage, National Nuclear Energy Series, div. 1, vol. 7 (Oak Ridge, Tenn.: USAEC Technical Information Service, 1951), p. 129, fig. 5.10.

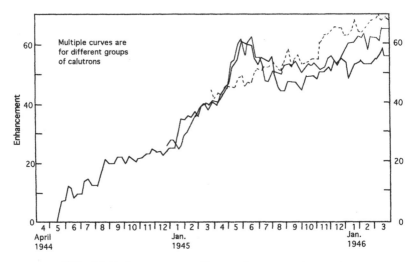

FIG. 46. Enhancement of beta calutrons at Oak Ridge
from 1944 to 1946. Multiple curves are for different groups of calutrons.

From R. S. Livingston, J. E. Rodgers, and E. G. Struxness, "Performance of the
Beta Ion Source," in *Separation of Isotopes in Calutron Units,* ed. H. Wesley Savage,
National Nuclear Energy Series, div. 1, vol. 7 (Oak Ridge, Tenn.:
USAEC Technical Information Service, 1951), p. 120, fig. 5.1.

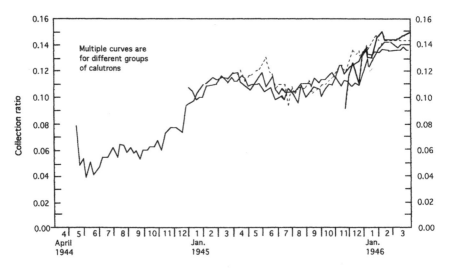

FIG. 47. Collection ratio of beta calutrons at Oak Ridge from
1944 to 1946. Multiple curves are for different groups of calutrons.

From R. S. Livingston, J. E. Rodgers, and E. G. Struxness, "Performance of the
Beta Ion Source," in *Separation of Isotopes in Calutron Units,* ed. H. Wesley Savage,
National Nuclear Energy Series, div. 1, vol. 7 (Oak Ridge, Tenn.:
USAEC Technical Information Service, 1951), p. 121, fig. 5.2.

calutron and consequently lost. The ratio of the U-235 collected to that put into the ion source is called the collection ratio, and, as figure 47 shows, in the beta units this increased about 5% to about 15% in two years. So even after two years, 85% of the U-235 ended up deposited all over the calutron. Deposits must be cleaned out after every batch run, and since the beta units separate partially enriched uranium, the deposited material is very valuable.

Some of the material is ionized and deposited near the collectors of the useful ion beams. It may be in the form of doubly ionized uranium (U^{++}), UCl^+, UCl_2^+, or UCl_3^+, or it may be in some other form.[4] The beams responsible for this material may, in combination, be equal to or stronger than the separation beams, and the size of these other beams partly determines the choice of UCl_4 as the source of uranium ions for separation. However large the amount of unwanted components produced with UCl_4, it is smaller than that produced with other compounds. The extraneous beams double the power requirement for the ion beams.

However, the ion source requires about ten times the power that the U-235 and U-238 beams require. This is estimated as about 75 kilowatts for the two-beam units, and 150 kilowatts for the four-beam alpha units.[5] The greatest power loss appears to be to leakage currents from the high-voltage units, either through small currents spread over large surfaces or by regular or irregular sparking. The current drains exceed 2 amperes at times.

Collection efficiency must also be considered. The beams of ions moving in the magnetic field would have a finite size, spreading out from the average trajectory because of the size of the initial source, imperfections in the initial focusing system, the ions' intrinsic thermal velocity, the effects of the ions' charges on one another (the space charge), and the scattering of the uranium atoms by gas molecules. The space charge and scattering effects are very important. A small beam in a chamber evacuated to a very good vacuum can be brought to an excellent focus, with almost pure U-235 incident on its collector. As the current is increased, however, the space charge will defocus the beam. To reduce this effect, some residual gas is left in the chamber, and the negative electrons, ionized from this gas by the passage of the uranium, partially neutralize the positive space charge, thus allowing a higher uranium current. There is an optimum amount of gas to be allowed in the vacuum chamber. If too little is allowed in, the useful beam will be reduced by space charge; if too much, it will be reduced by gas scattering. This scattering also caused the designers of the Oak Ridge system to

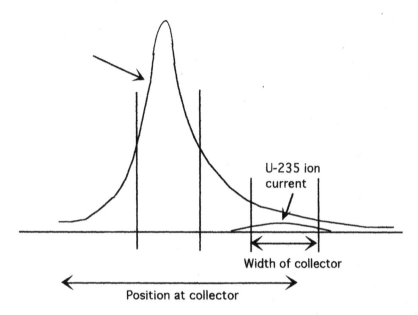

FIG. 48. Ion current as a function of isotope mass

From E. Gardner, "General Problems of Collecting Isotopes in Quantity," in
Sources and Collectors for Use in Calutrons, ed. R. K. Wakerling and A. Guthrie,
National Nuclear Energy Series, div. 1, vol. 6 (Oak Ridge, Tenn.:
USAEC Technical Information Service, 1953), p. 209, fig. 4.2.

place iron shims in the magnets to make the magnetic field partially
double-focusing.

Passage of uranium ions through a calutron does not result in pure U-
235. It does result in an enhancement of the U-235 concentration. The
deposit density as a function of isotope mass after separation as obtained
at Oak Ridge for an alpha unit is shown in figure 48. It appears that the
first stage of separation produced (in the collector) a concentration of as
high as 25% or even more, but generally about 15%. The second stage
(not shown here) went to about 90%. The separation might be much
smaller. At least two stages of separation are needed. If the enhancement
achieved at each stage is less, three or more stages will be needed. The
design of the second-stage (beta) separation unit necessarily differs from
that of the first-stage (alpha) because of its rich starting material.

In figure 48, the presence of the tails of the scattered U-238 beam at
the U-235 collector reduces the possible enrichment, so by selecting the

peak of the U-235 and leaving out the tails, the proportion of U-235 can be enhanced. This was done at Oak Ridge, at the expense of about a 30% loss in the amount of U-235 collected.

The second stage, which deals with the 15%-enriched U-235, will work on about one-twentieth of the uranium of the first stage. Taking into account actual beam currents and operating time plus collection losses at Oak Ridge, the amount collected there was about 35% of the amount that would ideally have been obtained with no losses and a beam current of 0.1 amperes. And this was after about two years of work. For a less-developed country, we could reasonably assume less than 25% effectiveness. If four beams were used, the result per four-beam unit in such a country would be about 54 grams of U-235 per unit per year. At 90% enrichment, this would give about 60 grams of weapon-grade uranium. Assuming that a nuclear weapon uses about 25 kilograms of highly enriched uranium, it would take a less-developed country about 450 four-beam calutrons to produce uranium for one bomb a year.

In my calculations, I have assumed a magnetic field of 4,000 gauss. It is relatively easy to attain a field of this strength because saturation effects in the iron of the magnets do not occur until about 15,000 gauss. With a field of this strength, its shape can be readily determined by the shape of the iron of the magnet pole tips, and the electric current and power required is for producing the magnetic field in the gap where the ion beams are propagating rather than in the iron.

To estimate the power required to produce the magnetic field, one has to know the size of coil used. Rather arbitrarily, I have assumed the cross section of the coil to be about 30 by 30 centimeters. Because the coil is wrapped around the iron of the calutron without overlapping the gap region, the coil thickness cannot be larger than that of the iron. By making the coil larger (also probably increasing the iron thickness), thus giving it a larger cross-sectional area, the power requirement could be reduced. With a coil 30 by 30 centimeters, about 60 kilowatts of electric power would be required for each magnet.[6]

Appendix C

Text of the Nuclear Non-proliferation Treaty

Signed at Washington, London, and Moscow, July 1, 1968
Ratification advised by U.S. Senate, March 13, 1969
Ratified by U.S. President, November 24, 1969
U.S. ratification deposited at Washington, London, and Moscow,
March 5, 1970
Proclaimed by U.S. President, March 5, 1970
Entered into force, March 5, 1970

The States concluding this Treaty, hereinafter referred to as the "Parties to the Treaty,"

Considering the devastation that would be visited upon all mankind by a nuclear war and the consequent need to make every effort to avert the danger of such a war and to take measures to safeguard the security of peoples,

Believing that the proliferation of nuclear weapons would seriously enhance the danger of nuclear war,

In conformity with resolutions of the United Nations General Assembly calling for the conclusion of an agreement on the prevention of wider dissemination of nuclear weapons,

Undertaking to cooperate in facilitating the application of International Atomic Energy Agency safeguards on peaceful nuclear activities,

Expressing their support for research, development and other efforts to further the application, within the framework of the International Atomic Energy Agency safeguards system, of the principle of safeguarding effectively the flow of source and special fissionable materials by use of instruments and other techniques at certain strategic points,

Affirming the principle that the benefits of peaceful application of nuclear technology, including any technological by-products which may be derived by nuclear-weapon States from the development of nuclear explosive devices, should be available for peaceful purposes to all Parties of the Treaty, whether nuclear-weapon or non-nuclear-weapon States,

Convinced that, in furtherance of this principle, all Parties to the Treaty are entitled to participate in the fullest possible exchange of scientific information for, and to contribute alone or in cooperation with other States to, the further development of the application of atomic energy for peaceful purposes,

Declaring their intention to achieve at the earliest possible date the cessation of the nuclear arms race and to undertake effective measures in the direction of nuclear disarmament,

Urging the cooperation of all States in the attainment of this objective,

Recalling the determination expressed by the Parties to the 1963 Treaty banning nuclear weapons tests in the atmosphere, in outer space and under water in its Preamble to seek to achieve the discontinuance of all test explosions of nuclear weapons for all time and to continue negotiations to this end,

Desiring to further the easing of international tension and the strengthening of trust between States in order to facilitate the cessation of the manufacture of nuclear weapons, the liquidation of all their existing stockpiles, and the elimination from national arsenals of nuclear weapons and the means of their delivery pursuant to a treaty on general and complete disarmament under strict and effective international control,

Recalling that, in accordance with the Charter of the United Nations, States must refrain in their international relations from the threat or use of force against the territorial integrity or political independence of any State, or in any other manner inconsistent with Purposes of the United Nations, and that the establishment and maintenance of international peace and security are to be promoted with the least diversion for armament of the world's human and economic resources,

Have agreed as follows:

ARTICLE I

Each nuclear-weapon State Party to the Treaty undertakes not to transfer to any recipient whatsoever nuclear weapons or other nuclear explosive devices or control over such weapons or explosive devices directly, or indirectly; and not in any way to assist, encourage, or induce any non-nuclear-weapon State to manufacture or otherwise acquire nuclear weapons or other nuclear explosive devices, or control over such weapons or explosive devices.

ARTICLE II

Each non-nuclear-weapon State Party to the Treaty undertakes not to receive the transfer from any transferor whatsoever of nuclear weapons or other nuclear explosive devices or of control over such weapons or explosive devices directly, or indirectly; not to manufacture or otherwise acquire nuclear weapons or other nuclear explosive devices; and not to seek or receive any assistance in the manufacture of nuclear weapons or other nuclear explosive devices.

ARTICLE III

1. Each non-nuclear-weapon State Party to the Treaty undertakes to accept safeguards, as set forth in an agreement to be negotiated and concluded with the International Atomic Energy Agency in accordance with the Statute of the International Atomic Energy Agency and the Agency's safeguards system, for the exclusive purpose of verification of the fulfillment of its obligation assumed under this Treaty with a view of preventing diversion of nuclear energy from peaceful uses to nuclear weapons or other nuclear explosive devices. Procedures for the safeguards required by this article shall be followed with respect to source or special fissionable material whether it is being produced, processed or used in any principal nuclear facility or is outside any such facility. The safeguards required by this article shall be applied to all source or special fissionable material in all peaceful nuclear activities within the territory of such State, under its jurisdiction, or carried out under its control anywhere.

2. Each State Party to the Treaty undertakes not to provide: (a) source or special fissionable material, (b) equipment or material especially designed or prepared for the processing, use or production of special fissionable material, to any non-nuclear-weapon State for peaceful purposes, unless the source or special fissionable material shall be subject to the safeguards required by this article.

3. The safeguards required by this article shall be implemented in a manner designed to comply with article IV of this Treaty, and to avoid hampering the economic or technological development of the Parties or international cooperation in the field of peaceful nuclear activities, including the international exchange of nuclear material and equipment for the processing, use or production of nuclear material for peaceful purposes in accordance with the provisions of this article and the principle of safeguarding set forth in the Preamble of the Treaty.

4. Non-nuclear-weapon States Party to the Treaty shall conclude agreements with the International Atomic Energy Agency to meet the requirements of this article either individually or together with other States in

accordance with the Statute of the International Atomic Energy Agency. Negotiation of such agreements shall commence within 180 days from the original entry into force of this Treaty. For States depositing their instruments of ratification or accession after the 180-day period, negotiation of such agreements shall commence not later than the date of such deposit. Such agreements shall enter into force not later than eighteen months after the initiation of negotiations.

ARTICLE IV

1. Nothing in this Treaty shall be interpreted as affecting the inalienable right of all the Parties to the Treaty to develop research, production and use of nuclear energy for peaceful purposes without discrimination and in conformity with articles I and II of this Treaty.

2. All the Parties to the Treaty undertake to facilitate, and have the right to participate in, the fullest possible exchange of equipment, materials and scientific and technological information for the peaceful uses of nuclear energy. Parties to the Treaty in a position to do so shall also cooperate in contributing alone or together with other States or international organizations to the further development of the application of nuclear energy for peaceful purposes, especially in the territories of non-nuclear-weapon States Party to the Treaty, with due consideration for the needs of the developing areas of the world.

ARTICLE V

Each Party to the Treaty undertakes to take appropriate measures to ensure that, in accordance with this Treaty, under appropriate international observation and through appropriate international procedures, potential benefits from any peaceful applications of nuclear explosions will be made available to non-nuclear-weapon States Party to the Treaty on a nondiscriminatory basis and that the charge to such Parties for the explosive devices used will be as low as possible and exclude any charge for research and development. Non-nuclear-weapon States Party to the Treaty shall be able to obtain such benefits, pursuant to a special international agreement or agreements, through an appropriate international body with adequate representation of non-nuclear-weapon States. Negotiations on this subject shall commence as soon as possible after the Treaty enters into force. Non-nuclear-weapon States Party to the Treaty so desiring may also obtain such benefits pursuant to bilateral agreements.

ARTICLE VI

Each of the Parties to the Treaty undertakes to pursue negotiations in good faith on effective measures relating to cessation of the nuclear arms race at an early date and to nuclear disarmament, and on a treaty on general and complete disarmament under strict and effective international control.

ARTICLE VII

Nothing in this Treaty affects the right of any group of States to conclude regional treaties in order to assure the total absence of nuclear weapons in their respective territories.

ARTICLE VIII

1. Any Party to the Treaty may propose amendments to this Treaty. The text of any proposed amendment shall be submitted to the Depositary Governments which shall circulate it to all Parties to the Treaty. Thereupon, if requested to do so by one-third or more of the Parties to the Treaty, the Depositary Governments shall convene a conference, to which they shall invite all the Parties to the Treaty, to consider such an amendment.

2. Any amendment to this Treaty must be approved by a majority of the votes of all the Parties to the Treaty, including the votes of all nuclear-weapon States Party to the Treaty and all other Parties which, on the date the amendment is circulated, are members of the Board of Governors of the International Atomic Energy Agency. The amendment shall enter into force for each Party that deposits its instrument of ratification of the amendment upon the deposit of such instruments of ratification by a majority of all the Parties, including the instruments of ratification of all nuclear-weapon States Party to the Treaty and all other Parties which, on the date the amendment is circulated, are members of the Board of Governors of the International Atomic Energy Agency. Thereafter, it shall enter into force for any other Party upon the deposit of its instrument of ratification of the amendment.

3. Five years after the entry into force of this Treaty, a conference of Parties to this Treaty shall be held in Geneva, Switzerland, in order to review the operation of this Treaty with a view to assuring that the purposes of the Preamble and the provisions of the Treaty are being realized. At intervals of five years thereafter, a majority of the Parties to

the Treaty may obtain, by submitting a proposal to this effect to the Depositary Government, the convening of further conferences with the same objective of reviewing the operation of the Treaty.

ARTICLE IX

1. This treaty shall be open to all States for signature. Any State which does not sign the Treaty before its entry into force in accordance with paragraph 3 of this article may accede to it at any time.

2. This Treaty shall be subject to ratification by signatory States. Instruments of ratification and instruments of accession shall be deposited with the Governments of the United States of America, the United Kingdom of Great Britain and Northern Ireland and the Union of Soviet Socialist Republics, which are hereby designated the Depositary Governments.

3. This Treaty shall enter into force after its ratification by the States, the Governments of which are designated Depositaries of the Treaty, and forty other States signatory to this Treaty and the deposit of their instruments of ratification. For the purposes of this Treaty, a nuclear-weapon State is one which has manufactured and exploded a nuclear weapon or other nuclear explosive device prior to January 1, 1967.

4. For States whose instruments of ratification or accession are deposited subsequent to the entry into force of this Treaty, it shall enter into force on the date of the deposit of their instruments of ratification or accession.

5. The Depositary Governments shall promptly inform all signatory and acceding States of the date of each signature, the date of deposit of each instrument of ratification or of accession, the date of the entry into force of this Treaty, and the date of receipt of any requests for convening a conference or other notices.

6. This Treaty shall be registered by the Depositary Governments pursuant to article 102 of the Charter of the United Nations.

ARTICLE X

1. Each Party shall in exercising its national sovereignty have the right to withdraw from the Treaty if it decides that extraordinary events, related to the subject matter of this Treaty, have jeopardized the supreme interests of its country. It shall give notice of such withdrawal to all other Parties to the Treaty and to the United Nations Security Council three months in advance. Such notice shall include a statement of the extraordinary events it regards as having jeopardized its supreme interests.

2. Twenty-five years after the entry into force of the Treaty, a conference shall be convened to decide whether the Treaty shall continue in force indefinitely, or shall be extended for an additional fixed period or periods. This decision shall be taken by a majority of the Parties to the Treaty.

ARTICLE XI

This Treaty, the English, Russian, French, Spanish, and Chinese texts of which are equally authentic, shall be deposited in the archives of the Depositary Governments. Duly certified copies of this Treaty shall be transmitted by the Depositary Governments to the Governments of the signatory and acceding States.

Notes

INTRODUCTION

1. An excellent source of information on the history of the atomic bomb is Richard Rhodes, *The Making of the Atomic Bomb* (New York: Simon & Schuster, 1986).

1. NUCLEAR CONFRONTATION

1. Bruce G. Blair, *The Logic of Accidental Nuclear War* (Washington, D.C.: Brookings Institution, 1993), pp. 168–218.

2. Ibid., p. 214, citing an interview by the *Moscow News* with Major General Boris Surikov, as reported in the *Bulletin of the Atomic Scientists*, June 1990, p. 47.

3. Scott D. Sagan, *The Limits of Safety: Organizations, Accidents, and Nuclear Weapons* (Princeton, N.J.: Princeton University Press, 1993), p. 176.

4. Ibid., p. 180.

5. Frank von Hippel, "How to Avoid Accidental Nuclear War," *Bulletin of the Atomic Scientists*, June 1990, pp. 35–37.

6. Sagan, *Limits of Safety*, p. 130.

7. Blair, *Accidental Nuclear War*, p. 188.

8. Ibid., p. 342.

9. Gary Milhollin, "Building Saddam Hussein's Bomb," *New York Times Magazine*, March 8, 1992, p. 32.

10. Kenneth N. Waltz, *The Spread of Nuclear Weapons: More May Be Better*, Adelphi Papers, no. 171 (London: International Institute for Strategic Studies, 1981). Most of the material in Waltz's book is also covered in Scott D. Sagan and Kenneth N. Waltz, *The Spread of Nuclear Weapons: A Debate* (New York: W. W. Norton, 1995); there Sagan discusses the hazards of nuclear weapons, which he also covers, in greater detail, in *The Limits of Safety*.

11. Bruce Bueno de Mesquita and William H. Riker, "An Assessment of the Merits of Selective Nuclear Proliferation," *Journal of Conflict Resolution* 26, no. 2 (June 1982), pp. 283–306.

12. Ibid., p. 302.

13. Steven J. Rosen, "A Stable System of Mutual Nuclear Deterrence

in the Arab-Israeli Conflict," *American Political Science Review* 71 (December 1977), p. 1367.

14. John J. Mearsheimer, "Back to the Future: Instability in Europe after the Cold War," *International Security* 15, no. 1 (1990), pp. 5–56.

15. Ibid., p. 36.

16. John J. Mearsheimer, "The Case for a Ukrainian Nuclear Deterrent," *Foreign Affairs*, Summer 1993, pp. 50–66; Steven E. Miller, "The Case against a Ukrainian Nuclear Deterrent," *Foreign Affairs*, Summer 1993, pp. 67–80.

17. William H. Kincade, "Nuclear Weapons in Ukraine: Hollow Threat, Wasting Asset," *Arms Control Today*, July-August 1993, p. 13.

2. INTRODUCTION TO THE TECHNOLOGY

1. Robert Serber, *The Los Alamos Primer* (Berkeley: University of California Press, 1992), p. 30.

2. John Wilson Lewis and Xue Litai, *China Builds the Bomb* (Stanford, Calif.: Stanford University Press, 1988), p. 244.

3. A useful reference is V. L. Mattson, "Uranium and Uranium Compounds," in *Encyclopedia of Chemical Technology*, 2d ed. (New York: Wiley Interscience, 1970), vol. 21, pp. 1–36.

3. PLUTONIUM PRODUCTION IN NUCLEAR REACTORS

1. Reactors can also be made that operate when fueled with thorium rather than uranium. These reactors produce another type of weapon material, U-233, rather than plutonium. Very few of them are in operation.

2. George S. Stanford, "Chernobyl, Moment by Moment," *Bulletin of the Atomic Scientists*, May-June 1997, p. 3.

3. Joint Committee on Atomic Energy, *Hearing with Regard to S1439, Export Reorganization Act of 1976*, 94th Cong., 2d sess., June 22, 1976, pp. 364–92.

4. For a description of the Brookhaven research reactor, see U.S. Atomic Energy Commission, *Research Reactors* (New York: McGraw-Hill, 1955), pp. 385–442.

5. The most important source is the decay of curium 242; this isotope undergoes α-particle emission and has a half-life of 163 days.

6. Frank von Hippel, David H. Albright, and Barbara G. Levi, "Quantities of Fissile Materials in U.S. and Soviet Nuclear Weapons Arsenals," in *PU/CEES Report no. 168* (Princeton, N.J.: Center for Energy and Environmental Studies, Princeton University, 1986), sec. 5, p. 1.

7. Frank von Hippel and Barbara G. Levi, "Controlling Nuclear Weapons at the Source: Verification of a Cutoff in the Production of Plutonium and Highly Enriched Uranium for Nuclear Weapons," in *Arms Control Verification,* ed. Kosta Tsipis, David Hafemeister, and Penny Janeway (Washington, D.C.: Pergammon-Brassey, 1986), p. 379.

8. J. Carson Mark, "Explosive Properties of Reactor-Grade Plutonium," *Science and Global Security* 4 (1993), pp. 111–24.

9. Ibid., p. 122.

10. National Academy of Sciences, Committee on International Security and Arms Control (John P. Holdren, chair), *Management and Disposition of Excess Weapons Plutonium* (Washington, D.C.: National Academy Press, 1995).

11. Frank von Hippel and Suzanne Jones, "The Slow Death of the Fast Breeder," *Bulletin of the Atomic Scientists;* September-October 1997, p. 46.

12. David Fisher, private communication.

13. An interesting example of this kind of computer study is described in "Radiation Dynamics of a Nuclear Explosion," by Andreas Pritzker and Walter Hälg of the Swiss Federal Institute of Technology (*Zeitschrift für Angewandte und Physik* 32 [1981]:1–11).

14. George Bunn and Roland M. Timerbaev, *Nuclear Verification under the NPT: What Should It Cover—How Far May It Go?* Program for Promoting Nuclear Non-proliferation, Study no. 5 (Southampton, England: Mountbatten Centre for International Studies, University of Southampton, 1994), p. 8. The requirements of the NPT with regard to weapons development are explored in some detail in this monograph.

4. URANIUM ENRICHMENT

1. Most of the material presented here on uranium enrichment and, in chapter 5, on assembly is covered in Robert F. Mozley, *Uranium Enrichment and Other Technical Problems Relating to Nuclear Weapons Proliferation* (Stanford, Calif.: Center for International Security and Arms Control, Stanford University, 1994).

2. In considering individual atoms or molecules, the following relationships are useful. Here E is energy, m is the mass of the individual atom or molecule, and v is its velocity. The subscripts refer to different isotopes.

$$E = mv^2/2$$
$$\text{Velocity} = v = \sqrt{2E/m}$$
$$\text{Momentum} = p = mv = \sqrt{2Em}$$

For two molecules of the same energy,

$$\Delta v = \sqrt{2E}(1/\sqrt{m_1} - 1/\sqrt{m_2}) \text{ and } \Delta p = \sqrt{2E}(\sqrt{m_1} - \sqrt{m_2}).$$

3. Information on the techniques described here can also be found in Allan S. Krass, Peter Boskma, Boelie Elzen, and Wim A. Smit, *Uranium Enrichment and Nuclear Weapons Proliferation* (New York: Taylor and Francis, 1983).

4. For a more detailed discussion of the material in this section, see appendix A.

5. R. K. Wakerling and A. Guthrie, eds., *Sources and Collectors for Use in Calutrons,* National Nuclear Energy Series, div. 1, vol. 6 (Oak Ridge, Tenn.: USAEC Technical Information Service, 1953); H. Wesley Savage, ed., *Separation of Isotopes in Calutron Units,* National Nuclear Energy Series, div. 1, vol. 7 (Oak Ridge, Tenn.: USAEC Technical Information Service, 1951).

6. R. Condit, "Insulators," in *Sources and Collectors for Use in Calutrons,* ed. R. K. Wakerling and A. Guthrie, National Nuclear Energy Series, div. 1, vol. 6 (Oak Ridge, Tenn.: USAEC Technical Information Service, 1953), p. 108.

7. When the original calutrons were built, their coils were much less efficient than those made by present methods, and the power cost could easily have been double that if modern methods of construction were used. The Iraqi coils are reputed to have been made with small tubing. Coils such as those are less efficient than coils made with larger, special "wire," and might use double the amount of power. The amount of power needed could be made very small by the use of superconducting coils, but this would require technology that a less-developed country would be hard-pressed to master. For more details concerning calutron power requirements, see appendix B.

8. George Anzelon, private communication.

9. F. J. Rahn, A. G. Adamantiades, J. E. Kenton, and C. Braun, *A Guide to Nuclear Power Technology* (New York: John Wiley and Sons, 1984), pp. 193–200.

10. An excellent description of the principles of separation physics, and of the centrifuge particularly, is to be found in Stanley Whitby, "Review of the Gas Centrifuge until 1962," *Reviews of Modern Physics* 56, no. 1 (1984), pp. 41–97.

11. Krass et al., *Uranium Enrichment,* p. 133.

12. *Holdup time* refers to the time material takes to pass through one stage of a cascade. A complicated formula involving per-stage and total

enrichment relates this time to the equilibrium time (the time needed to load a cascade).

13. E. J. Miles (director, Fuel Cycle Materials and Service Department, Westinghouse Electric Corporation), statement made before the Subcommittee on Energy Research and Development, Committee on Science, Space and Technology, House of Representatives, April 10, 1991.

14. For a detailed discussion of this history, see Dan Charles, "In the Beginning Was Uranium," *New Scientist,* October 24, 1992, pp. 30–35.

15. David Albright and Mark Hibbs, "Iraq's Shop-till-You-Drop Nuclear Program," *Bulletin of the Atomic Scientists,* April 1992, pp. 28–31, 34–36.

16. R. R. Eaton, R. L. Fox, and K. J. Touryan, "Isotope Enrichment by Aerodynamic Means: A Review and Some Theoretical Considerations," *Journal of Energy,* July–August 1970, pp. 229–31.

17. The energy unit *electron volt,* or *eV,* is commonly used in discussing atomic transitions. It is the energy required to move a single electronic charge through a potential of 1 volt. One electron volt equals 1.6×10^{-19} joules.

18. *Nominally* here means a fraction of the atoms equal to $(1 - 1/e)$, where e is the constant 2.718. The nominal number was that used to calculate the number of photons needed to excite the transition.

19. David L. Bodde (assistant director for Natural Resources and Commerce, Congressional Budget Office), statement made before the Subcommittee on Energy Research and Production, Committee on Science and Technology, House of Representatives, July 28, 1983.

20. I. Golovin, private communication, 1992. Dr. Golovin worked on the electromagnetic-separation project for the Soviet Union.

21. Paul J. Persiani, "Non-proliferation Aspects of Commercial Nuclear Fuel Cycles" (paper presented at the annual meeting of the Institute of Nuclear Materials Management, Orlando, Fla., July 1992).

6. EFFORTS TO PREVENT NUCLEAR PROLIFERATION

1. Quoted in William Epstein, *The Last Chance* (New York: Free Press, 1976), p. 8.

2. David Fischer, *Stopping the Spread of Nuclear Weapons: The Past and the Prospects* (London: Routledge, 1992), p. 41. Fischer quotes from Gerard Smith, "Nuclear Commerce and Non-proliferation: Some Thoughts" (paper presented at the USA Atomic Industrial Forum, Washington, D.C., April 29, 1982). Fischer's book is an excellent source of information

on the problems of proliferation, particularly with regard to the IAEA and the NPT.

3. A source of information on the origins of Euratom is Lawrence Scheinman, *Euratom: Nuclear Integration in Europe,* International Conciliation Series, no. 563 (Washington, D.C.: Carnegie Endowment for International Peace, 1967).

4. Excellent sources of information on the IAEA are Lawrence Scheinman, *The International Atomic Energy Agency and World Nuclear Order* (Washington, D.C.: Resources for the Future, 1987); David Fischer and Paul Szasz, *Safeguarding the Atom: A Critical Appraisal,* ed. Josef Goldblat (New York: Taylor & Francis, 1985); and Fischer, *Stopping the Spread of Nuclear Weapons.*

5. Scheinmann, *International Atomic Energy Agency,* p. 124.

6. Texts of the safeguards agreements can be found in Fischer and Szasz, *Safeguarding the Atom,* Appendix IV, pp. 186–211.

7. Ibid., p. 80.

8. George Bunn, *Arms Control by Committee* (Stanford, Calif.: Stanford University Press, 1992), p. 648.

9. "Hearings before the committee on Foreign Relations, United States Senate, Ninetieth Congress Treaty on the Non-proliferation of Nuclear Weapons, 1968, pp. 259–62.

10. The arcane phrase "source or special fissionable material" is defined by the IAEA to mean fissionable material that has been processed enough to be suitable for fuel fabrication, or any enriched fissionable material. It does not apply to ores, milled ores, or yellowcake. A more detailed explanation is to be found in "Statutes of IAEA" (Vienna: International Atomic Energy Agency, 1990) and "The Structure and Content of Agreements between the Agency and States Required in Connection with the Treaty on the Nonproliferation of Nuclear Weapons," INFCIRC/153 (Vienna: International Atomic Energy Agency, 1972).

11. George Bunn, *Does the Non-proliferation Treaty (NPT) Require Its Non-nuclear-weapon Members to Permit Inspection by the International Atomic Energy Agency (IAEA) of the Nuclear Activities That Have Not Been Reported to the IAEA?* (Stanford, Calif.: Center for International Security and Arms Control, Stanford University, 1992), p. 5.

12. A report on the NPT-extension conference is given in William Epstein, "Indefinite Extension—with Increased Accountability," *Bulletin of the Atomic Scientists,* July-August 1995, pp. 27–30.

13. In producing the explosion, India tried to avoid condemnation by asserting that its explosion was a peaceful one, that its device was not intended as a weapon. The NPT clearly forbids a nonnuclear nation to

receive help in producing any nuclear explosive device, not just a nuclear weapon.

7. THE WORLD'S NUCLEAR DEVELOPMENT

1. Two books were particularly helpful in preparing this material: Leonard S. Spector, with Jacqueline R. Smith, *Nuclear Ambitions* (Boulder, Colo.: Westview Press, 1990); and Leonard S. Spector and Mark G. McDonough, with Evan S. Medeiros, *Tracking Nuclear Proliferation* (Washington, D.C.: Carnegie Endowment for International Peace, 1995).

2. Henry DeWolf Smythe, *Atomic Energy for Military Purposes* (Princeton, N.J.: Princeton University Press, 1945).

3. Much of the material in this section came from two sources: William C. Potter, E. E. Cohen, and E. V. Kayukov, *Nuclear Profiles of the Soviet Successor States* (Monterey, Calif.: Program for Nonproliferation Studies, Monterey Institute of International Studies, 1993); and Spector and McDonough, with Madeiros, *Tracking Nuclear Proliferation*.

4. Frank von Hippel and Suzanne Jones, "The Slow Death of the Fast Breeder," *Bulletin of the Atomic Scientists,* September-October 1997, p. 49.

5. Most of the figures given here for amounts of plutonium are from David Albright, Frans Berkhout, and William Walker, *World Inventory of Plutonium and Highly Enriched Uranium, 1992,* SIPRI (New York: Oxford University Press, 1993).

6. Much of the material about Romania comes from Spector and McDonough, with Medeiros, *Tracking Nuclear Proliferation,* pp. 83–85.

7. "President Truman on Use of A-Bomb in Korea," *Bulletin of the Atomic Scientists,* December 1950, p. 381.

8. Lewis and Litai, *China Builds the Bomb,* p. 14. Lewis and Litai here refer to Sherman Adams's *First Hand Report: The Story of the Eisenhower Administration.* Reprint ed. (Westport, Conn.: Greenwood Press, 1974), p. 48.

9. Lewis and Litai, *China Builds the Bomb,* p. 20, citing the *New York Times,* December 27, 1953.

10. Quoted in Lewis and Litai, *China Builds the Bomb,* p. 32.

11. Ibid., p. 60. Lewis and Litai give detailed information about the extent of Soviet assistance in the Chinese atomic-bomb project.

12. von Hippel and Jones, "Slow Death," pp. 46–51.

13. Arjun Makhijani, "Open the Files, Please," *Bulletin of the Atomic Scientists,* January–February 1995, p. 4; See also Arjun Makhijani, "What 'Non-nuclear' Japan Is Not Telling the World," *Washington Post,* April 2, 1995, p. C1.

14. Gary Milhollin and Diana Edenswood, "Promises, Promises (While Building the Bomb)," *New York Times*, March 20, 1994, Week in Review section, p. 4.

15. Senate Committee on Armed Services, *The President's Report on the U.S. Military Presence in East Asia*, 101st Cong., 2d sess., 1990, pp. 77, 78.

16. Some of the U-238 in the fuel, when exposed to neutrons, is changed into Pu-239 (after an intermediate life as neptunium 239). After further exposure to neutrons, some of the Pu-239 is changed into Pu-240, and some of this, after even more exposure to neutron flux, is changed into Pu-241. By measuring the relative amounts of these isotopes, the total flux of neutrons to which the fuel has been exposed can be determined. Pu-241 decays, with about a thirteen-year half-life, into americium 241. If the plutonium has been chemically separated from other elements in the fuel, the only possible source of any americium present must be the postseparation plutonium. Therefore, the relative amounts of plutonium 241 and americium make it possible to tell when the chemical separation of the plutonium took place.

17. Bruce Cumings, "Spring Thaw for Korea's Cold War?" *Bulletin of the Atomic Scientists*, April 1992, pp. 18–19.

18. Lewis and Litae, *China Builds the Bomb*, p. 23.

19. "U.N. Says North Korea Will Face Famine As Early As This Summer," *New York Times*, May 14, 1996, pp. A1, A10.

20. Quoted in Gunnar Myrdal, *Asian Drama* (New York: Pantheon, 1968), p. 179.

21. A useful source of information on the India-China border war is Neville Maxwell, *India's China War* (London: Jonathan Cape, 1970).

22. Much of the information in this section comes from David Albright and Mark Hibbs, "India's Silent Bomb," *Bulletin of the Atomic Scientists*, September 1992, pp. 27–31.

23. David Albright and Mark Hibbs, "Pakistan's Bomb: Out of the Closet," *Bulletin of the Atomic Scientists*, July-August 1992, pp. 38–40.

24. Much of the material in this section comes from Seymour Hersh, "On the Nuclear Edge," *New Yorker*, March 29, 1993, pp. 56–73.

25. Ibid.

26. Devin T. Hagerty, "Nuclear Deterrence in South Asia," *International Security* 20, no. 3 (Winter 1995–96), pp. 79–114.

27. "South Asian Declaration," *New York Times*, Dec. 16, 1995, p. 4.

28. A great deal of information about Israeli nuclear-weapon development is given in Seymour Hersh, *The Samson Option* (New York: Vintage Books, 1991). However, Hersh provides little documentation, making it difficult to evaluate the accuracy of the convincingly written text.

29. David Fischer, private communication.

30. David Albright and Mark Hibbs, "Iraq's Bomb: Blueprints and Artifacts," *Bulletin of the Atomic Scientists,* January-February 1992, pp. 30–40.

31. A useful review of Iran's present situation is given in Ahmed Hashimi, *The Crisis of the Iranian State,* Adelphi Papers, no. 296 (Oxford: Oxford University Press, 1995).

32. Ibid., p. 19, quoting from the *Gulf States Newsletter,* no. 414 (July 1, 1991), p. 10.

33. David Fischer, private communication.

34. Speech by F. W. de Klerk to a joint session of the South African Parliament, March 24, 1993, in *Arms Control Today,* April 1993, pp. 27–28.

35. Hersh, *The Samson Option,* pp. 263–83.

36. A nuclear explosion at low altitude typically causes a double flash of light, the first flash occurring less than a millisecond after the initiation of the explosion and the second about 1/100 of a second later. This phenomenon is caused by the changing absorption and emission characteristics of the air surrounding the explosion as the temperature changes.

37. Waldo Stumpf, "South Africa's Nuclear Weapons Program: From Deterrence to Dismantlement," *Arms Control Today,* December 1995–January 1996, pp. 3–8. Much of this information is also to be found in an earlier article: David Albright, "South Africa and the Affordable Bomb," *Bulletin of the Atomic Scientists,* July-August 1994, pp. 37–47.

38. Stumpf, "South Africa's Nuclear Weapons Program," p. 7; Albright, "South Africa," p. 38.

39. Much of the information in this section comes from Greg Fry, "Toward a South Pacific Nuclear-Free Zone," *Bulletin of the Atomic Scientists,* June-July 1985, pp. 16–20.

40. The text of the treaty and some discussion of its provisions its given in appendix 21 of SIPRI, *SIPRI Yearbook 1986* (New York: Oxford University Press, 1986).

8. THE THEFT OF NUCLEAR MATERIALS AND THE EFFECTS OF UNCONTROLLED PROLIFERATION

1. There are a number of excellent sources of information on nuclear material theft in the former Soviet Union (FSU). The Program for Nonproliferation Studies, directed by William C. Potter, has had an ongoing program of gathering data on this subject. A useful release of the Monterey Institute of International Studies on this and other information about the FSU is William C. Potter, with Eve E. Cohen, and Edward Kayukov, *Nuclear Profiles of the Soviet Successor States* (Monterey, Calif.: Program for

Nonproliferation Studies, 1993). An excellent and complete review of the present situation is Graham T. Allison, Owen R. Coté, Jr., Richard A. Falkenrath, and Steven E. Miller, *Avoiding Nuclear Anarchy*, CSIA Studies in International Security No. 12 (Cambridge, Mass.: MIT Press, 1996). A more establishment examination of the problem is given in William H. Webster (Steering Committee Chair), Sarah A. Mullen (Task force Chair), *The Nuclear Black Market: An Interim Report*, Global Organized Crime Project (Washington, D.C.: Center for Strategic and International Studies, 1996). An excellent summary is given by Jack F. Matlock, Jr., U.S. Ambassador to the Soviet Union from 1987 to 1991, in "Russia's Leaking Nukes," *New York Review of Books*, February 5, 1998, pp. 15–18.

2. Graham T. Allison et al., p. 23.

3. Ibid. p. 8.

4. Ibid., p. 40, taken from testimony given by Lawrence Gershwin, House Committee on Appropriations, DOD Appropriations for 1993, Part 5, May 6, 1992, p. 498.

5. Ibid., p. 199.

6. Ibid., pp. 21, 22.

7. Sarah A. Mullen et al., p. 21.

8. Graham T. Allison et al., p. 102.

9. Ibid., p. 47. From *Boston Globe*, December 20, 1992.

10. Graham T. Allison et al., p. 130.

11. Apparently the smallest nuclear weapon in the U.S. Arsenal is the W54 warhead used for atomic demolition. It is described as weighing about 51 pounds and is 31 inches in length, 11 inches in diameter. It has a yield of about 0.25 kt and can be carried in a backpack by one soldier. *See* Thomas B. Cochran, William M. Arkin, and Milton M. Hoenig, *Nuclear Weapons Databook*, vol. 1, *U.S. Nuclear Forces and Capabilities*, Natural Resources Defense Council (Cambridge, Mass.: Ballinger Publishing 1984), p. 60.

9. IMPROVED CONTROL OF ATOMIC ENERGY

1. Spector, with Smith, *Nuclear Ambitions*, pp. 118–40.

2. Satellites two hundred miles above the earth's surface make a circuit of the earth in about ninety minutes. As the size of the satellite's orbit is increased, the satellite takes a longer time to circle the earth; at a distance of about 21,000 miles, it requires twenty-four hours. If the satellite is moving in the same direction in which the earth is revolving, it will stay in a fixed position relative to a point on the earth's equator.

3. If a 40,000-pound satellite is launched from the space shuttle, the

cost of putting it into orbit is about $500 million. If such a satellite is launched by an expendable rocket, the cost is about a third of that.

4. "Development and Control of Atomic Energy," in *Foreign Relations of the United States, 1945,* vol. 2, pp. 41–44 (Washington, D.C.: Government Printing Office, 1947).

5. Board of Consultants to Secretary of State's Committee on Atomic Energy (David E. Lilienthal, chairman), *A Report on the International Control of Atomic Energy* (Garden City, N.Y.: Doubleday and Company, 1946), p. 55.

6. Bernard M. Baruch, "The American Proposal for International Control," *Bulletin of the Atomic Scientists,* July 1, 1946, p. 4.

7. Ibid.

8. Ibid., p. 5.

9. Andrej Gromyko, "The Russian Proposal for International Control," *Bulletin of the Atomic Scientists,* July 1, 1946, p. 9.

10. J. Robert Oppenheimer, "The International Control of Atomic Energy," *Bulletin of the Atomic Scientists,* June 1, 1946, p. 4. This article is a condensation of the last of Oppenheimer's six "Messinger Lectures," which he delivered at Cornell University.

11. See Joseph Rotblat, Jack Steinberger, and Bhalchandra Udganonkar, eds., *A Nuclear-Weapon-Free World* (Boulder, Colo.: Westview Press, 1993).

12. His suggestions are to be found in Roland Timerbaev, "Evolution of the Soviet Approach to International Control of Nuclear Energy," paper presented at the symposium "Proliferation of Nuclear Weapons: Past, Present, and Future," Chicago, Ill., December 1992.

13. See Gerard C. Smith, "Take Nuclear Weapons into Custody," *Bulletin of the Atomic Scientists,* December 1990, pp. 12–13.

14. Jonathan Dean, "The Final Stages of Nuclear Arms Control," *Washington Quarterly,* Autumn 1994, pp. 131–52.

15. Ashton B. Carter, William J. Perry, and John D. Steinbruner, *A New Concept of Cooperative Security,* Brookings Occasional Papers (Washington, D.C.: Brookings Institution, 1992). Ashton Carter is Ford Foundation Professor of Science and International Security at the J. F. Kennedy School of Government, Harvard University; William Perry was secretary of defense in the first Clinton administration and is Berberian Professor of Engineering-Economic Systems and Operations Research at Stanford University; and John Steinbruner is senior fellow in foreign policy studies and holder of the Sydney Stein Chair in International Security at the Brookings Institution.

16. Ibid., p. 7.

17. Ibid., p. 63.

18. Roger D. Speed, *The International Control of Nuclear Weapons* (Stanford, Calif.: Center for International Security and Arms Control, Stanford University, 1994).

19. Ibid., p. ii.

20. Ibid.

21. Kosta Tsipis and Philip Morrison, "Arming for Peace," *Bulletin of the Atomic Scientists*, March–April 1994, pp. 38–43.

APPENDIX A. SEPARATIVE WORK UNIT

1. I have based much of what I say here on material contained in J. H. Tait, "Uranium Enrichment," in Marshall, *Nuclear Power Technology*, vol. 2, chap. 12. This chapter also contains much material on the various enrichment processes. Other useful descriptions are to be found in Krass et al., *Uranium Enrichment*, pp. 103–16; and Whitby, "The Gas Centrifuge," pp. 59–63.

APPENDIX B. SUPPLEMENTAL INFORMATION ON CALUTRONS

1. R. S. Livingston, J. E. Rogers, J. Rolland, and E. G. Struxness, "Performance of the Beta Ion Source," in *Separation of Isotopes in Calutron Units*, ed. H. Wesley Savage, National Nuclear Energy Series, div. 1, vol. 7 (Oak Ridge, Tenn.: USAEC Technical Information Service, 1951), pp. 117–41.

2. K. Korn and B. L. Moore, "Alpha I Receivers," in Savage, *Separation of Isotopes*, pp. 287–88.

3. Enhancement = $(100 - x)/x \times y/(100 - y)$ where x = % relative abundance of U-235 in input material and y = % relative abundance of U-235 in product material.

4. A. F. Clark, "Arcs in Magnetic Fields," in Wakerling and Guthrie, *Sources and Collectors*, p. 26.

5. H. W. Savage, "Electromagnetic Plant Specifications," in Savage, *Separation of Isotopes*, p. 41.

6. When the original calutrons were built, coils for such installations were much less efficient than those made by present methods, and the power cost could easily have been double. The Iraqi coils are reputed to have been made in Iraq using small tubing. Coils such as these are less efficient than those made with larger special "wire" and might use double the amount of power.

The amount of power needed for the coils could be made very small by the use of superconducting coils, but this technology would be very difficult for a less-developed country to master.

Glossary

AVLIS. For *atomic-vapor laser isotope separation.*

barn. A unit of area, 10^{-24} cm^2, used in expressing the effective area of atoms and nuclei for interactions.

BMEWS. For *ballistic-missile early-warning system.*

BWR. Abbreviation for *boiling-water reactor.*

calutron. An electromagnetic device used for isotope separation.

CANDU. For *Canadian deuterium uranium* (reactor).

cm. Abbreviation for *centimeter* (2.54 cm = 1 inch).

COCOM. Coordinating Committee, a group set up by the United States and its allies to prevent the Soviet Union and its allies from strengthening their military capabilities through East-West trade.

CFE. Conventional Forces in Europe (agreement).

CRISLA. For *chemical reaction by isotope-selective laser activation.*

critical mass. The mass of a fissile material that is sufficient to sustain a chain reaction. Critical mass depends on the shape of the material, its density, and the material surrounding it. The term is sometimes used to refer to the mass of a sphere of fissile material of normal density, with no material surrounding it.

cross section. The area for interaction of an atom or nucleus (often measured in barns). A cross section is determined as the ratio *a/bc* where *a* is the number of processes occurring, *b* the number of incident particles, and *c* the number of target nuclei per unit area.

curie. The quantity of any radioactive nuclide that undergoes 3.7×10^{10} disintegrations per second.

EEC. European Economic Community.

electron volt. The energy that an electron acquires in falling through a potential of 1 volt. Abbreviated *eV*. One electron volt is equal to 1.6×10^{-19} joules.

energy. The capability of doing work; force applied over a distance.

Euratom. European Atomic Energy Community.

eV. Abbreviation for *electron volt.*

gauss. A unit of magnetic-flux density or field; the earth's magnetic field is about 1/2 gauss.

gigawatt. One billion (10^9) watts.

half-life. The time required for a radioactive element to decay to half of its previous amount.

heavy water. Water with heavy hydrogen (deuterium) instead of normal hydrogen (D_2O rather than H_2O).

IAEA. International Atomic Energy Agency.

ICBM. For *intercontinental ballistic missiles*.

implosion. An explosion inward.

JCS. Joint Chiefs of Staff, an advisory group to the U.S. president, consisting of a chairman, a vice chairman, and the chief of each of the armed services.

joule. A unit of energy. One joule is equal to the force that would accelerate 1 kg at a rate of 1 meter per second, applied over a distance of 1 meter.

keV. One thousand electron volts.

kilogram. One thousand grams (2.205 pounds).

KWh. Abbreviation for *kilowatt hour.* One kilowatt hour is equal to the energy of 1 kilowatt of power for an hour.

KWh/SWU. Abbreviation for *kilowatt hours per separative work unit.* A measure of the efficiency of an isotope-separation system.

ln. Natural logarithm. A logarithm to the base "e" (e = 2.71828).

MAD. For *mutually assured destruction.* A term used to describe the nuclear deterrence policies of the United States and the U.S.S.R.

megawatt. One million watts. Abbreviated *MW.*

megawatt electric. The measure of the the electrical power output of a reactor; to be contrasted with megawatt thermal (abbreviated *MWt*), the measure of the heat generated by the reactor, generally three to four times greater than the electric power. Abbreviated *MWe.*

meter. A unit of length equal to 39.37 inches.

metric ton. One thousand kilograms. Abbreviated *mt.*

MeV. Abbreviation for *million electric volts.*

microgram. One millionth of a gram.

micron. One millionth of a meter (i.e., 10^{-6} meter).

milliampere. One thousandth of an ampere.

MLF. For *multilateral nuclear force.* An MLF was considered for NATO in the early 1960s, consisting of ships and submarines manned by crews drawn from all NATO powers and carrying nuclear weapons under NATO control.

moderator. Material used to slow down neutrons through collisions with its atoms.

MLIS. For *molecular laser isotope separation.*

MOX. Abbreviation for mixed-oxide fuel. Fuel for nuclear reactors made from a mixture of uranium and plutonium oxides.

MW. Abbreviation for *megawatt.*

MWe. Abbreviation for *megawatt electric.*

MWt. Abbreviation for *megawatt thermal.*

nanometer. One thousandth of a micron; 10^{-9} meter.

NORAD. North American Air Defense Command.

NPT. Nuclear Non-proliferation Treaty.

NSG. Nuclear Suppliers Group. Representatives of a group of nations capable of supplying nuclear technology. They set up supply restrictions to prevent nuclear proliferation.

Open Skies Treaty. A confidence-building treaty between twenty- seven states of Europe, the United States of Europe, the United States, and the former Soviet Union to allow low-level air surveillance of border regions to make surprise attack impossible.

OTH radar. Over-the-horizon radar.

PAL. For *permissive-action link.* A method of controlling the activation of a nuclear weapon so that it can be armed only with the proper authorization.

ppm. Abbreviation for *parts per million.*

PWR. Abbreviation for *pressurized-water reactor.*

rem. A unit used to express radiation dosage in terms of its biological effect.

roentgen. A unit of radiation measured in terms of ionization produced. One roentgen of radiation would produce 2.08×10^9 ion pairs per cubic centimeter of dry air at 0°C and 1 atmosphere of pressure.

SAC. Strategic Air Command.

separative work unit. A measure of the effectiveness of isotope-enrichment devices. About 200 SWU are required to enrich enough natural uranium, with its 0.72% of U-235, to produce 1 kg of 90%-enriched U-235 and a residue with 0.25% enrichment. Abbreviated *SWU.*

SIPRI. Stockholm International Peace Research Institute.

START. Strategic Arms Reduction Treaty.

SWU. Abbreviation for *separative work unit.*

Urenco. A European consortium for enriching uranium.

yellowcake. A marketable product of the early stages in the refinement of uranium ore. It is composed mostly of U_3O_8.

Bibliography

Albright, David. "South Africa and the Affordable Bomb." *Bulletin of the Atomic Scientists*, July-August 1994, pp. 37–47.

Albright, David, Frans Berkhout, and William Walker. *World Inventory of Plutonium and Highly Enriched Uranium, 1992.* SIPRI. New York: Oxford University Press, 1993.

Albright, David, and Mark Hibbs. "India's Silent Bomb." *Bulletin of the Atomic Scientists*, September 1992, pp. 27–31.

———. "Iraq's Bomb: Blueprints and Artifacts." *Bulletin of the Atomic Scientists*, January-February 1992, pp. 30–40.

———. "Iraq's Shop-till-You-Drop Nuclear Program." *Bulletin of the Atomic Scientists*, April 1992, pp. 28–31, 34–36.

———. "Pakistan's Bomb: Out of the Closet." *Bulletin of the Atomic Scientists*, July-August 1992, pp. 38–40.

———. "North Korea's Plutonium Puzzle." *Bulletin of the Atomic Scientists*, November 1992.

Allison, Graham T., Owen R. Coté, Jr., Richard A. Falkenrath, and Steven E. Miller. *Avoiding Nuclear Anarchy.* CSIA Studies in International Security, no. 12. Cambridge, Mass.: MIT Press, 1996.

Baruch, Bernard M. "The American Proposal for International Control." *Bulletin of the Atomic Scientists*, July 1, 1946, pp. 3–5, 10.

Blair, Bruce G. *The Logic of Accidental Nuclear War.* Washington, D.C.: Brookings Institution, 1993.

Bueno de Mesquita, Bruce, and William H. Riker. "An Assessment of the Merits of Selective Nuclear Proliferation." *Journal of Conflict Resolution* 26, no. 2 (June 1982), pp. 283–306.

Bunn, George. *Does the Non-proliferation Treaty (NPT) Require Its Non-nuclear-weapon Members to Permit Inspection by the International Atomic Energy Agency (IAEA) of the Nuclear Activities That Have Not Been Reported to the IAEA?* Stanford, Calif.: Center for International Security and Arms Control, Stanford University, 1992.

Bunn, George, and Roland M. Timerbaev. *Nuclear Verification under the NPT: What Should It Cover—How Far May It Go?* Program for Promoting Nuclear Nonproliferation, Study no. 5. Southampton, England: Mountbatten Centre for International Studies, University of Southampton, 1994.

_____
Carter, Ashton B., William J. Perry, and John D. Steinbruner, *A New Concept of Cooperative Security.* Brookings Occasional Papers. Washington, D.C.: Brookings Institution, 1992.

Charles, Dan. "In the Beginning Was Uranium." *New Scientist,* October 24, 1992, pp. 30–35.

Cumings, Bruce. "Spring Thaw for Korea's Cold War?" *Bulletin of the Atomic Scientists,* April 1992, pp. 18–19.

Dean, Jonathan, "The Final Stages of Nuclear Arms Control." *Washington Quarterly,* Autumn 1994, pp. 131–52.

"Development and Control of Atomic Energy." In *Foreign Relations of the United States,* 1945, vol. 2, pp. 41–44. Washington, D.C.: Government Printing Office, 1947.

Eaton, R. R., R. L. Fox, and K. J. Touryan. "Isotope Enrichment by Aerodynamic Means: A Review and Some Theoretical Considerations." *Journal of Energy,* July-August 1970, pp. 229–31.

Epstein, William. "Indefinite Extension—with Increased Accountability." *Bulletin of the Atomic Scientists,* July-August 1995, pp. 27–30.

———. *The Last Chance.* New York: Free Press, 1976.

Fischer, David. *Stopping the Spread of Nuclear Weapons: The Past and the Prospects.* London: Routledge, 1992.

Fischer, David, and Paul Szasz. *Safeguarding the Atom: A Critical Appraisal.* Edited by Josef Goldblat. SIPRI. New York: Taylor and Francis, 1985.

Fry, Greg. "Toward a South Pacific Nuclear-Free Zone." *Bulletin of the Atomic Scientists,* June-July 1985, pp. 16–20.

Gromyko, Andrej. "The Russian Proposal for International Control." *Bulletin of the Atomic Scientists,* July 1, 1946, pp. 8–10.

Hagerty, Devin T. "Nuclear Deterrence in South Asia." *International Security* 20, no. 3 (Winter 1995–96), pp. 79–114.

Hashimi, Ahmed. *The Crisis of the Iranian State,* Adelphi Papers, no. 296. Oxford: Oxford University Press, 1995.

Hersh, Seymour. "On the Nuclear Edge." *New Yorker,* March 29, 1993, pp. 56–73.

———. *The Samson Option.* New York: Vintage Books, 1991.

Kincade, William H. "Nuclear Weapons in Ukraine: Hollow Threat, Wasting Asset." *Arms Control Today,* July-August 1993, pp. 13–18.

Krass, Allan S., Peter Boskma, Boelie Elzen, and Wim A. Smit. *Uranium Enrichment and Nuclear Weapons Proliferation.* SIPRI. New York: Taylor and Francis, 1983.

Leventhal, Paul, and Yonah Alexander, eds. *Preventing Nuclear Terrorism.* Lexington, Mass.: Lexington Books, 1987.

Lewis, John Wilson, and Xue Litai. *China Builds the Bomb.* Stanford, Calif.: Stanford University Press, 1988.

Makhijani, Arjun. "Open the Files, Please." *Bulletin of the Atomic Scientists,* January-February 1995, p. 4.

————. "What 'Non-nuclear' Japan Is Not Telling the World," *Washington Post,* April 2, 1995, p. C1.

Mark, J. Carson. "Explosive Properties of Reactor-Grade Plutonium." *Science and Global Security* 4 (1993), pp. 111-28.

Marshall, W., ed. *Nuclear Power Technology.* Oxford: Clarendon Press, 1983.

Mattson, V. L. "Uranium and Uranium Compounds." In *Encyclopedia of Chemical Technology,* 2d ed., vol. 21, pp. 1-36. New York: Wiley Interscience, 1970.

Maxwell, Neville. *India's China War.* London: Jonathan Cape, 1970.

Mearsheimer, John J. "Back to the Future: Instability in Europe after the Cold War." *International Security* 15, no. 1 (1990), pp. 5-56.

————. "The Case for a Ukrainian Nuclear Deterrent." *Foreign Affairs,* Summer 1993, pp. 50-66.

Milhollin, Gary. "Building Saddam Hussein's Bomb." *New York Times Magazine,* March 8, 1992.

Milhollin, Gary, and Diana Edenswood. "Promises, Promises (While Building the Bomb)." *New York Times,* March 20, 1994, Week in Review section, p. 4.

Miller, Steven E. "The Case against a Ukrainian Nuclear Deterrent." *Foreign Affairs,* Summer 1993, pp. 67-80.

Mozley, Robert F. *Uranium Enrichment and Other Technical Problems Relating to Nuclear Weapons Proliferation.* Stanford, Calif.: Center for International Security and Arms Control, Stanford University, 1994.

Myrdal, Gunnar. *Asian Drama.* New York: Pantheon, 1968.

National Academy of Sciences. Committee on International Security and Arms Control (John P. Holdren, chair). *Management and Disposition of Excess Weapons Plutonium* (Washington, D.C.: National Academy Press, 1995).

Oppenheimer, J. Robert. "The International Control of Atomic Energy." *Bulletin of the Atomic Scientists,* June 1, 1946, pp. 1-5.

Organization for Economic Development and International Atomic Energy Agency. *Uranium: Resources, Production, and Demand.* Paris, 1982.

Potter, William C. "Nuclear Exports from the Former Soviet Union: What's New, What's True." *Arms Control Today,* January-February 1993, pp. 3-10.

Potter, William C., E. E. Cohen, and E. V. Kayukov. *Nuclear Profiles of the Soviet Successor States.* Monterey, Calif.: Program for Nonproliferation Studies, Monterey Institute of International Studies, 1993.

Pritzker, Andreas, and Walter Hälg. "Radiation Dynamics of a Nuclear Explosion." *Zeitschrift für Angewandte Mathematik und Physik* 32 (1981):1–11.

Rahn, F. J., A. G. Adamantiades, J. E. Kenton, and C. Braun. *A Guide to Nuclear Power Technology.* New York: John Wiley and Sons, 1984.

Rhodes, Richard. *The Making of the Atomic Bomb.* New York: Simon & Schuster, 1986.

Rosen, Steven J. "A Stable System of Mutual Nuclear Deterrence in the Arab-Israeli Conflict." *American Political Science Review* 71 (December 1977):1367–83.

Rotblat, Joseph, Jack Steinberger, and Bhalchandra Udganonkar, eds. *A Nuclear-Weapon-Free World.* Boulder, Colo.: Westview Press, 1993.

Sagan, Scott D. *The Limits of Safety: Organizations, Accidents, and Nuclear Weapons.* Princeton, N.J.: Princeton University Press, 1993.

Sagan, Scott D., and Kenneth N. Waltz. *The Spread of Nuclear Weapons: A Debate.* New York: W. W. Norton, 1995.

Savage, H. Wesley, ed. *Separation of Isotopes in Calutron Units.* National Nuclear Energy Series, div. 1, vol. 7, Oak Ridge, Tenn.: USAEC Technical Information Service, 1951.

Scheinman, Lawrence. *Euratom: Nuclear Integration in Europe.* International Conciliation Series, no. 563. Washington, D.C.: Carnegie Endowment for International Peace, 1967.

———. *The International Atomic Energy Agency and World Nuclear Order.* Washington, D.C.: Resources for the Future, 1987.

Serber, Robert. *The Los Alamos Primer.* Berkeley: University of California Press, 1992.

Shalter, J., E. Von Halle, and R. L. Hoglund. "Diffusion Separation Methods." In *Encyclopedia of Chemical Technology,* 2d ed., vol. 7, pp. 91–175. New York: Wiley Interscience, 1965.

SIPRI (Stockholm International Peace Research Institute). *Sipri Yearbook 1997.* New York: Oxford University Press, 1997.

Smith, Gerard C. "Take Nuclear Weapons into Custody." *Bulletin of the Atomic Scientists,* December 1990, pp. 12–13.

Smythe, Henry DeWolf. *Atomic Energy for Military Purposes.* Princeton, N.J.: Princeton University Press, 1945.

Spector, Leonard S., with Jacqueline R. Smith. *Nuclear Ambitions.* Boulder, Colo.: Westview Press, 1990.

Spector, Leonard S., and Mark G. McDonough, with Evan S. Medeiros. *Tracking Nuclear Proliferation.* Washington, D.C.: Carnegie Endowment for International Peace, 1995.

Speed, Roger D. *The International Control of Nuclear Weapons.* Stanford, Calif.: Center for International Security and Arms Control, Stanford University, 1994.

Stumpf, Waldo. "South Africa's Nuclear Weapons Program: From Deterrence to Dismantlement." *Arms Control Today,* December 1995-January 1996, pp. 3–8.

Timberbaev, Roland. "Evolution of the Soviet Approach to International Control of Nuclear Energy." Paper presented at the symposium "Proliferation of Nuclear Weapons: Past, Present, and Future," Chicago, Ill., December 1992.

Tsipis, Kosta, and Philip Morrison. "Arming for Peace." *Bulletin of the Atomic Scientists,* March-April 1994, pp. 38–43.

U.S. Atomic Energy Commission. *Research Reactors.* New York: McGraw-Hill, 1955.

U.S. Senate. Committee on Governmental Affairs. *Nuclear Proliferation Factbook.* Washington, D.C.: Government Printing Office, 1980.

von Hippel, Frank. "How to Avoid Accidental Nuclear War." *Bulletin of the Atomic Scientists,* June 1990, pp. 35–37.

von Hippel, Frank, David H. Albright, and Barbara G. Levi. "Quantities of Fissile Material in U.S. and Soviet Nuclear Weapons Arsenals." In *PU/CEES Report no. 168,* sec. 5, p. 1. Princeton, N.J.: Center for Energy and Environmental Studies, Princeton University, 1986.

von Hippel, Frank, and Barbara G. Levi. "Controlling Nuclear Weapons at the Source: Verification of a Cutoff in the Production of Plutonium and Highly Enriched Uranium for Nuclear Weapons." In *Arms Control Verification,* Kosta Tsipis, David Hafemeister, and Penny Janeway, eds. Washington, D.C.: Pergammon-Brassey, 1986.

Wakerling, R. K., and A. Guthrie, eds. *Sources and Collectors for Use in Calutrons.* National Nuclear Energy Series, div. 1, vol. 6. Oak Ridge, Tenn.: USAEC Technical Information Service, 1953.

Waltz, Kenneth N. *The Spread of Nuclear Weapons: More May Be Better.* Adelphi Papers, no. 171. London: International Institute for Strategic Studies, 1981.

Whitby, Stanley. "Review of the Gas Centrifuge until 1962." *Reviews of Modern Physics* 56, no. 1(1984), pp. 41–97.

Index

Hagerty, Devin T., 190, 191
Heavy water, 44, 127; reactor, 53
Helsinki Confidence- and Security-Building Measures, 20
Hersh, Seymour, 190, 191, 297n.35
Hindu, 184
Hydrogen: as atomic particle, 25, 27; as moderator, 44; as carrier gas, 108

Ideal cascade, 80. *See also* Cascade
Implosion weapon, 128–32; possible test under NPT, 75; possible gift to China by U.S.S.R., 170
India, 183–91; storage of weapons, 13; thorium, 53; U.S. and Canada, 136; NPT and, 145, 147; and China, 183–86; nuclear weapons and technology, 187–88; and Pakistan, 189–91
Indonesia, 148, 191–92
INFCIRC/153, 141, 144
INFCIRC/66, 140, 141
Innage, 276, 277
Inspection: reactor, 64, 65; IAEA and NPT, 139, 142, 144; North Korea, 173–76, 178, 235; border controls, 226–30; satellite, aerial, and intrusive, 235–40; Acheson plan, 243; Baruch plan, 246
International Atomic Energy Agency (IAEA), 137–42. *See also* International control; Nuclear Non-proliferation Treaty; Safeguards; *see under* individual nations
International control of atomic energy. *See* Atomic energy, plans for control of
Ions: in chemical processes, 62, 110; in calutrons, 89–93, 276–81
Iran, 182, 183, 192, 193, 197–200
Iraq, 193, 194–97; and bomb design, 12; calutron, 78, 94, 95; and centrifuge, 108
Ireland: NPT and, 142
Isotope, 27–28, 29–32. *See also* Enrichment technologies; Separative Work Unit
Israel, 193–94; and nuclear weapons, 13, 14, 17, 192, 193, 194; and NPT, 148, 150; and Iraq, 195, 196, 221; and terrorist threat, 229–31
Italy, 166; and fission discovery, 3; nuclear aid to other nations, 195, 207

Japan, 171; and reprocessing, 72; and ability to make nuclear weapons, 74–76; chemical enrichment, 110; and NPT, 148; and North Korea, 181, 182, 231
Jet-nozzle enrichment, 108–10
Joliot-Curie, Frédéric, 3, 163
Jordan. *See* Middle East
Joule, 31, 293n.17

Kashmir, 183–86, 189, 190
Kazakhstan, 159, 161–62, 217
Khamenei, Ayatollah, 197
Khan, A. Q., 189
Khatami, Mohammad, 197
Khomeini, Ayatollah, 197
Kincade, William H., 19
Korea: Korean war 168–69; South, 172; North, 173–83, 231, 234, 235, 241; Korean Peninsula Energy Development Organization, 177
Krass, Allan, 292n.3
Krushchev, Nikita, 170